the green traveller

Richard Hammond
greentraveller.co.uk

Richard Hammond

the green traveller

Conscious adventure that doesn't cost the earth

With special photography by **James Bowden**
illustrations by **Naomi Wilkinson**
and design by **Tina Hobson**

First published in the United Kingdom in 2022 by
Pavilion
43 Great Ormond Street
London
WC1N 3HZ

ISBN 978-1-911682-21-9

A CIP catalogue record for this book is available from the British Library.
10 9 8 7 6 5 4 3 2 1

Reproduction by Rival Colour Ltd., UK
Printed and bound by Toppan Leefung Printing Ltd., China

www.pavilionbooks.com

Commissioning editor: Sophie Allen
Design: Tina Hobson
Production manager: Phil Brown
Illustration: Naomi Wilkinson
Photography: James Bowden
(except see Picture Credits on page 176)

Contents

Introduction

Along a short stretch of the towpath outside Bath, the Kennet and Avon Canal, River Avon, A36 trunk road and the Great Western Railway all run parallel with one another. It is a remarkable snapshot of how modes of transport have evolved over the last 200 years, from the early nineteenth-century heyday of canals and waterways to the golden age of the Victorian railways and the countrywide expansion of road building in the twentieth century. Today, we are living through another transition, but this time it is a wholesale change in energy supply, replacing fossil fuels with hydrogen and other renewables that is not just influencing the way we travel, but is a transformation in how we power the entire country. It is a profound development driven by necessity in response to the global climate crisis.

Over the coming years there will be other large-scale technological changes as well as regulation, backed up by extensive, legally binding legislation, to make the transition to net zero. These changes will take a time, and the reality is that we don't have much time. Since the Industrial Revolution of the mid-eighteenth century, carbon dioxide levels have risen by more than 30 per cent, causing global average temperatures to rise by 1°C. This might seem a small increase, but we are already seeing the effects on our climate in the form of extreme weather events – heatwaves, floods and severe storms – as well as the loss of polar ice and rising sea levels. The concentration of carbon dioxide currently in the atmosphere is well over 400 parts per million, higher than at any time in at least 800,000 years – and it is still increasing. In addition, other greenhouse gases such as methane and nitrous oxide are also being released through human activities and contributing to climate change. Global temperatures are predicted to increase by several more degrees, yet the consensus is that temperature rises of just 1.5°C will cause dangerous warming of the planet. The stability of our world's climate hinges on whether we can keep this small rise in global temperatures in check. This is the decade that counts.

Commensurate with the climate emergency is the nature emergency. Worldwide, 1 million animal and plant species are threatened with extinction due to the intensification of agriculture and forestry, resource extraction, hunting, invasive species, urban sprawl, pollution and climate change. Yet this is not just about the disappearance of remote rainforests or polar bears at the extremities of the planet – habitat and biodiversity loss is happening on a colossal scale in the UK, to our hedgerows and forests, our garden birds and the fish in our seas. Over 15 per cent of all wildlife in the UK is threatened with extinction.

The green traveller

This book is about how to travel in a way that is sensitive to the climate and nature emergencies. It is primarily focused on experiences that have a lower carbon footprint and provide a positive effect on the conservation of biodiversity. It is also focused on individual actions that can make a significant difference to the impact of how we travel.

Being a green traveller is not about making grand, one-off gestures, it is a state of mind, an ongoing attitude to conscious adventure that influences all aspects of how we holiday, including what we pack in our luggage and how we travel out to destinations, as well as the choice of hotels and activities we take part in while we're there. Addressing the three Rs of the circular economy (Reduce, Reuse, Recycle) is a useful steer, and there are several other 'Rs' that can be helpful: 'Rethinking' transport; 'Refusing' single-use plastic; 'Repairing' clothes, and so on. Just as the 'slow food' movement is all about savouring the taste of food, so green travel is about savouring the journey, relishing local food and appreciating different cultures while cherishing those sponteneous moments away from home with friends, family and others that make holidays so special.

Travelling with a lower carbon footprint

The average annual carbon footprint in the UK is currently over 10 tonnes per person, which needs to be brought down drastically to help contribute to the halt in the rise of global temperatures. Holidays can be a significant slice of a person's annual carbon footprint, and the actual travel portion is often responsible for at least 70 per cent of the carbon emissions of the entire trip. Therefore, the most effective way for a green traveller to reduce the carbon footprint of a holiday is to cut down on those emissions caused by travelling to and from the destination. The easiest way to achieve to this is to reduce the distance travelled and to travel in a way that burns less, or even better, no fossil fuels, using more sustainable modes of transport; or by not travelling in a vehicle at all, choosing instead to travel on foot, by bike or under sail. In particular, there is a steep difference in terms of the amount of carbon dioxide emitted by aeroplanes compared with most land-based vehicles. There are concerted efforts to decarbonize air travel using alternative fuels and methods of propulsion (such as via electricity and hydrogen), but even the most optimistic predictions support that this change is at least a decade away for most airlines. For the time being, flying within the UK produces about nine times as much carbon dioxide as travelling by bus, and 5–6 times as much as travelling by train. Emitting carbon dioxide at the higher altitudes planes reach is

Travelling by train through the mountains of
North West Wales on the Cambrian Coast Line

Comparison of carbon emissions by mode of transport for a return trip London to Glasgow

Coach	40kg CO2e
Train	64kg CO2e
Small electric car (driver only)	148kg CO2e
Small efficient petrol car (driver only)	237kg CO2e
Plane (economy class)	368kg CO2e
Large SUV (driver only)	1,020kg CO2e

Source: *How bad are bananas, the carbon footprint of everything* by Mike Burners-Lee, published by Profile Books, 2020

also thought to have more of an effect on climate change than when it is released at ground level. These figures do depend on a variety of factors, such as the age and type of aircraft or vehicle, how you travel to and from airports, railways and coach stations, and so on, but generally speaking, the emissions from taking a flight are a dramatic leap up from those of most forms of overland travel.

There are also differences in emissions depending on the vehicle you are in and how many people you are travelling with. For instance, one person driving in a small, efficient petrol car emits about four times as much carbon as travelling by train; but if there are four people in the car, then the emissions are on a par with the train. Because of the amount of carbon that is emitted in producing electric cars, they are not carbon neutral, as is sometimes reported, but they are significantly less polluting than a standard petrol car, as long as the energy used to charge the electric car is sourced from renewable energy. If there are at least two people in a small electric car then the emissions are generally about the same as travelling by train. In terms of ferry travel, travelling as a foot passenger has a carbon footprint that's about half that of taking the train, though the carbon footprint of one driver taking a small petrol car on a ferry is several times that of taking the train. There are new ships being built that are powered by liquified natural gas, which produces about 25 per cent less carbon dioxide emissions.

While reducing the carbon emissions from travelling to your holiday destination will likely have the most dramatic

impact on your holiday's emissions, there are other factors that will affect your carbon emissions when you're at the destination, including your choice of hotel, food and activities, as well as how you travel around. The average carbon footprint of a night in a typical hotel in the UK is about 31.1kg CO2, according to the Hotel Carbon Measurement Initiative, so choosing a hotel that has lower than average carbon emissions can make a significant difference to your holiday's footprint. There are also significant emissions of carbon and other greenhouse gases arising from the production of meat and dairy, so choosing a plant-based diet can help, so too can choosing local, seasonal food to minimize food miles. If you're travelling on your own or as a couple or in a group, it's also greener to take a bus or local train rather than a taxi; but if you do take a taxi, choose a firm that uses electric vehicles. It is better still to hire a bike and explore the locality on two wheels instead of four. Many of the accommodations featured in this book provided information on how to arrive by public transport. Some even offer significant discounts if you arrive without a car.

Holidays in the UK

This book includes many experiences in the UK that can be reached car-free – on foot, by bike or by public transport as well as those that are on the radar for electric car drivers. There are so many wonderful holidays in the UK that can be reached using sustainable transport: visiting age-old villages, world-famous cities, protected landscapes, historic coastline and beautiful islands. Green travellers can visit any number of heritage attractions run by the National Trust, English Heritage, Cadw and Historic Environment Scotland as well as hundreds of forests managed by Forestry Commission England, Natural Resources Wales and Forestry and Land Scotland; there are hundreds of former railway lines that have been converted to 'greenway' walking and cycle paths, and dozens of characterful community-run pubs, museums and galleries. We have some of the finest sandy beaches in the world reachable on foot; and an ever-increasing number of beach shacks, off-grid campsites and glampsites that are popping up all over the country.

The food revolution across the UK over the past 20 years has helped change the appeal of holidaying at home – thanks in no small part to the rise of the celebrity chef and the popularity of television programmes profiling amateur chefs and bakers, such as MasterChef and The Great British Bake Off. As the quality of cooking has improved, so too has the recognition of the provenance of ingredients, connecting menus with the farmers and growers from the region. Creating local dishes doesn't just benefit the environment by cutting down on the emissions created by transporting ingredients ('food miles'), there's also an obvious appeal of a meal where the ingredients may be only a few hours old. Eco-labels, such as the blue label administered by the Marine Stewardship Council help us understand what food to eat and when, while certification schemes such as the Sustainable Restaurant Association guide us to ethical eateries.

Flight-free holidays

This book also includes many holidays that can be reached without flying from the UK. We are lucky to have the rich cultural and geographical diversity of Europe on our doorstep, especially given that an overland trip across the Irish Sea, North Sea or the English Channel results in a fraction of the carbon emissions of a long-haul flight. So many great European cities can be reached overland within hours from the UK, including Dublin, Paris, Lille, Brussels, Nantes, Amsterdam, Avignon, Toulouse and Geneva. Low-impact winter activities, such as snowshoeing and ski-touring in the Pyrenees and the Alps are less than a day's train journey away; the beautiful islands of the Balearics, Corsica, Sardinia and Sicily are all accessible by rail and sail. There are also any number of low-impact holidays on the water, in the water and below the water, including paddle-boarding, canoeing and surfing; electric boat trips in nature reserves and swimming in the natural pools of innovative eco hotels; hiking, cycling, and wild swimming in the mountains, and snorkelling and scuba diving along the Atlantic coast.

The UK's rich maritime heritage means there is no shortage of departure points to Ireland and the continent by yacht, boat, ship and ferry. Many are well served by public transport,

and so too are the corresponding ports in Ireland, France, the Netherlands and Spain, so foot passengers can make a seamless transition between train, coach and ferry. The Rail & Sail initiative has made it easy and more affordable to travel by train and ferry to Ireland from all over the UK. So too has the Rail & Sail Dutchflyer made the train and ferry combination from Harwich to the Hook of Holland (and on to Rotterdam, Amsterdam and beyond by train) one of the most popular ways to travel to Northern Europe, certainly from the east of England.

Thanks to the connection of Eurostar with the modern, efficient, high-speed rail networks of Europe, it is also possible to travel comfortably by train to all corners of Europe and beyond. For very long-distance journeys, flying is of course the quickest way to get from A to B, but train journeys of less than 6 hours can work out to be a similar duration to a flight, once you've factored in the transit to out-of-town airports, the time taken to go through airport security and the final leg of the journey from the airport to your holiday location. Cities such as Paris, Amsterdam, Lyon and Strasbourg can all be reached in less than 6 hours from London. Many regions can be reached within a day, such as the south of France and northern Spain. You can then stay overnight and continue the journey the following day, for example, taking the train to Marseille or Nice and catching the ferry the next morning to Corsica or Sardinia; or stopping off in several places en route to far-flung cities like Istanbul or Moscow. There has also been a resurgence in overnight sleeper trains, such as the night trains within Italy, the sleeper services from Brussels to Vienna, Munich to Venice, Paris

Thanks to the connection of Eurostar with the modern, high-speed rail networks of Europe, it is possible to travel comfortably by train to all corners of Europe and beyond

There is now ample information and sustainable products on the market that make it easy to be a green traveller

to Moscow and Berlin to Malmö, as well as other overnight services within the Nordic countries and between Croatia, the Czech Republic, Hungary, Poland and Slovakia. Travelling overnight not only brings an added sense of excitement, but it enables you to travel overland to the far reaches of Europe without paying to stay overnight in hotels along the way.

Another great advantage of travelling by rail and coach for a city break is that the stations are often transport hubs, conveniently located in the centre of cities, from where it's just a short walk, cycle, bus or tram ride to and from your city break hotel or to connect with other journeys. You can also stop off, eat in a great restaurant and leisurely explore places along the way, whether in the immediate vicinity of the railway station or further afield. Detours I have made while waiting for onward train connections have included going to the beach in Barcelona, eating tapas in Algeciras, drinking a cappuccino in a quiet little square in Milan, admiring the yachts in Marseille's harbour, and cycling around Copenhagen. These little mini adventures can really help make the journey part of the holiday.

Positive impact travel

There's much urgent work that needs to be done to protect nature – in villages, towns and cities, as well as rural areas, in nature reserves, the countryside and vast rewilding areas. In this book, I have featured citizen science and other projects in the UK that desperately need the help of volunteers, ranging from just a few hours of your time to a residential weekend or longer. I have also included a chapter on medium- to long-term volunteering overseas, focusing on projects where you can contribute to nature conservation and humanitarian work that require at least a month's commitment. If you have the time, relevant skills and resources, volunteering can bring much-needed help to these important projects.

There is also a chapter on a range of positive-impact holidays overseas that support regenerative projects, which aid nature conservation and socio-economic work in non-industrialized countries. Many of these are in remote places and may require flying to reach them, so you do have to weigh up the benefits of supporting their work with the pollution of a return flight. If you do fly to these kinds of positive impact holidays, be wary of some of the green claims bandied around by airlines. While planes continue to burn huge amounts of fossil fuel (some of the larger planes get through a gallon of fuel a second), it is hard to see how they can be framed as 'green', but there is quite a large disparity between aircraft and the operating procedures of airlines, with some being more carbon efficient than others. For more information on the extent of carbon emissions associated with flying, see the atmosfair Airline Index (**atmosfair.de**) and the associated document, the Flight Emissions Calculator, which explains its methodology.

While the aviation industry continues to be such a large polluter, surely there needs to be a cultural shift in treating flying so casually. While jumping on a plane is still a luxury for many, for others it's too easy to fly off on a shopping trip to New York for the weekend, and Milan the next. Some advocate a more selective approach to flying: just as with the flexitarian approach to food where you eat a mainly plant-based diet and only occasionally eat lean meat and sustainably sourced fish, a similar attitude to flying could be

that you mainly travel overland and only occasionally fly with one of the less polluting airlines, staying for longer, and choosing to make the most of the flight by taking part in a volunteering or a positive-impact holiday that benefits nature conservation and humanitarian work.

Going green

A rapidly increasing number of travel companies are addressing the climate and nature emergencies. However, there are also unscrupulous businesses that are jumping on the 'eco' travel marketing bandwagon. In this book, I've included tips to help you tell the green from the greenwash, plus I have included as many experiences as possible I have encountered in over 20 years of writing and filming about green travel to help shine a light on those guides, businesses and organizations that are going the extra mile to reduce their impact on climate change and provide a positive impact on nature conservation.

Thankfully, there is now ample information and sustainable product on the market so it is much easier to be a green traveller, from packing plastic-free alternatives to finding and booking eco-friendly hotels and local guides, using public transport, contributing to rewilding, selecting locally sourced, seasonal food, and taking part in a huge range of low-impact outdoor adventures. As the world makes the transition to cheaper, alternative energy, low carbon mass transit as well as electric car journeys are fast becoming competitively priced for short to medium distances. Futhermore, the modernization of cross-channel ferry services and the renaissance of rail (including the revitalization of night trains across Europe) means long-distance overland travel is becoming ever more practical and attractive.

The experiences featured in this book are just a snapshot of the huge range of joyful, healthier, green travel experiences available at home and abroad. I hope you enjoy the journey. Less carbon, more fun!

Richard Hammond

Planning

Preparing to go green

Low carbon travelling around the UK

Travel by train, bus, ferry, electric car, bike, or on foot, here's how to make the most of the increasing number of sustainable transport options available across the country.

Trains

The best thing about train travel is that you can use the time to do something other than stare at the miles of road ahead. You can play cards, read the newspaper or a book, catch up on emails and text, watch a film, enjoy a meal, or just gaze out of the window and enjoy the views of the great British countryside. It's a great way to cover large distances across the country: you can travel from London to Bristol in less than 80 minutes, from Edinburgh to Birmingham in 4 hours, and from Exeter to London in just over 2 hours. Most railway stations are in city centres, so on arrival you can disembark and quickly reach the heart of the city without the hassle of parking.

Railcards and passes

FRIENDS AND FAMILY RAILCARD
Save a third on rail tickets and 60 per cent off children's fares with the Friends and Family Railcard. It's valid for up to four adults and four children aged 5–15 (plus you can have two adults named on one card, so if one cardholder isn't using it, the other can) so long as it's used after morning peak times. It can also be used for the Caledonian Sleeper and also on some rail/sea journeys with

Wightlink and Red Funnel Ferries to stations on the Isle of Wight (as well as Hoverport services to and from Ryde Hoverport), and Stena Line ferries to Ireland – where it's part of a train and ferry journey (familyandfriends-railcard.co.uk).

TWO TOGETHER RAILCARD

For adults who travel together, the Two Together Railcard provides one-third off train tickets when those two people travel on the same journey. It can used for both standard or first class tickets after morning peak times, and any time at weekends and on Public Holidays (twotogether-railcard.co.uk).

REGIONAL 'ROVER' TRAVEL PASSES

If you're planning to spend a few days travelling by train then regional travel passes can make train travel much more affordable than buying individual tickets. They can often be used in conjunction with bus travel. There are 60 passes in the UK, such as the North of England Rover, which gives you four days unlimited rail travel between Liverpool, Manchester, Leeds and Hull, and the Great West Way Discoverer Pass, which gives you unlimited rail and bus travel along a 125-mile (200-km) touring route between London and Bristol, including Bath, Salisbury and Windsor.

The All Line Rover pass provides unlimited rail travel throughout Great Britain for seven or 14 consecutive days, so it's great for longer journeys. It includes travel on the Ffestiniog Railway as well as the Welsh Highland Railway, and is also valid on the UK's overnight sleeper services. The GB Rail Rover Guide has information and links to rover tickets available throughout Britain (railrover.org).

Buying train tickets

National Rail publishes the fares for all rail tickets so there's no need to shop around for the best price, though there can be a small booking fee that can vary depending on the agent, such as **thetrainline.com**, **raileasy.com**, **mytrainticket.co.uk** and **redspottedhanky.com**. Agents that don't add a booking fee include **trainsplit.com**, **railsmartr.co.uk**, and the Transport for Wales website (**tfwrail.wales**), which sells tickets for all rail routes in Britain (except sleepers). For every ticket booked on **trainhugger.com**, they plant a tree in the UK.

SET UP A 'TICKET ALERT'

Rail tickets for are usually released 8–12 weeks ahead of travel, but you can set up a free email 'ticket alert' at **thetrainline.com/ticketalert** to let you know as soon bookings open for your chosen route so you can snap up the cheapest tickets as soon as they become available.

Connecting journeys

PLUSBUS

The PlusBus ticket gives you discounted travel on buses and trams to travel to and from railway stations, which can be used on over 200 bus companies across Britain, and on trams in Birmingham, Blackpool, Edinburgh, Nottingham, Sheffield and Wolverhampton. Buy it with your train ticket at any National Rail station ticket office or online (from train company websites and most other online rail ticket retailers). Young people (aged 16–30), students and most other Railcard holders get one-third off the normal day ticket prices, and children (aged 5–16) pay half the adult price day ticket price (plusbus.info).

TRAIN TAXI

If you need to take a taxi for the final leg of a journey, the TrainTaxi website lists taxi firms that serve railway stations through the UK (traintaxi.co.uk).

Overnight rail services

Travelling overnight on a train is a great way to travel long distances without having to stay in a hotel en route. There are two main overnight sleeper services in the UK: the Caledonian Sleeper between London Euston and Scotland (stopping at several Scottish railway stations); and the Night Riviera between London Paddington and Penzance railway station in Cornwall. These 'hotels on rails' have lounge cars with a bar, and beds in private sleeping cabins.

The Caledonian Sleeper is actually the collective name for several overnight services from London to Scotland: the Lowlander route travels directly to Glasgow and Edinburgh (the train splits in the early hours of the morning, taking passengers to Edinburgh Waverly or Glasgow Central); while the Highlander travels further, connecting London with popular destinations such as Aberdeen, Inverness, Aviemore and Fort William. You can also board

The scenic train journey at Criccieth on the Cambrian Coast Line along the west coast of Wales

the train at Watford Junction, Carlisle, Crewe and Preston. It's a brilliant way to travel up from England to the mountainous fresh and wild of Scotland, and vice versa. One of my favourite trips by Caledonian Sleeper is to alight at Corrour station (four stops before Fort William) and walk a mile (1.6km) to the wonderful, off-grid Loch Ossian Youth Hostel on the northern edge of Rannoch Moor (see p71). Another is to continue further up to Fort William and catch the connecting train to the port of Mallaig; from there you take a ferry over to the beautiful Knoydart Peninsula – a fantastic place for wild camping and walking – and home to The Old Forge pub, the most remote pub on mainland Britain, and the stunning Inverie Bay (see p95).

One of the great things about the Night Riviera service to Cornwall is that you can use it to connect with the ferry service from Penzance to the Isles of Scilly. It's just a 10-minute walk from the railway station to the check-in at Penzance Harbour for the Scillonian Ferry departure to Hugh Town on St Mary's; just enough time to grab yourself a pasty before you set off for one of the country's best flight-free adventures.

Taking bikes on trains

In general, most rail companies will let you take your bike on board for free at most times of the day, as long as you have reserved it for a specific train, usually 24 hours in advance (there are sometimes restrictions on busy commuter trains). If you miss that particular train and it's the fault of the rail operator (for example your connecting train was late or cancelled), then you should be able to board the next available train, so long as there is space (check with the station staff and/or the guard). Folding bikes are, however, usually regarded as luggage, so you can take one on board whenever you like, even at peak times, as long as it fits on the luggage rack and doesn't inconvenience other passengers.

There are some rail services that don't require a bike reservation, so you can just turn up at the station with your bike and board the train, but it is risky: if the train's available bike spaces are taken the guard can refuse you boarding with your bike (there are usually limits to how many bikes the guard can allow to be carried on board, depending on the service). It's wise to check with the train company you intend to travel with to find out the latest information regarding taking bikes on trains – there's a handy link to the cycling pages of each train operator on the National Rail website (nationalrail.co.uk/stations_destinations/cyclists.aspx). You can also look for the PlusBike information on the National Rail website when you select a particular journey. It will tell you the cycle carriage rules for the specific train(s), and also includes information on bike facilities at the railway stations and the number of available cycle parking spaces (nationalrail.co.uk/PlusBike).

Coaches

National Express (nationalexpress.com), Megabus (uk.megabus.com) and Flixbus (flixbus.co.uk) are the three main operators that run intercity coach travel services across the UK, while Scottish Citylink (citylink.co.uk), TrawsCymru (trawscymru.info) and Ulsterbus (translink.co.uk) run services in Scotland, Wales and North Ireland respectively. For the three services that run across the UK, you can reserve your own seat on most routes and the coaches usually have free Wi-Fi and USB charging points. All three operators have a luggage allowance of up to 44lb (20kg) that you put in the hold (underfloor lockers) at the start of the journey, as well as space for 'soft hand luggage' (i.e. not hard-shelled or wheeled luggage, which has to go in the hold), to store items in overhead luggage racks or on your lap/under the seat in front of you (or under your own seat) to access essentials during the journey. You can pay extra to take up to three additional items of luggage on National Express coaches. Toilets are available on all coaches. Most coach operators will only take a bike if it packs down into a suitable box or bag to be put in hold, as long as it conforms with their hold luggage specifications.

Buses

Britain has historically been blessed with a vast bus network and although subsidies – particularly for rural services – have been cut in recent years, there are still many wonderful bus journeys that can take you to remote villages, visitor attractions and the coast. Many bus operators provide day/weekly tickets as well as family/group tickets, which can save you money on multiple journeys.

In many parts of the country, there are smart new buses that accept contactless payment and have comfortable seats and Wi-Fi. A survey in 2018 by many of the leading bus companies in the UK unveiled the three most popular bus routes in the UK: the 840 Coastliner, which runs from Leeds to York and Whitby via the North York Moors; the 914/915/916 Glasgow to Fort William to Skye via Loch Lomond, Rannoch, Glencoe and Great Glen; and the Purbeck Breezer, from Bournemouth to Swanage via Sandbanks, Shell Bay and Studland.

Other popular routes include the 5/5C/X5 Caernarfon to Llandudno along the coast of North Wales, the 39 from Brecon to Hereford via the Golden Valley, and the 919 Fort William to Inverness via Great Glen and Loch Ness.

One of my favourite journeys is the X18 south from Newcastle along the Northumberland coast, passing by the wonderful castles at Warkworth and Alnwick then to the lovely fishing village of Craster, before snaking round the coast to Seahouses (the gateway to the Farne Islands) past the historic coastal castle of Bamburgh and ending at the beautiful town of Berwick-upon-Tweed.

The bus network along the coast of Pembrokeshire is a brilliant way to connect up travelling to the coastal villages and towns, and the region's fabulous beaches with the world-class Pembrokeshire Coast Path; five bus routes operate seven days a week during the summer.

There are also lots of open-top bus journeys that can take you to some of the finest visitor attractions in the country. Some of my favourites are the Needles Breezer on the Isle of Wight that climbs up to the Needles Battery; the New Forest Tour that passes through ancient woodland; the Stonehenge Tour, which travels from Salisbury via Old Sarum to Stonehenge; and the tour of the City of Bath, which provides wonderful views of the city's parks, gardens and Georgian architecture.

Electric cars

It wasn't very long ago that electric vehicles (EVs) were the butt of jokes up and down the land for their minimal range and poor performance. How things have changed in the last few years. Nowadays, range anxiety is fast becoming redundant as the technology and efficiency of electric cars has developed exponentially. The UK is the second largest electric car market in Europe (after Germany), and with the prospect of cheaper, second-hand electric cars coming on to the market, the future is bright for EVs. The charging network has struggled to keep up with the increasing number of electric cars on the roads, but significant developments are underway to make the electric car charging infrastructure as efficient as multi-pump petrol stations.

Charging networks

There are specific areas within the UK where the charging network is widespread, such as on Orkney in the north of Scotland, the City of London, parts of Wales and the north-east of England, but with the sale of new petrol and diesel engines predicted to end by 2030, the race is on to cover the entire country with charging stations. Two of the most popular apps to help map your EV journey are Zap Map (zap-map.com) and Google Maps, which has previously shown Tesla charging stations and is now rolling out charging stations for other car types, showing shops and eateries near charging stations. The RAC (rac.co.uk) and Automobile Association (theaa.com) provide lots of useful information on driving electric cars in the UK, including the latest details on the roll-out of rapid charging points that accept both debit and credit cards.

Developments are underway to make the electric car charging infrastructure as efficient as multi-pump petrol stations

Lift sharing

There are a number of car clubs that allow you to have the use of a car on an hourly basis, and lift sharing schemes where you share your car journey in the UK with another passenger – it's a great way to reduce the cost and carbon footprint of travelling by car. Some are managed locally, for commuters, sharing the school run, etc. and others nationally, for festivals and other long-distance travel. Here are some examples: liftshare.com, blablacar.co.uk, gocarshare.com, co-wheels.org.uk.

Cycling

The success of cyclists Chris Hoy, Bradley Wiggins and Laura Kenny at the London Olympics in 2012, as well as the high-profile stage of the 2014 Tour de France held in Yorkshire, paved the way for a renaissance in British cycling, not just at the top level, but also at the grassroots, thanks also in small part to organizations such as Sustrans (sustrans.org.uk), Love to Ride (lovetoride.net), British Cycling (britishcycling.org.uk) and Cycling UK (cyclinguk.org).

Millions of people now ride a bike in the UK – for commuting to work, for family days out on car-free paths at the weekend, and for multi-day tours on the UK's many long-distance cycling routes. Every year, Cycling UK runs the Women's Festival of Cycling (cyclinguk.org/womensfestival), which publishes a list of 100 women who are encouraging others to experience the joy of cycling, from mountain bikers and endurance cyclists to community group leaders, parents and carers who cycle to school with their kids and industry entrepreneurs. It's a wonderful celebration of the breadth of involvement in cycling throughout the

country that's backed up by an increasingly sophisticated cycling infrastructure, from cycle hire and bike repair shops to cycling cafés, cycling clubs and festivals, as well as the development of the National Cycle Network (sustrans.org.uk/national-cycle-network) – more than half the UK population lives within a mile of the National Cycle Network. You can plan a route almost anywhere in the UK with Google Maps or Cycle Streets (cyclestreets.net), which allows you to select three types of journeys (fastest – the quickest way to cycle from A to B; quietest – away from busy traffic; and balanced – a mix between the two). There are also excellent guides to cycle routes in the UK at sustrans.org.uk and cycle-route.com. Find the reports of routes that others have done on apps such as Bikemap (bikemap.net), Mapmyride (mapmyride.com), Komoot (komoot.com) and Strava (strava.com).

If you're planning a multi-day trip, you can find overnight accommodation that welcomes cyclists at Beds for Cyclists (beds4cyclists.com) and Cyclists Welcome (cyclistswelcome.co.uk/accommodation). There are excellent bike storage and other cycle-friendly facilities at many hostels in the Independent Hostels Association as well as the Youth Hostel Association, such as YHA Dartmoor, YHA Eyam in Derbyshire and YHA Keswick in Cumbria. Also, all 800 hotels that are part of the hotel chain Premier Inn welcome cyclists – they allow you to keep a (clean) bike in your room and receptionists should be able point the way to local cycling facilities. There are also many cycling holiday operators that organize guided and self-guided cycling holidays, such as Contours (contours.co.uk), Cycle Breaks (cyclebreaks.com), Cycling for Softies (cycling-for-softies.co.uk), Headwater (headwater.com), Inntravel (inntravel. co.uk), Macs Adventure (macsadventure.com), Open Road Open Skies (openroadopenskies.co.uk), Skedaddle (skedaddle.com) and Wheely Wonderful Cycling (wheelywonderfulcycling.co.uk).

Electric bikes

The only difference between an electric bike and a conventional bike is that it has an electric battery and motor to power the wheels, but what a difference it can make to a hilly climb or a long commute. A small digital display allows you to monitor the battery and switch between lower or higher amounts of motor assist as you cycle. Just as the technology for electric cars has become ever more sophisticated, so too has the technology for electric powered bikes – some now have the battery hidden inside the frame of the bike. Electric bikes have been particularly popular with people who need that little bit of help going uphill (such as the older generation, or for parents carrying young children) or just for those travelling longer distances, for example on a multi-day itinerary.

All the major retailers now stock electric bikes including Chain Reaction Cycles, Decathlon, Evans, Halfords, Rutland Cycles and Wiggle, and you can often find electric bikes available in cycle hire outlets. Increasingly, electric bike trips are now an option provided by cycling tour operators, such as Compass Holidays (compass-holidays. com), Cycling for Softies (cycling-for-softies.co.uk), Drover Holidays (droverholidays.co.uk), Freedom Treks (freedomtreks.co.uk), Freewheel Holidays (freewheelholidays.co.uk), Headwater (headwater. com), Hooked on Cycling (hookedoncycling.co.uk), Inntravel (inntravel.co.uk), Love Velo (lovevelo. co.uk), Skedaddle (skedaddle.com), Utracks (utracks.com) and Wheel to Wheel Holidays (wheel2wheelholidays.com).

There are also an increasing number of region-specific operators that focus entirely on providing electric bike breaks, such as Quiet Lanes, which runs ebike holidays in the Brecon Beacons (quietlanes.co.uk), National Forest EBike Holidays (ebikeholiday.co.uk) and Cotswolds Electric Bike Tours (cotswoldelectricbiketours.co.uk).

Walking

Britain is a nation of walkers. According to the Ramblers Association, 26.9 million British people walk for leisure and travel. As well as being able to walk along the country's rights of way (footpaths, bridleways and byways), there is also the right, in certain places, to walk off these paths, across privately owned land known as 'open access land'; this right was introduced in 2004–5 and opened up areas of open country and registered common land in England and Wales. For details of where you can walk without fear of falling foul of trespass laws, visit the website of the Ramblers Association (ramblers.org.uk) as well as the Natural England (openaccess.naturalengland.org.uk), which has a facility for you to search for those areas of open access land, coastal margins and the new England Coast Path. Open access land is marked on Ordnance Survey maps as a yellow wash (coastal margin is marked as a magenta wash).

Scotland has different open access rights to England and Wales, where everyone has statutory rights of access to most land and inland water, as long as these rights are 'exercised responsibly' following three main principles: respect the interests of other people; care for the environment; and take responsibility for your own actions. Guidance on this is provided in the Scottish Outdoor Access Code (outdooraccess-scotland.scot).

Travelling out of the high season

Is there anywhere quite like the UK in the summer? Wildflower meadows, butterflies and bumblebees, camping and firepits, wild swimming, coves and sandy beaches, long summer days, cricket, tennis, festivals, strawberries, and any number of watersports, from sea-kayaking to sailing. Yet there's much to commend travelling in the UK out of the peak summer season, when you can avoid the crowds, especially in popular places such as Cornwall, the Lake District and North Wales; it helps create year-round jobs, and you might find that you have that special place to yourself. Here are some of the sights, sounds and activities to enjoy travelling year-round:

Spring: woodland wildflowers, wild garlic, bluebells, apple and cherry blossom, spring veg, waterfall walks, the return of winter migrating birds and morning birdsong, longer evenings and sunlight through the windows.

Autumn: autumn colours, blackberry picking, harvest, bonfires, picking pumpkins, mellow mist and lingering wood smoke, crunchy leaves underfoot, foraging for seafood, chestnuts and mushrooms.

Winter: Wrapping up for winter walks, pubs, crackling fires, hot soup and hot chocolate, wood-fired hot tubs, Christmas markets, surfing, snowfall, sledging, snowshoeing, cross-country skiing and ski-touring.

The main long-distance walks in England and Wales are the 16 National Trails, most of which are accessible by public transport, including the South Downs Way, Pennine Way and the South West Coast Path. My favourite is the Pembrokeshire Coast Path, a 186-mile (300-km) mostly clifftop walk along the stunning coast of South West Wales (nationaltrail.co.uk). One of the least known is the wonderful Glyndŵr's Way, through the open moorland and forests of mid Wales, from Knighton to Welshpool. In Scotland, there are 29 Great Trails, including the John Muir Way, Moray Coast Trail and the West Highland Way – Scotland's first long-distance route, from Glasgow along the shores of Loch Lomond, across the wilderness of Rannoch Moor to Fort William at the foot of the UK's highest mountain, Ben Nevis (scotlandsgreattrails.com).

An excellent source of information about walking in Britain is walkingbritain.co.uk, which provides information on 2,000 walks for all levels of ability and fitness, from easy circular walks to challenging mountain hikes. So too is walkersarewelcome.org.uk – a community-led scheme of over 100 towns and villages across Britain committed to the maintenance of footpaths and facilities for walkers, as well as promoting the health benefits of walking, and encouraging the use of public transport. The Slow Ways project (slowways.org) also aims to create a national network of walking routes connecting all of Great Britain's towns and cities, as well as thousands of villages (see also p121).

The main long-distance walks in England and Wales are the National Trails, most of which are accessible by public transport

Walking holiday companies

There are dozens of holiday companies offering guided walks, solo and family holidays, as well as itineraries for self-guided walks, plus other services such as luggage transport for those walking longer trails. The following three companies are long established:

HF HOLIDAYS has been running walking holidays in the UK for over a hundred years, including walks island hopping on the Isles of Scilly, Channel Islands and Hebrides, festive breaks and family holidays. The company also offers guided day walks from its 17 country houses throughout England, from classic challenges such as climbing Catbells in the Lake District, to gentle strolls in Shropshire's Carding Mill Valley or between the Slaughters in the Cotswolds (hfholidays.co.uk).

RAMBLERS WALKING HOLIDAYS has run guided, small group walking holidays since 1946, including special interest trips, such as birdwatching, flora, skills and navigation, and 'rail and walk', as well as walking trips from Hassness Country House on the shores of Lake Buttermere in the western Lake District. It also runs a staff-managed initiative called Heart & Sole, which supports communities in the places that it visits, including animal welfare issues as well as smaller, more personal ventures, such as providing equipment for schools (ramblersholidays.co.uk).

FOOTPATH HOLIDAYS is a family-run business in Wiltshire (footpath-holidays.com) that has been organizing walking breaks for 40 years, including guided and self-guided trips, as well as heritage tours with a Blue Badge Guide – tour guides who have been examined on their knowledge and communication of heritage. For more information on the hundreds of Blue Badge members, see: britainsbestguides.org

Ferries

Britain has several domestic ferry operators that take foot passengers, here are the main destinations they serve:

West Coast of Scotland

Caledonian MacBrayne, known as Calmac, operates passenger and vehicle ferries between the mainland of Scotland and 22 of the major islands on its west coast. You can travel as a foot passenger on most of its journeys – reservations can be made online except for the service to Mallaig–Small Isles–Canna, Muck, Eigg and Rum, where you have to call the Mallaig office on 01687 310240. The main railway stations that connect directly to ports are at Mallaig, Oban, Gourock, Wemyss Bay, Largs, Ardrossan, and Troon, which all connect by train with Glasgow. There are over 30 types of island-hopping tickets, so you can plan your own trip at your own pace (calmac.co.uk).

Isle of Man

The Steam Packet Company runs services to the Isle of Man from Liverpool in 3 hours 45 minutes and from Belfast in under 3 hours (steam-packet.com).

Isle of Scilly

The Scillonian Ferry crosses from Penzance to St Mary's (the gateway to the islands) in about 2 hours and 45 minutes. Thankfully, for those travelling down to Penzance on the overnight sleeper, there's plenty of time from the morning arrival at Penzance railway station to walk to the ferry terminal to check in (islesofscilly-travel.co.uk).

Isle of Wight

Two major operators run ferries to the Isle of Wight – Wightlink Ferries and Red Funnel, plus Hovertravel runs a high-speed hovercraft service.

Wightlink Ferries operates a year-round service from Portsmouth to Ryde (a high-speed catamaran ride for foot passengers only, once or twice hourly), Portsmouth to Fishbourne (once or twice hourly ferry, 40-minute ride) and Lymington to Yarmouth (hourly, 40-minute ride). Bikes can be taken on board free of charge, although space on the catamaran is limited (wightlink.co.uk).

Red Funnel runs a year-round service from Southampton to East Cowes (hourly, 55-minute ride) and a high-speed foot passenger service from Southampton to West Cowes (every 30 minutes peak time, 25-minute ride). Bikes can be taken aboard the East Cowes ferry free of charge but not on the high-speed West Cowes ferry, unless they're foldaways (redfunnel.co.uk).

Hovertravel runs a year-round hovercraft for foot passengers from Southsea to Ryde. The journey takes just 10 minutes and it runs every 30 minutes, plus they have a handy shuttle service between the Hard Interchange Bus Station in Portsmouth and the Hoverport (hovertravel.co.uk).

Channel Islands

Condor Ferries runs the services to the Channel Islands – there are mutiple sailings each week from either Poole or Portsmouth to Guernsey and Jersey: Poole to Guernsey takes about 3 hours, 4 times a week; Poole to Jersey takes about 4 hours, 4 times a week. Portsmouth to Guernsey takes about 7 hours, 6 times a week; Portsmouth to Jersey take about 10 hours 20 minutes, 6 times a week (condorferries.co.uk).

The Gosport Ferry is a quick and convienient alternative to the 14-mile journey by road between Gosport and Portsmouth

Public transport to ferry ports

How to travel by train or coach to the ferry ports that serve the Isle of Wight and Channel Islands.

LYMINGTON

By coach: National Express coaches serve Lymington bus station, which is just off the high street, then walk to Lymington Pier, else you can hop on the train at Lymington Town station for the 2-minute ride to Lymington Pier.
By train: National Rail and South West Trains operate trains to Lymington Pier, which is opposite the ferry terminal.

PORTSMOUTH AND POOLE See pp36–37.

SOUTHAMPTON

By coach: National Express via Southampton, which includes the ferry to Ryde with Wightlink.
By train: Trains run from London Waterloo and Victoria every 20 minutes or so, then take free CityLink shuttle to Red Funnel's ferry terminals.

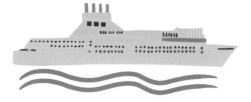

Foot ferries

There are dozens of foot passenger ferries that provide a handy short-cut across rivers, estuaries and harbours, or cross over to small islands. Most take bikes too, though do check with the operator before you travel. Here are some examples:

Suffolk Coast and Heaths has four foot ferries at Walberswick, Butley, Felixstowe to Bawdsey, and Harwich Harbour Ferry (thesuffolkcoast.co.uk).
Normanton-on-Soar is a chain ferry across the River Soar. It's been operating since 1771 and is run by volunteers at the weekends, April to September (normanton-on-soar.co.uk/chain-ferry).
Coniston Launch is a passenger cruise ferry around Coniston Water, but you can use it to get to landing stages, space permitting. The Northern cruise calls at The Coniston Inn jetty, Torver and Brantwood, while the Southern cruise calls at Torver, Lake Bank, Sunny Bank and Brantwood (conistonlaunch.co.uk).
Helford River Boats Ferry between Helford Passage and Helford Village, Cornwall, is part of the South West Coastal Path (helford-river-boats.co.uk).
Lundy Island The MS Oldenburg crosses in just less than 2 hours from Bideford or Ilfracombe to Lundy (landmarktrust.org.uk).
Mevagissey to Fowey ferry across St Austell Bay (mevagissey-ferries.co.uk).
Horning Foot Ferry, Norfolk Broads, is a short trip across the river between the Ferry Inn and Woodbastwick Staithe. You can also go to Horning (Swan Green), down to Cockshoot Dyke and St Benet's Church (horningfootferry.co.uk).
Gosport Ferry between Gosport and Portsmouth. A combined bus-ferry ticket offers unlimited travel on any First buses across Hampshire and one return ferry trip (gosportferry.co.uk).
Hythe Ferry (hytheferry.co.uk) from Hythe to Southampton. You can use it to connect with the New Forest Tour (thenewforesttour.info).

Travelling overland to Europe and beyond

The modernization of cross-channel ferry services, the revitilization of rail networks along with the development of high-speed rail and overnight sleeper services have opened up flight-free travel. Here's how to plan and book overland journeys to the continent.

There are many ways to travel to Europe from the UK without flying. The shortest route is by ferry across the English Channel from Dover to Calais, but choosing between the other options comes down to ease of access, preference for the mode of transport and journey duration, and price. Here is a summary of the mainstream flight-free options:

By train on Eurostar through the Channel Tunnel.

As a foot passenger on a ferry across The English Channel or North Sea.

By coach or electric car onboard a ferry across the English Channel or North Sea, or on a Eurotunnel Le Shuttle vehicle-carrying train through the Channel Tunnel (often called the 'Chunnel').

By train

The Eurostar is an international high-speed rail service through the Channel Tunnel that runs direct from the magnificently renovated London St Pancras International railway station (adjacent to Kings Cross mainline station) to Lille, Brussels, Paris, Disneyland Paris, Rotterdam and Amsterdam. During the summer there's also a direct service to Lyon, Avignon and Marseille, and in the winter, there's a direct Ski Train service to Moûtiers, Aime-la-Plagne and Bourg-Saint-Maurice (subject to restrictions or cancellations).

On Eurostar there's no weight limit for your luggage, but you should be able to carry and lift your bags safely. Each bag can be up to 33½in (85cm) long at its widest point. There are three types of tickets: Standard, which has a few tables that are ideal for families or groups of friends; Standard Premier, which has roomier seats and a cold light meal with a round of drinks served at your seat; and Business Premier, with benefits that include a three-course hot meal, champagne and other drinks served at your seat, a later check-in, a flexible ticket and access to the smart business lounges in London, Paris and Brussels, and the NS International Lounges on platform 1 at Amsterdam Centraal and platform 2 at Rotterdam Centraal.

On board Eurostar, there's free Wi-Fi and power sockets, plus you have access to two bar-buffet carriages that sell a range of hot and cold, alcoholic and non-alcoholic drinks, including champagne, as well as snacks and wholesome, hearty dishes. It's about 30 minutes from London to the Channel Tunnel, then, after about 20 minutes in the tunnel, you emerge for the quick onward journey through the beautiful countryside of northern France.

Travelling to Eurostar from outside London

Eurostar has negotiated with rail companies throughout the UK, so that you can buy a train ticket to get you to London to connect seamlessly with your Eurostar departure, as well as with local rail operators abroad for travelling beyond Eurostar's destinations. If you've already bought your Eurostar ticket, it's worth mentioning this to the staff at the ticket office at your local railway station to see if there are any discounts on your train journey to London.

Going further afield

From the main Eurostar arrival terminals, Lille, Brussels and Paris, it's possible to take a connecting train much further into Europe and beyond. Transferring trains in Lille and Brussels is usually fairly straightforward as you just need to find the platform of the connecting train, but in Paris you may have to cross the city. The Eurostar train arrives in to Paris at Gare du Nord, which is in the 10th arrondissement (district) near the Canal Saint-Martin and the historic Place de la République, which has many bars, restaurants and cafés. Gare du Nord has many connections within the station to northern France and onwards by Thalys trains to Belgium, Germany and the Netherlands, but if you're going elsewhere, such as to the south and west of France, you'll have to transfer to one of the other stations. If you're not used to Paris, this may seem daunting, but in practice the transfer between stations is pretty seamless – all are well connected by the city's metro system (which is very similar to the London underground) or overground rail network RER.

Tip for Eurostar

You can buy a Navigo Easy card to use on the Paris metro at the bar buffet on board Eurostar – it will save you time on arrival at Gare du Nord where the queues at the staffed counters can be long.

Train times to Europe

PASSPORT

UNDER 6 HOURS
(from London)
Lille
Brussels
Paris
Ghent
Amsterdam
Cologne

WITHIN A DAY
(from London)
Avignon
Zurich
Geneva
Munich
Milan
Barcelona

—— Rail connection
········ Ferry connection

Kiruna
Bodo
16:15
9:30
Trondheim 3:40 Ostersund
6:30 5:05
Bergen
6:45 Oslo Stockholm
7:30 5:00
Aarhus
Copenhagen
4:25 4:40
Rostock
Aberdeen
0:50 2:20
Glasgow Edinburgh
4:00 4:25
Belfast
Westport York
3:10 2:10 Hollyhead 1:50
Dublin 3:50 Birmingham
Cork 2:45 1:25 Gdansk
Bristol 1:45 Hamburg 5:35
Amsterdam 5:15 1:40 Berlin 2:40 Warsaw
London 6:10 5:15
Brussels 1:50 Cologne 4:20 7:20
Penzance 5:05 1:05 3:40 9:00 Katowice 2:10 Krakow
2:35 1:50 3:10 Prague 5:20 1:25 3:10 Przemysl
2:50 3:10 4:05 4:28
Paris Frankfurt 6:00 Vienna 6:45
Rennes 2:10 1:25 3:20 Munich 4:00
3:55 3:05 Basel 4:00 2:30 Budapest
1:55 Bern Zurich 7:40
Lyon 3:50 7:30 Ljubljana 8:05 15:00
Bordeaux 3:15 Milan 2:35 Venice 6:30 Zagreb 12:00 Bucharest
6:15 1:40 6:20
Santiago Santander Montpelier Nice Genoa Bologna 2:20 6:00 Belgrade Craiova
Vigo 2:40 2:35 Bastia 6:00 Split 9:50 8:50 Sofia
Porto Hendaye Marseille Ajaccio Florence 5:20 Dubrovnik 8:20 2:20
5:10 Pamplona 3:00 Rome Bar Skopje 9:40 Istanbul
4:30 3:00 Olbia Naples Bari 5:00
13:30 2:30 Barcelona Porto Torres 1:05 4:00 Durres Thessaloniki
Lisbon 10:30 Madrid 3:10 Palma Cagliari 7:30 Igoumenitsa 5:25 Patras
2:20 Valencia Palermo 4:10 Athens
3:00 2:25 3:15 Ibiza Town
Faro Seville Granada Cantania
Algerciras Malaga

To Tangier   To Tangier   To Algiers   To Tunis

How to transfer between stations in Paris for rail connections

GARE DU NORD TO GARE DE L'EST

For Basel, Strasbourg, Reims, Zurich, Frankfurt and Munich.

It's actually quicker to walk the 10 minutes from Gare du Nord to Gare de l'Est than taking the metro: exit Gare du Nord, turn left, then at the main intersection turn right (slightly downhill) along Rue du Faubourg Saint-Denis for about 440 yards (400m) then left along Rue de Chabrol to Gare de l'Est.

GARE DU NORD TO GARE DE LYON

For Grenoble, Nice, Lyon, Chambery, Avignon, Marseille, Perpignan, Geneva, Lausanne, the high-speed TGV trains to Barcelona, Milan and Turin.

Follow the signs for RER line D (which is signposted 'direction' 'Melun', 'Malesherbes' or 'Corbeil-Essonnes'). It's just two stops from Gare du Nord to Gare de Lyon and takes a little over 10 minutes (plus there's a short 5-minute walk to the connecting TGV departure platforms), but I recommend you leave at least 50 minutes for the entire transfer.

GARE DU NORD TO GARE D'AUSTERLITZ

For Cahors, Rodez, Montauban, St Gervais, Chamonix and Carcassonne.

Follow the signs for Metro line M5 to Gare d'Austerlitz (which is signposted 'direction Place d'Italie'). It's nine stops from Gare du Nord to Gare d'Austerlitz and takes 20–30 minutes, but I recommend you leave at least 50 minutes for the entire transfer.

GARE DU NORD TO GARE MONTPARNASSE

For the west and southwest of France for high-speed TGV trains to Agen, Angers, Biarritz, Bayonne, Bordeaux, Le Mans, Nantes, Pau, Poitiers, Rennes, St-Nazaire, Tours, Toulouse, and for discount high-speed Ouigo trains to Poitiers, Bordeaux and Rennes.

Follow the signs for Metro line M4 to Montparnasse Bienvenue (which is signposted 'direction Porte d'Orléans'). It's 14 stops from Gare du Nord to Montparnasse and takes 25–35 minutes, but I recommend you leave at least 50 minutes for the entire transfer time.

GARE DU NORD TO GARE DE BERCY

For Vichy and Clermont-Ferrand and TER regional trains to Lyon and Dijon.

Follow the signs for RER Line D (which is signposted 'direction' 'Melun', 'Malesherbes' or 'Corbeil-Essonnes') for two stops to Gare de Lyon then it's just one stop on Metro line 14 to Bercy (it will be signposted 'M14 direction Olympiades'). Allow 50 minutes for the transfer. Alternatively, you can walk from Gare de Lyon: exit the station and walk onto the forecourt, turn left into the rue de Bercy, running alongside the station. Gare de Bercy is about 800 yards (700–800m) along the road.

GARE DU NORD TO GARE SAINT LAZARE

For Évreux, Lisieux, Caen, Vernon, Rouen, Le Havre, Cherbourg and Trouville-Deauville.

Follow the signs for RER Line E (which is signposted 'direction Haussmann–St Lazare') and it's just one stop to 'Haussmann–St Lazare' station but I recommend you leave at least 30 minutes for the entire transfer time.

Transfer times

The transfer times given are the minimum amount of time you should allow between the scheduled arrival of your Eurostar in Paris and the scheduled departure time of your connecting train from Paris. Don't forget – when you take the return Eurostar back to London, you should factor in the compulsory Eurostar check-in time in addition to the transfer time.

Handy map

There are handy downloadable PDF colour-coded maps of the Metro, RER, Transilien (the commuter rail network), tramway and bus lines of the entire Paris transport network on the transport website: ratp.fr/plans.

The seamless connection of Eurostar with Europe's high-speed rail networks means that you can reach many wonderful European cities within 24 hours of leaving the UK. Barcelona, for instance, is reachable in one day, so too are Geneva, Milan and Munich. You can also use the high-speed rail networks to Nice and Marseille to connect with ferries to the Mediterranean Islands of Corsica, Sardinia and Sicily; to Barcelona to connect with ferries to the Balearic Islands of Ibiza, Mallorca and Menorca; and to Algeciras and Tarifa to connect with ferries to Morocco. You can go further still, to Greece and Turkey, or even travel all the way across Russia to Vladivostok on the Trans-Siberian Express from Moscow, or take the branch line – the Trans-Mongolian – across Siberia, Mongolia and the Gobi Desert to Beijing in China (the journey from Moscow takes six nights).

Overnight trains

Long distance trans-continental journeys, like the Trans-Mongolian, do take some planning (you'll need to sort out visas, for instance, for entering Russia and China), but there are many overnight trains in Europe that are as easy to organize as day trains, taking you across huge distances within Europe while you sleep. The advantage of the overnight train is that you save on a night in a hotel, and it can be a wonderful way to travel long distance. There are two types of berths, depending on the night train: 'sleepers' are basically hotel rooms on rails, with proper beds, mattresses, sheets and a washbasin; 'couchettes' are more basic, with padded bunks, a rug and a pillow. While many overnight train services were cut several years ago, in recent years some have made a comeback in response to a resurgence in demand for long distance rail travel, and there are some wonderful routes available, such as the Nightjet

sleeper train from Brussels to Vienna (nightjet. com), the French Intercités de Nuit service from Paris to Nice (sncf.com), and Trenitalia's Intercity Notte service from Milan to Syracuse, Sicily (trenitalia.com).

Trains to ski areas

The most accessible of the Scottish ski areas is the Nevis Range; the mountain gondola up to it is a 10-minute bus ride from the railway station in Fort William (trains run from Glasgow direct to Fort William, plus there's the overnight train from London to Fort William). It is also possible to reach many European ski areas by train. Eurostar has run a Ski Train for many years, which travels direct from London to the French Alps, stopping at Moûtiers, Aime la Plagne and Bourg-Saint-Maurice. (The service was halted during the Covid pandemic and is subject to restrictions or cancellations.)

With a generous baggage allowance and two services a week (overnight or daytime), it's a great low-carbon way to travel to the slopes. If you travel down on the Friday night service (and back on the Saturday night service), you can fit in two extra days' skiing on the relatively quieter Saturday changeover days without having to pay for the extra nights' accommodation (when you arrive on the Saturday morning, once you've wiped the sleep from your eyes, you can hit the slopes before lunch; and on the final Saturday, the departing train isn't until the evening, so you can fit in almost a full days' skiing). Another major benefit of taking the Eurostar Ski Train to the Alps (as and when service resumes) is that there is an extended baggage allowance with no weight restrictions. Each passenger can take an extra item of luggage on top of the standard two cases measuring up to 33½in (85cm) at their longest length, plus one item of hand luggage. Eurostar have also set aside an area in each carriage dedicated to stowing your large luggage, so you can keep your expensive skis or snowboard close at hand. It's worth bearing in mind though that the Ski Train overnight service does not provide sleeper carriages, you travel on normal seats of whichever ticket you buy (Standard or Standard Premier). Even if Eurostar's Ski Train doesn't run or it is booked up, check to see if ski operators, such as Travelski (uk.travelski.com) have inclusive train packages, or you can take regular, scheduled trains running daily: take the Eurostar to Paris then you can take either a daytime TGV train or an overnight train with couchettes. Many extra trains run on Fridays, Saturdays and Sundays during the ski season. There's a wealth of information about taking the train to many European ski resorts on snowcarbon.co.uk and skiflightfree.org.

Booking European train tickets

All Eurostar tickets can be bought on Eurostar.com. If you want to go further afield, there are two main pan-European ticketing agencies, both of which allow you to buy tickets for multiple train operators in multiple European countries. They both charge a small booking fee. Thetrainline.com is best known for selling UK train tickets but has now expanded into Europe. RailEurope.com is owned by French Railways and is a consolidation of all the various RailEurope websites.

Both agencies offer a free email alert service to let you know as soon as bookings open for your chosen route so you can snap up the cheapest tickets when they become available. Sign up for the 'ticket alert' at thetrainline.com/ticketalert; while on

The Man in Seat Sixty-One

The best online resource for information on booking train travel worldwide is the website set up and run by Mark Smith – seat61.com. It is so-named because Seat 61 in Eurostar's first-class compartments 7, 8 or 11 is an individual seat that lines up with the window. It's this sort of attention to detail that is makes his site such a useful resource. It provides up-to-date detail on the complexities and intricacies of booking train travel, including tips on how to find and book the best tickets via the myriad of ticketing agencies worldwide. It's especially useful if you're planning multi-stage journeys across international borders.

RailEurope.com search for the route and dates that you want on its booking page and, if booking hasn't opened yet, you will get a message recommending that you set up a 'booking alert'.

A great place to check rail timetables is the German railways website (bahn.de/en), which covers all of Europe. While many trains in Europe can't be booked more than 2–4 months in advance, Eurostar can now be booked 6 months in advance. If you're planning to travel beyond Paris, Brussels or Lille, you might want to hold off buying a non-refundable Eurostar ticket until you know you can get the ticket for the onward European leg of the journey.

Interrail pass

Interrail is a rail pass that provides unlimited train travel on scheduled train services across most of Europe. It started in 1972 as a rail pass for young people, but there are now Interrail passes for children, youths, adults and seniors. There are several types of Interrail passes based on the number of trips you can take within a particular timeframe, such as a 3-month global pass that covers 33 countries and a one-country pass, for example in Switzerland, where for varying prices, you can travel for three, four, five, six or eight travel days within one month (interrail.eu).

Rail holidays

Travelling by train is a great way to get from A to B, but it can also be a wonderful way to go sight-seeing. There are lots of companies that organize escorted rail holidays where you travel each day by train along a designated route with a tour manager who can explain the historical and social context of the sights along the way. Others simply organize the travel, hotels and rail tickets and provide detailed documentation, leaving you free to explore at your own pace. Perhaps the best-known rail journey is the Orient Express, the luxury train from Paris to Venice, but there are hundreds of other fantastic rail journeys through incredible scenery. One of most visited countries for a rail holiday is Switzerland, where there are any number of wonderful routes through spectacular alpine scenery, such as the Gornergrat (for views of the Matterhorn and Lauterbrunnen Valley), the Jungfrau (the highest railway in Europe), Mount Rigi Railway (the first ever mountain railway), the Glacier Express, and the Bernina Express (from Chur to St Moritz – the route is actually a UNESCO World Heritage Site – where you pass Pontresina up to the breathtaking Bernina Pass, along alpine creeks in view of the Morteratsch Glacier before ambling up through the Upper Engadine lake region in the canton of Graubünden). One of my favourite routes in Spain is the Ferrocarriles de Vía Estrecha (FEVE) train that trundles along the north coast of the Basque Country, Cantabria, Asturias and Galicia – there are over 100 stops along the route providing access to wonderful coastal walks, gorgeous beaches and excellent cafés and restaurants offering exquisite seafood lunches. I also love the steep Flåm Railway in Norway, which descends almost 3,000ft (886m) over just 12½ miles (20km) passing huge waterfalls and deep ravines on its way to the head of Aurlandsfjord, one of Norway's most picturesque fjords.

The advantage of booking a rail holiday through a rail specialist operator, rather than organizing the trip yourself, is that you'll be benefiting from their experience of travelling by train; they're used to deciphering the complexities of booking multiple train tickets in different countries, the nuances of rail timetables, and they know the most picturesque routes and the most suitable and conveniently located hotels en route. Companies that run these kinds of rail holidays will likely have some sort of financial protection in place so that should something go wrong, you will be well cared for, though do check before you book.

● **Great Rail Journeys:** The grandfather of rail holidays, this York-based company has been running escorted rail trips for 45 years all over the world, including the UK and Ireland, as well as river cruises, mostly in Europe (greatrail.com).

● **Rail Discoveries:** Run by the same team as Great Rail Journeys offering rail holidays on a smaller budget (raildiscoveries.com).

● **Inntravel:** Based in North Yorkshire and recognized as one of the UK's leading UK specialist tour operators, it runs non-group, self-guided rail holidays in Europe (inntravel.com).

● **Ffestiniog Travel:** Based in Tremadog, Wales, this is a small, independent company established in 1974 offering up to 40 high-quality escorted rail tours each year as well as tailor-made train travel, specialist steam tours and heritage railway holidays (ffestiniogtravel.com).

● **Planet Rail:** Specializes in tailor-made first class rail holidays, such as The Orient Express and other luxury train journeys (planetrail.co.uk).

● **Railbookers:** London-based agency selling customizable rail holidays (railbookers.co.uk).

● **Rail Trail:** A family-run firm based in Staffordshire (railtrail.co.uk).

● **Tailor Made Rail:** Based in London and arranges independent, unescorted rail holidays (tailormaderail.com).

By ferry

The modernisation of ferry services has revolutionized the experience of travelling across the Irish Sea, North Sea and The English Channel. Especially for longer overnight crossings to the continent where you can travel in style on spacious ships, enjoy fine dining in à la carte restaurants, spa treatment rooms, and comfortable en suite cabins, so on arrival you freel refreshed for the onward journey. There also plenty of facilities to keep children entertained during the crossing, including soft play areas, games rooms, live entertainment and cinema. Europe has never felt closer.

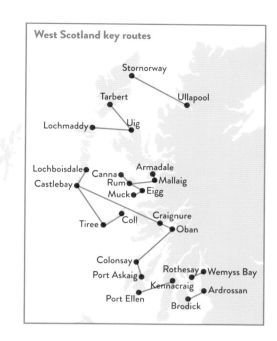

West Scotland key routes

Isle of Wight routes

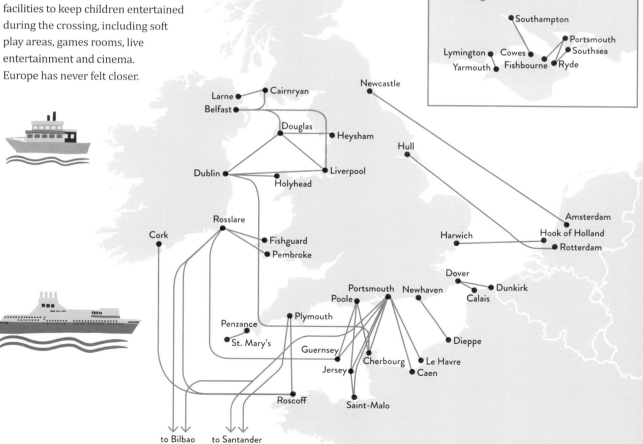

Public transport to ferry ports

Here's a guide to how to reach each of the main ferry ports by public transport, including how to transfer to the ferry check-in on departure (UK ports) and how to connect with public transport on arrival abroad:

DOVER

By train: From Dover Priory Station there is a regular shuttle bus service to the port terminal building, or you can take a taxi (5 minutes) or walk (15–20 minutes).

By bus/coach: There is a National Express coach stop just outside the ferry terminal, which comes from London Victoria Coach Station. If you wanted to travel onwards from Calais to Amsterdam, Bruges, Brussels or Paris you could board the coach at this stop outside the terminal (there is a ticket office next to the coach stop).

HARWICH

By train: Stena Line sells a Sail & Rail ticket to Holland, known as the Dutchflyer, which is a combined train and ferry ticket from London Liverpool Street (or any National Express East Anglia station, such as Cambridge, Colchester, Ipswich and Norwich) to Harwich International port, from where you can catch either the morning or overnight Stena Line ferry service to the Hook of Holland, and take any onward train to any station in Holland. Harwich International railway station is immediately adjacent to the port, so it is a quick transfer from the train platform to the ferry check-in, and on the other side, it's the same quick transfer off the ferry to the Hook of Holland railway station, which has train services to Rotterdam, Amsterdam and beyond (stenaline.co.uk/ferry-to-holland/rail-and-sail)

HULL

By train and bus/coach: From Hull Paragon Interchange (home to the coach and railway station) there's a shuttle bus to the ferry terminal building. Alternatively, there's a taxi rank outside Hull Paragon Interchange.

NEWCASTLE

By train: From Bewick Street opposite Newcastle Central Station there's a shuttle bus that takes 20–30 minutes to the port terminal that is timed to coincide with ferry departures.

By bus/coach: From Newcastle coach station it's a 5-minute walk to where the shuttle bus departs on Bewick Street opposite the railway station (as above).

NEWHAVEN

By train: From Newhaven railway station it's a 3-minute walk to the ferry terminal building.

By bus/coach: There's a local bus service from Brighton, Seaford, Peacehaven, Dover, Bexhill, Rye, Folkestone and Hastings to Newhaven bus stop, from where it's a short walk to the ferry terminal building.

PORTSMOUTH

By train: From Portsmouth Harbour railway station it's a short 10-minute taxi ride to the ferry departure terminal. NB between May and September, there is a shuttle bus from Portsmouth and Southsea railway station to the ferry departure terminal.

By bus/coach: The National Express coach stops right outside the ferry departure terminal.

POOLE

By train: It's a 25-minute walk from Poole Railway Station to Poole Ferry Terminal.

By bus/coach: It's a 25-minute walk from Poole Bus and Coach Station (in the Dolphin Centre) to the Poole Ferry Terminal. Taxis are available at most times from both the railway and coach stations. A shuttle bus runs between the passenger terminal and the ship for foot passengers.

PLYMOUTH

By train: From Plymouth railway station it's about a 20-minute walk to the ferry terminal, or 5 minutes in a taxi.

By bus/coach: From Plymouth coach station it's about a 25-minute walk to the ferry terminal, or 5 minutes in a taxi.

CAEN, FRANCE

Although the route is called Caen, the ferry port is at Ouistreham about 10 miles (16km) north of Caen. Thankfully, there's an excellent shuttles bus service (Bus Verts du Calvados line 1), which is scheduled to meet ferry arrivals at the port and run to Caen's main railway station and the city centre – the journey takes around 40 minutes. Gare de Caen (railway station) has services to many destinations throughout France, including Paris (journey time around 2 hours).

CHERBOURG, FRANCE

It's a few minutes' walk to Cherbourg's main railway station (follow the quayside south along the side of the harbour), a short taxi ride, or bus number 8 runs between the ferry port and the station. Gare de Cherbourg (railway station) is well connected to the French national rail network, with regular services to various local and long-distance destinations, including Paris (around 3 hours away).

ROSCOFF, FRANCE

The charming fishing port of Roscoff is a great entry point in France, especially if you're travelling to Brittany, the Loire and Aquitaine. On arrival, it's about a mile (1.6km), a 15-minute walk or short taxi ride to Roscoff railway station where there are trains to Morlaix for connections to Paris and high-speed TGVs to destinations across France.

ST MALO, FRANCE

It is approximately 10 minutes' walk to St Malo town centre or coach station and 25 minutes to the train station.

By bus: It's a short 3-minute walk to a bus stop (by the swimming pool 'La piscine du Naye') for a shuttle bus into town, which stops at 'Gare Routière' (bus station) just opposite the railway station in the modern part of St Malo, from where there are trains to the rest of France. Alternatively, there's a taxi rank outside the ferry terminal.

SANTANDER, SPAIN

In the heart of the city, Santander port is just one block along Avenida Castilla to Santander's main railway station (a few minutes in a taxi) where there are trains running to major centres in the region and the rest of the country. Santander is the gateway to the Picos de Europa.

BILBAO, SPAIN

The port of Bilbao is 10 miles (16km) north-west of Bilbao-Abando railway station, from where there are regular train services to major centres across Spain, including Madrid and Barcelona. There is no public transport direct from/to the ferry terminal, however there is a taxi rank outside the ferry terminal, or you could walk just under 2 miles (3km) to Santurtzi metro station to take the metro to Bilbao-Abando station (Santurtzi is the last stop on Line 2 and goes direct to Bilbao city centre).

Foot passengers

You can travel as a foot passenger on many of the ferry services out of the UK and enjoy all the benefits of modern ferry travel – bars and restaurants, plenty of entertainment and facilities for families, comfortable overnight cabins and no bag restrictions. The ports on both sides of the crossing are well connected by public transport, so it's easy to travel by bus or train to the ports in the UK, as well as disembark on the other side and continue the journey overland.

The following services allow foot passengers; check-in for foot passengers is usually at least 90 minutes before departure:

Brittany Ferries: Poole to Cherbourg; Portsmouth to Cherbourg; Portsmouth to St Malo; Portsmouth to Bilbao; Portsmouth to Santander; Plymouth to Santander; Plymouth to Roscoff; Portsmouth to Le Harve; Portsmouth to Caen (brittany-ferries.co.uk).

Stena Line: Harwich to Hook of Holland (stenaline.co.uk).

P&O Ferries: Dover to Calais; Hull to Rotterdam. Check-in time is 60 minutes before departure for foot passengers on P&O ferry services (poferries.com).

DFDS: Dover to Calais; Newhaven to Dieppe; Newcastle to Amsterdam (dfds.com).

There's a wealth of information about ferry services from the UK on the website run by Discover Ferries – an industry body representing 13 ferry operators in the UK, Ireland and the British Islands. It includes the latest news from its members and information on changes to ferry regulations, such as those being rolled out post Brexit (discoverferries.com). It also runs campaigns, such as Ferry Fortnight, usually at the end of February, which celebrates ferry travel and includes promotions, special offers and prizes (bigferryfortnight.com).

Ferries to Ireland from the UK

There are several ferry options for travelling between the UK and Ireland: you can choose a 'fast' or 'slow' ferry and travel as a foot passenger or a car passenger to Dublin, Cork and Rosslare in the Republic of Ireland, or Larne and Belfast in Northern Ireland. In most cases, when travelling as a foot passenger, you can buy a Sail & Rail ticket that combines both the rail and ferry legs of the journey (see below).

Irish Ferries runs slow ferry services between Pembroke in Wales to Rosslare on Ireland's south-east coast, and between Holyhead in Wales to Dublin Port. Dublin Port is 3¾ miles (6km) from Dublin city centre. Foot passengers are welcome on most of these crossings. Irish Ferries also has a high-speed catamaran service, Dublin Swift, on the Holyhead to Dublin route, which takes 2 hours, although it is more prone to cancellation if the sea is choppy, in which case you will be put on the next slower crossing. It is often taken out of service during winter months, with more regular services offered from April onwards. Bikes may be taken on the ferry for a small fee, which you can add to your booking (irishferries.com).

Stena Line runs slow ferry crossings from Holyhead in Wales to Dublin Port, from Fishguard in Wales to Rosslare in south-east Ireland, from Liverpool in England to Belfast, and from Cairnryan in Scotland to Belfast, all of which are available for both foot and car passengers. Bikes can be taken on the ferry for a small additional fee each way. Choose the option for 'bicycle' when you book rather than 'foot passenger'. There are train stations at Fishguard and Rosslare with easy transfers to the ferry. For Cairnryan: take a train to Ayr, then a Stena Line shuttle bus to the port – this service is available to passengers who have booked using the Sail & Rail facility on Stena Line's website – see the Sail & Rail section below (stenaline.co.uk).

P&O Ferries runs fast and frequent crossings between Cairnryan in Scotland to Larne in Northern Ireland, as well as between Liverpool and Dublin. The Liverpool-Dublin route does not carry foot passengers, however the Scotland to Ireland services carry both foot and car passengers. If you are bringing a bike, choose the 'bicycle' option when booking instead of 'foot passenger' – there is a small additional fee for cyclists. The Liverpool to Dublin crossing is one of the longest Irish crossings at 8 hours and 30 minutes, with cabins available.

SAIL & RAIL TO IRELAND

Both Stena Line and Irish Ferries allow you to book both the rail and ferry legs of your journey in one go, known as a Sail & Rail ticket, at a price that is much lower than if you booked the two legs separately. This combined train and ferry ticket can be for journeys from anywhere in Great Britain to anywhere in Northern Ireland and Republic of Ireland via UK ferry ports of Holyhead, Fishguard or Cairnryan. The Sail & Rail option is also available back from Ireland to the UK. There is no option to upgrade with these special Sail & Rail fares, but one of the distinct advantages of this Sail & Rail package is that the fares come at a fixed price which don't increase with peak travel periods or depending on how far in advance you book. You can book the Sail & Rail tickets on the website of Transport for Wales (tfwrail.wales/ticket-types/sailrail), which manages Sail & Rail fares on behalf of all British train operators. There's a 50 per cent discount for children aged 5–15, while those aged 0–4 travel free. You can also buy Sail & Rail tickets online at trainsplit.com and avantiwestcoast.co.uk.

BUYING FERRY TICKETS

Ferries can be booked via the websites of the individual ferry operators as well as via the following ticketing agents:

aferry.com; ferrysavers.co.uk; directferries.co.uk.

By coach, electric car, bike, or lift sharing

By coach

The major coach operators from the UK to Europe are Flixbus (flixbus.co.uk), which runs coach trips from Manchester, Birmingham and London to multiple cities in Europe, and National Express, which runs a service from London to Brussels, Paris and Amsterdam (nationalexpress.com); if you're travelling from outside London, you can travel to London to connect with the international service. National Express runs coaches from most major cities in the UK. Luggage allowance is one medium-sized suitcase and one piece of hand luggage per person. As with coaches operating in the UK, there's free Wi-Fi, charging sockets, and onboard toilets. You can also book Flixbus and National Express tickets through Omio (omio.co.uk), which also sells tickets for Alsa (the coach operator in Spain), and Eurolines, which works with 29 coach companies throughout Europe (eurolines.de).

By electric car

Cars can be taken on all the major ferry routes described in the foot passenger section above, as well as the Dover to Calais route run by DFDS (which doesn't take foot passengers). There are electric car charging facilities on the following services:
Eurotunnel Le Shuttle: Has rapid chargers for universal electric and hybrid cars, as well as dedicated Tesla chargers at both terminals so if you can recharge before you head through the tunnel on either side.

Irish Ferries: Provides charging facilities for POD Point Type II chargers on its Holyhead to Dublin ferry. You have to pre-book the charging point as an upgrade option when booking your trip and a nominal fee may apply. You're also asked to check in at least 1 hour in advance of the sailing time if you intend to recharge your vehicle during the crossing.

Hiring an electric car in Europe

There has been a huge increase in the production of electric cars in recent years and many of the large car rental companies, such as Avis, Europcar, SIXT and Enterprise now hire electric cars. Do make sure you hire a car that has the appropriate mileage per battery that's relevant for your use. Public charging networks provide a mixture of slow, fast and rapid charging points operated by either a national or regional network, so do check the location of the charging points as well as the charging time and payment methods. The car hire company may be able to advise on this when you hire the car – some may have arrangements with energy partners and can provide you with a charge card that you can use at a number of locations in Europe.

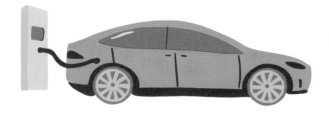

Charging electric vehicles in Europe

Electric vehicle (EV) charging networks are expanding very quickly across Europe. As in the UK there are different companies providing chargers, but the market is much more fragmented on the continent – if you think it's complicated in the UK, in Europe there is a bewildering number of providers. In most cases, you need to log in using a network RFID card, a key fob or an app, some of which need to be pre-loaded with funds. Chargers that accept a contactless debit or credit card are still not widespread. Thankfully, there are aggregators who can provide an RFID card that works on several different networks, reducing the number of cards or apps you need to obtain.

As in the UK, there are chargers at many motorway service areas and are also generally found where cars are likely to be parked for a while, such as supermarkets, shopping centre car parks, hotels and tourist attractions. The Automobile Association (theaa.com) has a handy guide to recharging in Europe, including the latest information on the charging networks in each country and breakdown cover for electric vehicles in Europe.

The situation is changing rapidly, so it's always worth checking the AA's website again just before you embark on a journey in Europe. Also, keep an eye on the website zap-map.com for the latest news about electric vehicles and the expansion of charging networks throughout the continent.

Charging networks
The following websites/apps provide information on where you can charge throughout Europe:

- openchargemap.org
- my.newmotion.com
- plugshare.com
- chargemap.com
- plugsurfing.com
- nextcharge.app

It is possible to take a bike on Eurostar, Eurotunnel Le Shuttle, and many of the ferries out of the UK

How to take a bike to Europe

On Eurostar, you can take a bike as regular luggage so long as it is less than 33½in (85cm) long when bagged up (it will be considered one of your allowed items of luggage). If your bike is over the limit, you can use Eurostar's luggage delivery service (subject to restrictions or cancellations – this service was put on hold following COVID-19 so do check the latest information with Eurostar), which is a reservation service that includes a charge, the amount varies depending on how you pack up your bike and how far in advance you make the booking. There's a limited number of spaces for fully assembled bikes (usually just two per train), so most people take their bike bagged or boxed up. For the latest information on charges and conditions, see 'Luggage and bikes' under the Travel Info section on the Eurostar website (eurostar.com).

Eurotunnel Le Shuttle provides a chargeable cycle-carrying facility whereby you put your bike on a vehicle with a driver who takes you through the shuttle. You need to book the service at least 48 hours in advance and they take a maximum of five cyclists per group booking. The pick-up/drop-off point is conveniently at the Holiday Inn Express in Folkestone, which is a short walk from Folkestone West railway station. In France, the pick-up/drop-off point is Ciffco, Boulevard de l'Europe, 62904 Coquelles, from where it's a 20-minute cycle to Calais train station, which has trains to and from Lille.

On most ferries from the UK to Europe, you can take your bike on with you as a foot passenger without having to bag or box it up. You check in at the same time as foot passengers, and you must dismount and push your bike up the same vehicle ramps used by cars. On arrival, you just wheel it down the same ramps and cycle off. Many ferry operators actively encourage cyclists, providing tips on their websites for cycling adventures abroad (there's also lots of advice for cycling routes on the website of the European cycling network Eurovelo: eurovelo.com/en).

Taking a bike with you is free on Brittany Ferries but on some of the other ferry companies there can be a small additional charge – instead of the usual foot passenger fare you pay a bicycle passenger fare.

Once in Europe, you can take a bike on many coaches and trains (especially outside peak hours), though as in the UK the arrangements vary between the operators so it's worth checking on the website of the individual coach or rail operator to check their bike policy. Small folding bikes usually count as normal luggage – you can take them with you on the coach or train, though it is advisable to put them in a cover. Similarly, you can usually take a bike on a train (or put it in the hold of a coach) if it is semi-dismantled and put in a zipped-up bike bag with the wheels and pedals removed and the handlebars turned sideways (especially if it is less than 47¼ × 35½in (120 × 90cm).

Many local and regional train services in Europe, such as the TER in France (but not the fast intercity services) have specific bike compartments for which there can be a small charge. For intercity trains in Germany, you will need a bike ticket and reservation that you can book online - most storage spaces for bikes are usually in the second class carriages.

You can check out the drivers' profiles and if you need more information about them or the trip, you can message them

Lift sharing in Europe

As in the UK, there are several lift sharing schemes in Europe whereby you join a car journey with another passenger – it's a great way to reduce the cost and carbon footprint of travelling by car, especially for long distances. The France-based company BlaBlaCar has 70 million members worldwide and facilitates carpooling across Europe. Once you've signed up as member, you just input where you're heading, where you're leaving from and when, and they show who is driving on a similar journey and an associated price that includes a fixed contribution to the driver's fuel. You can check out the drivers' profiles and, if you need more information about them or the trip, you can message them before booking (blablacar.co.uk).

Carbon offsetting

Carbon offsetting is a means of paying for 'credits' from projects that prevent or remove the emissions of an equivalent amount of greenhouse gases elsewhere. This is often done by planting trees to absorb carbon out of the atmosphere as they grow, or by delivering energy-efficient technologies, such as cooking stoves to communities in developing countries. Offsetting projects like these take time to absorb the carbon, and some people see the process as a dangerous distraction from the critical work of reducing carbon emissions – a band-aid solution that allows people and companies to continue to pollute the environment with a convenient 'get-out-of-jail-free' card. Others say it is a useful way of at least doing something to mitigate carbon emissions.

The idea is that you work out the associated carbon emissions using online tools and pay the offset yourself or choose a company that will do this for you. Offsetting is not limited to flying, you can use it to offset carbon emissions from almost anything, including rail and ferry journeys, as well as those resulting from day-to-day living, such as commuting. Regarding holidays, some operators include carbon offsetting as part of the price of the flight or holiday itself. While airlines have been providing the option for users to offset their flight for many years, some are now automatically offsetting their emissions from the fuel they use for every flight themselves. Increasingly travel companies, too, are measuring the carbon footprint of their holidays – the online portal for ethical adventure travel, muchbetteradventures.com, shows the carbon emissions on the listings of all its holidays so you can see immediately how much carbon the trip will emit. The small group adventure tour operators Intrepid and Explore! offset all their trips, so too does Pura Aventura, which includes in its calculations the emissions from international travel to and from the destination, whether that is by air, sea or rail.

If you choose to offset yourself, first you need to work out your emissions using an online calculator, then find a project that compensates for these emissions via one of the offsetting organizations, such as Gold Standard (goldstandard.org), ClimateCare (climatecare.org), C Level (clevel.co.uk), and Atmosfair (atmosfair.de). Or you could just donate directly to an organization that works on projects to absorb carbon or generate renewable energy, paying an amount equivalent of your carbon emissions. Try Forests Without Frontiers (forestswithoutfrontiers.org), the Woodland Trust (woodlandtrust.org.uk) and the World Land Trust (worldlandtrust.org). It's important to remember though, that while offsetting can work, the best strategy must be to reduce your own emissions first by foregoing carbon intensive modes of transport, such as aeroplanes and SUVs, and choosing more sustainable forms of transport, greener hotels, sustainable food and low-impact activities, examples of which are provided throughout this book.

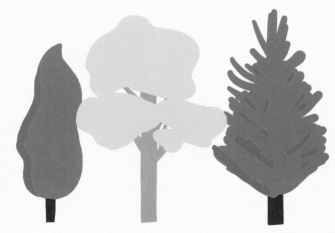

Green places to stay

Camping out under the stars in a bivvy bag is the ultimate
low-impact, back-to-nature way to bed down for the night.
Bothies, refuges, tents and tipis can be just as rewarding,
but finding green accommodation with a few more bells and
whistles can be tricky – there are lots of businesses flying
the green flag in name only. Here's our guide to what to
can expect at genuine eco-friendly places to stay.

Wild camping

One of the joys of camping in the wild is sleeping under the stars in a beautiful tranquil location. All you need is basic – but reliable – gear, including a tough, light tent, a decent mattress and sleeping bag, a good outdoor stove, refillable water bottle and head torch. It can be great to combine your stay with canoeing or paddle-boarding, but there are rules you should follow.

Permission: Check before you go whether it is in fact legal to wild camp wherever you intend to go. It is likely that in England, Wales and Ireland someone will own that piece of land, so you should seek permission from the landowner before you go. In Scotland, you can wild camp in many areas so long as you are away from dwellings and roads, but in some areas, you may still need permission, so do your research before you go. For the latest details of the Scottish Outdoor Access Code see outdooraccess-scotland.scot. The Mountaineering Council of Scotland has helpful guidelines for wild camping whether you intend to do it in Scotland or elsewhere: mountaineering.scot.

Leave no trace: Stay just one night at each location to reduce disturbing it – pitch late and leave early in a way that no one can tell you've been there. Once you've packed everything away and are about to leave, do one last slow survey of the site to check for anything you may have missed, such as tent pegs and litter – make sure you take everything away with you.

Fire: Only light an open fire if it's permitted and safe to do so – many sites don't allow fires, so check before you go.

Minimize your presence: Camp in small groups, try to blend in with the landscape (e.g., take a subtle-coloured tent), keep noise levels down and reduce the use of lights so wildlife is disturbed as little as possible.

Campsites

Sleeping under canvas is by its nature low impact, but campsites can have an environmental footprint arising from on-site amenities and infrastructure, such as the lighting, heating and maintenance of shower blocks. The greenest campsites use alternative energy to provide electricity and heating for the hot water, provide recycling bins for plastic, paper, card, tins and glass, and compost bins for organic matter. Some even provide discounts if you arrive by public transport. Many campsites on farms provide essentials, such as milk, bread and eggs, and some might even have a farm shop selling local produce.

Trailblazer: Abbey Home Farm, Cirencester, Gloucestershire

A family-friendly organic farm campsite where you can camp in a car-free field with basic amenities (compost loos and cold tap water) and views across the Cotswolds, or stay in a yurt camp (great for groups), a shepherd's hut or a stone cottage. It's a 5-minute stroll through the woods to the onsite farm shop and café, and there are lots of activities for children. Bus 881/855 runs from Kemble railway station to Cirencester from where it's a 40-minute walk or 10-minute cycle to the campsite (theorganicfarmshop.co.uk).

Delux den for two:
a hand-crafted yurt at
Mallinson's Woodland
Retreat, Devon

Glampsites

Glamorous campsites cover a wide range of accommodation, from canvas bell tents, tipis and yurts to more rigid structures, such as rustic log cabins, pods, huts and treehouses. They typically provide more facilities than traditional turn-up-and-pitch campsites, and these inevitably draw more resources, such as electricity for lights and small kitchens, running water for showers, and fuel for hot water and heating. An increasing number of glampsites provide hot tubs, which can require a lot of energy to heat – wood-fired hot tubs are preferable, as long as the wood is sourced and gathered sustainably. The amount of energy required for small-scale operations can usually be supplied by simple alternative energy technologies such as photovoltaic panels, self-contained wood burners, biomass boilers that use sustainably sourced wood pellets, and thermal solar panels, so many glampsites can run effectively off the grid.

Trailblazer: Penhein, Monmouthshire

Splendid isolation in a secluded woodland 850ft (260m) high on a 450-acre (182-ha) farm in the heart of the Monmouthshire hills in South Wales – on a clear day you can see both Severn bridges and beyond to Bristol. There are just a handful of Persian high-domed tents each with its own loo, kitchen, wood-burning stove and shower, and the owners have ensured sustainability runs right through the site's day-to-day operations, from the local crafting of the tents to the spring-fed filtered water (**penhein.co.uk**).

Bed & breakfasts

If glampsites are about back-to-nature luxury, then B&Bs are about a decent bed for the night and a breakfast to set you up for the day. The popularity and convenience of Airbnb and online DIY home-sharing sites, such as Homestay, Vrbo, and Plum Guide, has forced many owner-managed B&Bs to put greater emphasis on promoting the personalization of their homely service and, of course, their stellar breakfasts. The greenest will tell you the names of the local businesses they source their breakfast ingredients from and provide vegetarian and vegan options. As B&Bs are, by definition, run by live-in owners, many provide home-made jams, preserves and bread and can give you invaluable tips about the best local pubs and restaurants, and what to do locally.

Trailblazer: Milden Hall, Suffolk

A farmhouse B&B on a seventh-generation 500-year-old working farm that takes a holistic approach to farming and conservation. There are rooms in the main house for up to six, plus you can go self-catering in a glorious sixteenth-century Tudor barn, which sleeps up to 23, or in the Old Brooder – a 20-bed modern bunkhouse with oak beds and colourful kantha bedspreads. Sustainability runs through all its operations – energy is solar and sustainable timber-powered – and it runs a range of creative art weeks and group activities for children, including a science and natural history day. There are 20 bikes available to borrow and guests

Self-catering

The single largest draw on energy at self-catering cottages is likely to be for the provision of central heating and hot water, and the greenest places supply this through their own alternative energy systems, such as solar thermal, biomass or geothermal and ground-source heating, and they either provide their own electricity from wind turbines or photovoltaic panels or they buy it in from renewable energy suppliers, such as Bulb, Good Energy, Octopus and Ecotricity. Swimming pools require a lot of maintenance, but even these can be run in a greener fashion, for example by using salt water instead of chlorine and using alternative energies to heat the water. As for the interior, a growing number of self-catering places are using recycled or second-hand furniture and implementing certified Cradle-to-Cradle products, from toiletries to flooring, water bottles and window treatments.

Trailblazer: Wheatland Farm, Devon

Four eco lodges and a cottage on a wildlife-rich nature reserve in beautiful central Devon, close to the Tarka Trail, the Granite Way, Dartmoor and North Devon's beaches. The idea is that the income from your stay funds the conservation of the nature reserve – the owners use traditional management techniques in consultation with Natural England and the Devon Wildlife Trust and one-third of the farm, Popehouse Moor, is a Site of Special Scientific Interest for its culm grassland habitats and rare plants and animals. The farm has a a swimmable wildlife pond, a tree plantation and fields for you to explore. Bikes are available to borrow, plus electric bikes can be hired (**wheatlandfarm.co.uk**).

Bothies & refuges

Bothies are typically small, stone buildings, such as former shepherd's dwellings, that are temporary shelters for walkers in remote, mostly hilly areas. There is usually just a roof, four walls, a dry floor and few – if any – facilities: no beds, lights, running water or electricity, though many are equipped with fireplaces (fuel is not always provided). In the UK, there are about a hundred bothies, mostly in mountainous areas of Scotland, though there are a few in out-of-the-way places in the north of England and in some of the mountainous areas of Wales.

The Mountain Bothy Association (mountainbothies. org.uk), a charity that was founded in 1965, manages the UK's bothies (its website pinpoints their location on an OS map and provides a grid reference). Other than Over Phawhope in Southern Scotland and Glenpean in the Western Highlands of Scotland, the MBA doesn't own the bothies; they are 'fostered' through the encouragement of their owners; any renovation work on the bothies is usually financed through membership subscriptions or donations, and is carried out by volunteers.

There are other kinds of refuges, shacks and shelters in Europe run by individual organizations in each country; some are not as well maintained as those in the UK while others are more like designer cabins and have many more facilities, so do check before you go what you're likely to find. Here are some of the most popular organizations and resources that can help you find low-impact refuges in rural areas of Europe:

FRANCE: Over the last decade, the French Federation of Alpine and Mountain Clubs has been renovating many of mountain shelters, adding solar photovoltaic and solar thermal panels as well as wind turbines. You can book many of these through its website (ffcam.fr), although those on the Tour du Mont Blanc have to be booked on the site montblanc.ffcam.fr. The website of Gîte d'étape et Refuges (gites-refuges.com) lists 4,000 places to stay in mountain areas throughout France, aimed at hikers, mountaineers, skiers, cyclists, canoeists and horse-riders. The Gîte de France website (gites-de-france.com) includes over 170 gîtes that have earned the Gîte Panda label, which is given to owners, mainly in regional or national parks, who have committed to protecting their local area and provide guests with educational packs to help you observe local flora and fauna.

White Laggan bothy in the Galloway Hills, Scotland

SPAIN: In the north of Spain there are several networks of refuges: for the 30 mountain refuges in Andorra, see: visitandorra.com; for the small collection of refuges in the Picos de Europa, see reservarefugios.com; in Asturias, see fempa.net/refugios; in Catalonia, you can book high mountain refuges via the website of the Centre Excursionista de Catalunya (cec.cat). In the south, the mountaineering agency Spanish Highs is an excellent resource for information about mountain huts, shelters and refuges in the Sierra Nevada (spanishhighs.co.uk).

ITALY: There are nearly 3,000 alpine huts and refuges listed on the Italian website rifugi-bivacchi.com, which was set up by Giuseppe 'Popi' Miotti, a mountaineer, alpine guide and journalist. The site includes huts on other Alpine countries as well as on the Mediterranean islands of Sardinia and Sicily.

THE ALPS: Across the Eastern Alps of Austria, Germany, Italy and Switzerland, there are more than 1,000 huts that belong to a various Alpine Associations as well as private owners. The CAA-Club Arc Alpin is an umbrella organsation of the following 8 mountaineering associations, coordinating work on nature protection and planning in the Alps: alpenverein.it, cai.it, ffcam.fr, alpenverein.de, alpenverein.li, alpenverein.at, pzs.si and sac-cas.ch. In Austria, the Austrian Alpine Club provides members with reduction in bed charges in all their huts as well as those operated by the German Alpine Club. Across the Julian Alps in Slovenia, the Alpine Association of Slovenia manages about 180 huts, shelters and refuges, see en.pzs.si. There are over 200 mountain lodges and huts along the Via Dinarica, a series of long-distance trails across the Dinaric Alps from Slovenia to Albania through Croatia, Bosnia and Herzegovina and Montenegro (viadinarica.com).

Trailblazer: Mountain Bug

Qualified International Mountain Leaders Robert and Emma Mason have over 18 years of experience guiding and arranging mountain holidays. They now specialize in guiding in the mountains of the French and Spanish Pyrenees, including the Cathar region of the Eastern Pyrenees. Their trips are designed to reach the wildest and most beautiful parts of the mountains without leaving any trace. Some of the more intrepid trips include staying overnight in mountain refuges, which have communal dormitories or sleeping platforms. They guide low-impact holidays all year round for all abilities: hiking, cycling, and canyoning in the summer, and alternative winter sports, such as snowshoeing and ski-touring, in the winter (**mountainbug.com**).

NORDIC COUNTRIES: There are 550 cabins on foot and ski trails operated by the Norwegian Trekking Association across a network of about 13.5 miles (22,000km) of marked foot trails and about 4.5 miles (7,000km) of branch-marked ski tracks (english.dnt.no). The Swedish Tourist Association runs simple mountain cabins spaced 6–12 miles (10–20km) apart along skiing and walking trails (swedishtouristassociation.com). In Finland, there's a large network of 'open wilderness huts' mostly in the northern and eastern parts of the country (nationalparks.fi/huts).

Mountain huts in Europe

outdooractive.com lists thousands of mountain huts and refuges across Europe, from simple shelters to serviced cabins. mountainhuts.info features over 670 mountains huts in central Europe, and gives hut reviews based on the experience of hikers who have stayed there.

Hostels, cabins & bunkhouses

Hostels have come a long way from rickety bunks and daily chores – the modern hostel has comfortable beds and smart linen, bathrooms, a licensed bar and menus of locally inspired, seasonal food. In addition to spacious shared dorms, many have private, double and family rooms – basic but clean – and an increasing number have campsites where you can bring your own tent or stay in a tipi, bell tent, pod, safari tent, shepherd's hut or Airstream for a fraction of the price of an upmarket glampsite. Most hostels are geared up for walkers and cyclists and provide plenty of leaflets, maps and guidebooks on local routes, and many provide facilities for cyclists, such as safe-storage and overnight drying rooms.

Hostels are also no longer just for 'youths'. Although it still goes by its original name, the Youth Hostel Association of England and Wales (YHA) caters for people of all ages, from schools to backpackers, couples and families. So too do the many independent hostels that are popping up all over the country in stunning locations, many of which can be found via the Independent Hostels Guide network – an eclectic range of independently run hostels, bunkhouses and camping barns across England, Wales and Scotland. The network has a dedicated section on its website listing those hostels that are particularly eco-friendly (independenthostels.co.uk/eco-hostels). Another excellent resource is Kash Bhattacharya's website budgettraveller.org, which has a wealth of information on hostels based on ten years of his travels to budget accommodation worldwide. Both the main directories for hostels also feature eco hostels: hostelworld.com and hostelbookers.com.

Trailblazer:
Lazy Duck, Inverness-shire

Owners Phil and Sarah are breathing new life into three off-grid cabins, a safari tent and bunkhouse in the heart of the Cairngorms National Park. The site was run for 20 years by David and Valery who made this eco haven a bit special. Spread over 6 acres (2.4ha) there are wood-fired hot tubs and sauna, as well as yoga and massage in the wellbeing studio. Don't miss the hamper of homegrown goodies, including bread, eggs, granola, and veg and salad from their garden (lazyduck.co.uk).

Lazy Duck's Woodman's Hut in a centuries-old Scots Pine Forest

Hotels

As with self-catering accommodation, central heating and hot water are likely to be the largest draw on a hotel's energy supply, and particularly laundry services. The average carbon emissions of a UK hotel is 31.1kg CO2 per room night, according to the Hotel Carbon Measurement Initiative (HCMI). Hotels that have large-scale electricity generating systems can, during times of reduced demand, generate more electricity than they need and feed it into the grid for others to use.

The carbon footprint of Battlesteads, a family-run hotel and restaurant near Hexham, is just 4.9kg CO2 per room night thanks to the owners installing a biomass heating and hot water system that uses sustainable fuel from forestry only a mile away, and whose surplus heat is used to heat two polytunnels that provide fresh fruit and vegetables for the kitchen through the year (battlesteads.com).

Finding green places to stay

Increasingly accommodation websites group green businesses in collections, such as 'Eco-retreats' (**coolplaces.co.uk**), 'Eco Stays' (**hostunusual.com**), 'Eco' (**i-escape.com**), 'Eco-Houses' (**oneoffplaces.co.uk**), 'Eco Friendly' (**coolstays.com**), and 'Sustainable Spaces' (**canopyandstars.co.uk**). Some provide filters for green facilities, such as 'electric vehicle charging station' (**booking.com**), 'accessible by public transport' (**sawdays.co.uk**), and 'vegetarian-friendly' (**goodhotelguide.com**). Several websites specialize in green accommodation, providing details about the businesses' eco credentials:

- biostays.com
- bookdifferent.com
- bouteco.co
- ecobnb.com
- ecohotels.com
- greenpearls.com
- myecostay.eu
- organicholidays.com

Trailblazer
The Scarlet Hotel, Cornwall

Pool with a view: the natural swimming pool and wood-fired hot tub at The Scarlet Hotel

The Scarlet Hotel sets the standard for small, luxury hotels in the UK. All of the heat for the 37-bed hotel comes from a biomass boiler, which is run on wood pellets from a local company. Solar panels are used to heat the indoor pool, with any excess used to top up the boiler, while the air-to-air heat exchanger uses heat from air being expelled to heat the fresh air being drawn in from outside. The rooms are well-insulated, using a combination of hardboard and mineral wool, and there is comprehensive recycling of glass, plastics, cans, paper and cooking oil, and a variety of water-saving devices ranging from a blending valve to aerators that regulate water usage to irrigate the sea-thrift roofing, wash cars and rinse wetsuits and other outdoor equipment (scarlethotel.co.uk).

How to know if a hotel is genuinely green

Thankfully, a rapidly increasing number of hoteliers are going to great lengths to reduce the impact of their business on the environment, reduce or even eliminate their carbon emissions, maximize the conservation of local biodiversity, and play a contributing role in safeguarding the culture and livelihoods of their local communities. Sustainability is at the heart of these businesses. Unfortunately, there are also lots of unscrupulous businesses that are jumping on the 'eco' marketing bandwagon, and it can be difficult to tell the 'green' from the 'greenwash'. Here are a few questions to help steer you in the direction of those hotels where the owners are going the extra mile to help you sleep green.

The website

As a first port of call, check the hotel's website to see if they address these questions; there may be a formal document set out as a 'green policy' – the best hotels include this information embedded throughout all their messaging, not just tucked away in one section. For instance, in the 'Rooms' section, they'll mention their recycling facilities; in the food section, they show you where and how to buy local, seasonal food; and on the 'How to find us' page, they will show how to travel there by public transport and won't just assume you'll fly or drive. Some may have a Green Guest charter that provides information on how you can be a greener visitor while staying at their property. They may also include logos of ecolabel certification schemes that

have inspected their green credentials (see Ecolabels and certification schemes, pp64–67). Bear in mind it often costs businesses quite a lot of time and money to go through the certification process, so many genuinely green places, especially small hotels, may not have the funds or the inclination to do this, so don't judge a business purely on whether or not they have an ecolabel.

The building

Does the building fit into the local landscape? Is the siting and design of the building unobtrusive and sympathetic to the colours and aesthetics around it? Have they cleared trees, redirected water sources, or eliminated any other biodiverse habitat in order to build it? Keep an eye out for its Energy

The sensitive siting and design of Finca Can Marti, Ibiza

Performance Certificate, which shows
a) the overall energy efficiency of the building and
b) the overall environmental impact of the building in terms of CO_2 emissions. They are rated A–G, with the higher rating (A) the most efficient for energy and the least environmental impact.

The design

Has the hotel been designed in an environmentally sensitive fashion? Hoteliers are increasingly using the concept of biophilia to make their buildings' architecture and design be more in tune with nature, using natural lighting and ventilation, natural materials, including wood and stone, and natural landscaping in the form of living roofs and wildlife friendly outdoor spaces. You may also see examples of Slow Design aesthetics, which draws on the approach of the Slow Food Movement, slowing resource consumption and extending the value and life of products.

The rooms

Are they furnished with eco interiors? Do they use second-hand and/or upcycled furniture? Is the bedding and linen organic cotton? Is there natural air-conditioning? If they do have air conditioning, do they provide clear instructions on how to reduce your draw on energy and encourage you to turn it off when you leave the room?

Chemicals

Have they reduced or eliminated the use of less volatile compounds (VOCs) throughout the building? Have they used natural, mineral, breathable paints and oils; do they use chemical-free alternatives to phosphates; do they use natural control methods for their garden instead of herbicides and pesticides? Do they use a chlorine-free agent for cleaning the swimming pool or have a natural swimming pool? Eco-labelled products with third party certifications, such as the EU Ecolabel, Nature Plus, NF, The Nordic Swan Ecolabel, and the Blue Angel can help determine if the cleaning chemical is eco-friendly.

Energy sources

Do they utilize solar gain and/or alternatives to fossil fuels for their heating and electricity supplies? Do they have ground-source heat pumps/ geothermal, biomass boilers or solar thermal panels for heating, and/or photo-voltaic panels or wind turbines for generating electricity? If not, is their electricity supply from a utility provider that sources its electricity from renewable sources? Do they have wood burners using wood from sustainable sources or from their own land?

Energy use

How do they reduce their draw on energy? How well insulated is the building? Are their appliances, such as fridges and kettles, A-rated or better? Do they set targets for how much less energy they use over time? Do they use low-energy lightbulbs, have motion sensors for lighting in corridors and/or toilet/ shower blocks and encourage you to turn off standby button.

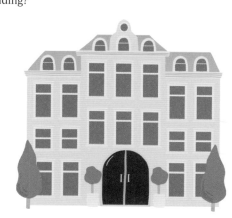

Waste

How do they minimize the amount of waste they send to landfill? Do they encourage you to follow the three Rs: 'reduce, reuse, recycle'? Do they encourage you to bring refillable water bottles/ coffee cups and reusable bags for shopping? Do they provide recycling bins for guests, and if so, are they separated into: plastic; paper and magazines; card; aluminium; and glass? Are they free of single-use plastic, such as straws and cups? Do they have bulk dispensers instead of miniatures for toiletries, bathroom soaps and shampoo? Do they provide organic toiletries, use green suppliers, such as Who Gives a Crap, and support zero waste campaigns such as Guardians of Grub? Do they provide separate bins for food compost, such as vegetables peelings?

Water

How do they reduce their consumption of water? Do they meter and monitor their water supply? Do they have low-flow water savers in cisterns, flow restrictors in showerheads and taps? How do they reduce the amount of washing (do they encourage you to reuse towels and sheets to save laundry)? Do they harvest rainwater for use in toilets and/or the garden? Do they recycle their grey water (water used in sinks, dishwashers, showers and bath), which can be cleaned and plumbed back into toilets, washing machines and outside taps? Water conservation is particularly important in hotter Mediterranean countries where large-scale tourism development has been a major contribution to the degradation and destruction of water ecosystems with river courses being fragmented, groundwater levels sinking and wetlands drying out.

Locally grown fruit and veg on sale at a farm shop in Wiltshire

Food

How much of the food they provide and/or serve is sourced locally? Do they provide local and/or seasonal and/or organic food? This both supports the local economy and reduces food miles. Do they offer vegan and/or vegetarian food? It's worth checking what they mean by 'local' ... do they give figures in metres or miles or counties? It's often a good indication as to how genuine their local procurement is if they give the actual names of the local businesses (and their geographical location) that they source their products from. Do they provide information on the timings and location of nearby farmers' markets, as well information on local farm shops, village stores, pubs and cafés, particularly those specializing in local, home-grown or freshly caught produce.

Low-carbon travel

Do they actively encourage guests to arrive on foot, by bike and by public transport? Do they provide information for guests on how to arrive by bike and/or public transport and provide transfers from the nearest railway station/bus stop? Even better, do they offer a discount for guests arriving on foot, by bike or by public transport? Do they provide high-speed chargers for electric cars (check that the electricity is from a renewable energy source) and information on local charging networks? Do they provide standard and/or electric bikes for you to use?

Employment

How many of the owners/employees are local? Are the owners local and if so, do they own or have shares or some sort of ownership in the business, or are they merely managing the business (and providing profits) for someone far away? Do they employ people from the local community, and do they train them? Do they provide information about their social and cultural impacts?

Wildlife

Do they actively encourage the conservation of biodiversity? Are their gardens wildlife-friendly, attracting bees, butterflies and other indicator species (without using insecticides or artificial fertilizers)? Do they plant native flora? Do they weed by hand, rather than using weedkillers? Do they reduce light pollution at night? Do they contribute financially or otherwise to local wildlife charities or community groups?

People power

Even though a hotel may not look like it is doing much for the environment, it may be doing some of the important large-scale changes behind the scenes. However, if you feel a hotel's green claims are dubious; for instance, the absence of any recycling facilities whatsoever or the blatant

Hoteliers are increasingly using the concept of biophilia to make their buildings' architecture and design be more in tune with nature

over-use of energy and water, it is worth pointing out what you have seen in the feedback form, on social media or on review sites following your stay. These kinds of observations are an important signal to the hotel that visitors are increasingly interested in their commitment to low carbon living, biodiversity and the use of local resources.

The little things

Sometimes it's the little touches that can help signal the owner's heartfelt commitment to the environment and local community, such as providing jugs of water and home-grown wildflowers on the table; the upcycling of things like flowerpots in the garden; a logbook for documenting wildlife. Penhein glampsite in Monmouthshire (see p46), asks guests to leave behind any full tins of food that they don't want to take home, so that they can donate them to a local food bank.

How to be a greener guest

Camping

Use compostable or recyclable cooking and eating equipment.

Use environmentally friendly washing products.

Use a large water container that can be refilled on site, rather than buying lots of plastic bottles of water.

If you're taking extra supplies of toilet roll, check whether campsite requires it to be biodegradable, and buy from ethical suppliers, such as uk.whogivesacrap.org

Check if the campsite allows open fires and if it does, use designated fire pits if available (or take your own), and avoid disposable barbecues.

Sort your rubbish and put it in relevant recycling bins on site before you leave.

If you have camping gear that you no longer need, rather than sending it to landfill, consider sending it to organizations such as Gift Your Gear and the Continuum Project, or share it on Freecycle.

Bothies

The Bothy Code requests that you leave the bothy as you would hope to find it, clean and tidy with dry kindling for the next visitors (who may arrive in foul weather and need the warmth of a fire as soon as possible). Make sure that watercourses are not polluted and that you don't cut firewood from living trees, adhere to the estate's restrictions on use of the bothy, for example during stag stalking or at lambing time, and respect the restriction on numbers – groups of six or more should not use bothies to ensure that there is room for any walker relying on the shelter provided by the bothy.

Self-catering

It's all too easy to forget about what food you're going to need for a self-catering break until the last moment, at which point you make an emergency dash to the nearest supermarket, buy everything in bulk, and then end up throwing the surplus food and associated packaging in the bin at the end of the week. Far better to plan ahead and buy fresh, seasonal food, or order it from a local supplier who can deliver it to you before you reach your accommodation. Increasingly farm shops are providing local delivery services – there's a handy guide to over 8,800 farm shops across the UK at bigbarn.co.uk – places such as the Loch Arthur Farm Shop in Dumfries and Galloway, that pride themselves on the quality of artisan food. Online marketplaces such as magaroo.com can help you find local independent businesses, while local veg box schemes provide a new revenue stream for independent growers and producers, and reduce the need for single-use plastics. There are an increasing number who enable you to order on a one-off basis, so if you don't ordinarily have an order for your home, you can still order a box for your self-catering break. Schemes that offer one-off use and deliver nationwide include Eversfield Organic, Boxxfresh, Riverford Organic Farmers, Abel & Cole, Pikt and The Veg Box Company, but there may well be local schemes, such as localfooddirect.co.uk, which delivers fresh, local and ethically sourced food across Somerset, shropshiresown.co.uk, which delivers throughout Shropshire, and food4myholiday.com, a family-run service specifically for self-catering guests in Cornwall and West Devon.

Hotels

On entering the room, read the information pack to understand how you can support the hotel's eco initiatives, for example, by preventing your laundry from being washed every day or making sure you sort your rubbish in accordance with the hotel's recycling scheme. Also, look out for any tips on how you can support the local economy, such as where you can eat locally. Turn off the air-conditioning unit/heating or adjust it to a sensible temperature: personal preferences vary, but generally somewhere between 21 and 23°C (70–74°F) is comfortable for most.

On leaving the room, turn off the air-con, heating or other electric devices that are on standby if the hotel hasn't given you a key card that does this automatically.

On check out, give your hotel feedback on how eco-friendly you think it is; if you think it could do more, encourage the hotel to go greener in the future.

Sustainable food & drink

Feasting on local, seasonal food washed down with the local tipple conveys a sense of place better than any travel brochure. It's also one of the most effective ways to keep your carbon emissions down. There can be a surprising number of hidden emissions embedded within the provenance of food and drink, especially when it is shipped, or worse, flown in from overseas. Over 25 per cent of all greenhouse gases are based on the food industry. Whether it's freshly baked bread for breakfast, salad from the kitchen garden for lunch, or the catch of the day for dinner – choosing local isn't just good for the planet, it's also enjoyable and a great way to put money into the local community.

Be aware that the term 'local' can be used disingenuously: I've seen it used to describe a radius of hundreds of miles, stretching the concept to render it virtually meaningless. It's best if the description of food includes the name and location of the local business. Prawn on the Lawn, a sustainable seafood restaurant in Padstow, Cornwall (prawnonthelawn.com), goes one step further and names the people behind their products, for example: 'Ross supplies us with veg, salad and herbs that he grows on his family's farm less than a mile from Padstow' and 'Johnny's a fifth-generation Padstow fisherman supplying the freshest crab and lobster from his day boat PW132. Look out for him popping into the restaurant in his oilskins.'

It is just as important to avoid food that comes from intensive farming, which has had a devastating environmental cost over the past 70 years. While yields have skyrocketed, fossil fuel-derived fertilizers and pesticides have polluted our air and waterways, wiping out many insects and wild plants, while other intensive farming practices have destroyed wildflower meadows, ponds and hedges up and down the land. Numbers of bees, butterflies and birds across the UK countryside have plummeted: in particular, hedgehogs, tree sparrows and turtle doves have all declined by over 90 per cent. Poor soil management has led to increasingly severe flooding and precious soil is being washed away at an alarming rate.

We should also avoid seafood from intensive fishing. According to the Marine Conservation Society (MCS), 90 per cent of world fish stocks are currently fully or overexploited, so it is vital to choose seafood from sustainable sources – whether that is fish that is farmed sustainably or caught in the wild sustainably. The MCS has produced a Good Fish Guide to help you choose sustainable fish by understanding three key things: where it was sourced; whether it was farmed or wild-caught; and how this was done, such as whether it was hand-gathered, dredged, bottom-trawled, mechanically harvested, caught by hook and line, or by a net. It also includes a handy guide to what is in season – the most unsustainable fish is red-rated.

Other organizations that can help point the way to more sustainable food and drink include:

Food Made Good is an initiative of the Sustainable Restaurant Association, which asseses restaurants on how sustainable they are, based on how they rate regarding three pillars:
Sourcing: using local and seasonal produce to support British business, reduce haulage costs and the environmental impact of transport; increasing the proportion of veg-led dishes to combat environmental damage and purchasing high welfare meat and dairy products; supporting global farmers by sourcing fairly traded produce to ensure farmers in the developing world have access to a trade system based on justice and fairness.
Society: providing equal opportunities, training and policies to keep employees happy and productive; engaging with the local community; offering balanced menu options, reasonable portions and healthy cooking options to cater for customers' needs.
Environment: improving energy efficiency and managing water usage; reducing food wastage and eliminating waste that goes to landfill.

It awards three stars to the best, such as: Lussmans in Hertfordshire, St Albans, Harpenden and Hitchin; Where The Light Gets In (WTLGI) in Stockport; and BuJo Burger Joint in Ireland. The food served on Eurostar is also three-star rated. One of my favourite three-star restaurants overseas is at Hôtel les Orangeries in Lussac-les-Châteaux, just south of Poitiers, France, which designs dishes using edible flowers, wild herbs and oils for flavourings supplied from a local garden.

Pasture for Life is a certification scheme for meat and dairy that comes from animals raised only on grass and pasture (pastureforlife.org).

The menu at Prawn on the Lawn, Cornwall, names the people behind their products

Marine Stewardship Council (MSC) has a blue fish label for those products that come from well-managed, sustainable fisheries. Over 150 fish and chip shops in the UK have this label, including Rockfish in Brixham, Devon, and Cod's Scallop in Nottingham, so too do several chippies that operate out of mobile vans, such as The Whitby Fish and Chips Company and Kingfisher On The Go in Plymouth (msc.org).

Farm Wilder selects and labels produce from farms where wildlife still thrives – birds such as cuckoos that have vanished from much of Britain, or rare butterflies like the marsh fritillary. It works with charities including Butterfly Conservation, The Wildlife Trusts, RSPB and the Farming and Wildlife Advisory Group to help these farmers nurture endangered species, restore biodiversity and farm more sustainably (farmwilder.org).

Soil Association is a British charity that campaigns on a range of issues related to the way we eat, farm and care for the natural world (soilassociation.org).

Could this café be a glimpse of the future? Insects can be a wonderful source of protein and it's thought they could be used as a food source for the world's growing population. Grub Kitchen is based on a 300-year-old farm that is also home to an invertebrate zoo, wildlife walks and guided bug safaris. After becoming more familiar with the world of insects, feast on dishes such as a 'cricket falafels', 'black ant and olive crusted goat cheese', and 'smoked chipotle cricket' (**grubkitchen.co.uk**).

Local food tours

Connecting with a local guide to show you around is a great way to get to know the local food scene, especially in cities where the breadth of choice can be bewildering. They can take you to the lesser-known places that serve local signature dishes based on age-old recipes that the locals swear by. There are several websites that can point you to local food tours, such as **spottedbylocals.com**, **toursbylocals.com**, Airbnb (select the 'Food and drink' filter in its 'Experiences' section), and **culinarybackstreets.com**, which specializes in culinary food tours in several European cities, such as Lisbon, Porto, Naples, Barcelona and Marseille.

One of my favourite foodie tours was with Alternative Athens, a half-day tour to the best street food stalls and the shops of heartfelt producers in the Greek capital, where I was given a wide range of fabulous tastings of the city's vibrant food scene including an oregano-perfumed pork souvlaki and a nut-packed baklava oozing with honey (**alternativeathens.com**).

An award-winning range of ketchups, mayos and relishes, sold nationwide, made from ingredients that would otherwise have been wasted because they're the wrong shape, size or colour, from over-ripe bananas to curly cucumbers and other 'wonky' veg (**rubiesintherubble.com**).

Sustainable wine

The UK now has a sophisticated wine scene with hundreds of vineyards producing all manner of wines, from award-winning sparkling whites to velvety reds. Keep an eye out for the Sustainable Wines of Great Britain label awarded to those producers that promote biodiversity on their vineyards, manage them sustainably with minimum pesticides and fertilizers, and reduce water- and non-renewable energy consumption (**winegb.co.uk**). Natural wine is made from organically farmed grapes that have been grown using permaculture practices; crucially, it is made without adding or removing anything during the wine-making process, both in the vineyard and in the winery (**rawwine.com**).

Booking green holidays

While it's perfectly possible to book all elements of a holiday yourself, if you'd like to draw on the knowledge, experience, and protection of booking through a travel company, here is a selection of booking platforms, travel agencies and tour operators – as well as curated collections and advisories – that specialize in green travel and positive impact holidays:

Adventure Alternative was founded by British mountaineer Gavin Bate in 2001 and specializes in adventure travel, including climbing expeditions, trekking holidays, school trips abroad and charity treks (adventurealternative.com).

Byway is an online travel agent that organizes and sells flight-free holidays in the UK and Europe (byway.travel).

Earth Changers is a travel advisory that showcases positive impact holidays worldwide (earth-changers.com).

Exodus Travels (exodus.co.uk) and **Explore!** (explore.co.uk) have for decades led the way in the UK running small group adventure tours worldwide. Both focus on low impact adventures led by experienced guides, often using small, locally owned accommodation.

G Adventures and **Intrepid** are the two largest adventure tour operators that have done a lot to run their operations sustainably and share best practice with the industry. G Adventures (gadventures.com) also runs the non-profit 'Planeterra', funding projects in social enterprise, healthcare, conservation and emergency response (planeterra.org), while Intrepid (intrepidtravel.com) is certified by B Corp ensuring that it is committed to balancing profit and purpose.

Much Better Adventures is an online platform that sells low-impact small group adventure holidays worldwide (muchbetteradventures.com).

Inntravel specializes in self-guided walking, cycling and activity holidays in the UK and Europe (inntravel.com).

Natural Britain sells a range of low-impact travel experiences in Britain (natural-britain.com).

Nature Travels runs ecotourism holidays in Sweden, Finland and Norway (naturetravels.co.uk).

Pura Aventura, sells positive impact holidays in Spain, Portugal and Latin America (pura-aventura.com).

Steppes Travel runs adventure holidays that support women's empowerment and wildlife conservation (steppestravel.com).

Sunvil is a London-based operator that has been an advocate of sustainable tourism for over 40 years (sunvil.co.uk)

Travel Matters organizes family holidays that focus on conservation and local communities (travelmatters.co.uk).

Undiscovered Mountains specializes in sustainable activity breaks in the Alps and Norway (undiscoveredmountains.com).

Wild Europe Travel specializes in flight-free travel to Europe's wild places (wildeuropetravel.com).

Wilderness Group runs small group active and adventure holidays across the UK and Ireland (wildernessgroup.co.uk).

Others:
- Expertafrica.com
- Joroexperiences.com
- Justice.travel
- Kynder.net
- Niarratravel.com
- Regenerativetravel.com
- Theblueyonder.com
- Travellingwhale.com
- Tribes.co.uk
- Upnorway.com
- Urbanadventures.com
- Wildfrontierstravel.com

What to pack

Travelling light is the greenest way to go: it reduces the chances of having to dispose of items; it makes it much easier to travel around, especially on foot, by bike or on public transport; and it's more fuel efficient – especially noticeable if you're travelling in an electric car. A useful device for packing economically is to consider the three Rs:

Reduce: What can I get away with not taking; are there items that can double up for several uses?
Reuse: What can I take that I can reuse over and over again?
Recycle: What can I take that can be recycled once I've finished using it?

Refill

City to Sea, an environmental organisation on a mission to stop plastic pollution, has produced a handy app (**refill.org.uk**) to help you locate:

● over 400 local refill schemes across the UK
● refill stations where you can refill water bottles
● places with discounts if you bring your own cup
● eateries where you can take your own lunchbox
● shops selling refills of groceries, toiletries, etc.

Five essential items for plastic-free travel

The problem with single-use plastics, such as plastic straws and inflatable toys, is that they break down over time into the tiny microplastics that we're already seeing consumed by marine wildlife, both on land and in the ocean. These microplastics not only kill wildlife, but they then enter the food chain and ultimately cause serious health issues for humans. According to the World Wide Fund for Nature, without action, by 2050 there could be more plastic in the sea than fish. Here are five reusable items that you can easily pack in your luggage to reduce the use of single-use plastic:

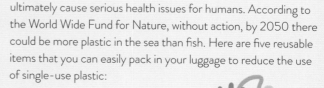

|  | |  |  | |

Water bottle
Fill it up from refill stations or from the water supply in your hostel/B&B/hotel room so you don't have to buy plastic water bottles each time you want a drink.

Coffee cup
Take on train, coach and car journeys so you have it to hand when you stop at a service station or pop into a coffee shop – some offer a discount if you provide your own cup.

Food container
Pack in your daysack for storing food to take on a walk or to the beach, or for taking to street food stalls and festivals – ideally with your own reusable or compostable cutlery.

Toiletries container
Pop all your toiletries into a single container, including a bottle of shampoo and shower gel (or even better, a bar of shampoo/soap) to avoid having to use mini toiletries.

Shopping bag
Keep one handy (ideally with handles) not just as a replacement for buying a plastic bag at a supermarket, but also when you're out buying food and groceries at a local market.

Kit with a conscience

Search online for 'ethical outdoor clothing' and there will be dozens of options showing you how get more of an ethical bang for your buck. Look for products made with renewable energy, certified organic and natural fabrics, that have used as little chemical intervention as possible, are packaged with biodegradable/recyclable material, and are listed in ethical directories, such as on ethicalconsumer.org and thegoodshoppingguide.com. Keep an eye out for the following labels, certification schemes and common terms associated with ethical outdoor gear:

B Corp is a certification system for businesses that commit legally to balance profit with purpose.
Bluesign is a certification system for the manufacturing process and supply chain of sustainable textiles, approving products that are safe for the environment, workers and customers.
Earth Positive is a label for organic clothing manufactured solely using sustainable energy from wind and solar power.
Fair Wear Foundation works with brands within the textile industry to ensure fair pay and conditions for workers in garment factories.
Global Organic Textile Standard sets a range of criteria including the harvesting of the raw materials and environmentally and socially responsible manufacturing, as well as standards for labelling organic textiles.
1% for the Planet is a network of businesses worldwide that donate 1 per cent or more of sales (or for individuals, 1 per cent of their salary) to environmental projects.
STANDARD 100 by OEKO-TEX® is a worldwide certification system that tests textiles for harmful substances.

'PETA-approved vegan' label highlights clothing, accessories, furniture, and home décor items made of vegan alternatives to animal-derived materials such as leather, fur, silk, feathers or bone.
PFC-free means products that are free from man-made per- or poly-fluorinated chemicals that accumulate in soil, rivers, drinking water, and in the bodies of humans and wildlife and can lead to adverse human health effects.
Responsible Down Standard (RDS) is a standard created by North Face in partnership with Textile Exchange and Control Union Certifications to safeguard the welfare of birds used for down and feathers, from farm to finished garment.
Textile Exchange Organic Content Standard verifies that a product contains organically grown material.

Packing for camping

Tips for upcycling, reusing and recycling kit for camping:

Dental floss has several other uses: it's great for hanging up light clothing (it's amazing how strong it is) and it's also useful for dividing up food, such as cheese or sponge cakes, if you've mislaid the knife.
A tarpaulin is great in a sudden rain shower, to put over tables, chairs and logs, and can also act as a handy shade from the sun.
Kids' school lunch boxes are handy beach cool boxes – and don't forget to pack a freeze block to keep sandwiches cool.

A dry bag is useful not just to keep phones, wallets, etc. from getting wet, but also to prevent wet things, like swimming kit, making everything else wet.
Old washing machine drums make great fire bowls – stand them on an old Christmas tree stand to keep them from burning the grass. Make sure you are allowed to have a fire – some campsites don't allow them.
Always take a multi-tool kit, such as a Swiss Army knife, not just for the knives, but for the tweezers for extracting ticks and the toothpick for getting out that annoying piece of apple stuck between your teeth.

Buy less, repair more

It's easy to be seduced into buying the next great piece of clothing or kit, but before you click on 'go to checkout', ask yourself whether you actually need new gear, or could your old belongings be repaired? The most sustainable products are actually those you already own. Prolonging the lifespan of what you have, keeping it out of landfill and doing what it was designed to do for as long as possible until it's finally worn out, will preserve resources, reduce chemical pollution and save unnecessary carbon emissions. Sometimes there are simple patches and fixes you can make yourself to rips and tears (see ifixit.com for tips on how to repair everyday items), but if you're unable to, several well-known outdoor brands now offer to repair and reproof damaged outdoor clothing and equipment you've brought from them, such as Alpkit, Berghaus, Cotswold Outdoor and Patagonia (make sure you keep your proof of purchase). There are also specialist repairers that can make good any outdoor clothing and equipment, from footwear to waterproof jackets, trousers and fleeces to sleeping bags, backpacks and even tents. Lancashire Sports Repairs (lancashiresportsrepairs.co.uk) repairs boots, outdoor clothing, sleeping bags and tents; Feet First (resoles.co.uk) mends outdoor footwear; Scottish Mountain Gear (scottishmountaingear.com) repairs clothing, tents and rucksacks; Mountaineering Designs (mountaineering-designs. co.uk) specializes in repairing down-filled clothing and sleeping bags.

Some gear you may want to buy new, such as safety equipment, or nearly new, such as waterproof outer garments, but there are lots of items of clothing and equipment that you can buy second-hand that will prolong the life of those items and save you some money. There are many places to find second-hand outdoor gear, such as the Outdoor Gear Exchange Group on Facebook Marketplace, on Freecycle, as well as on eBay and Amazon, and from brands that sell refurbished kit, such as Vango's Camping Recycled, North Face Renewed, and Arc'teryx Used Gear.

Once you've decided that you no longer have need for particular items of clothing or equipment, it's great to recycle your own kit, such as on Freecycle, by donating it directly to a homeless charity (especially warm jackets and sleeping bags), by giving it to Gift Your Gear (giftyourgear.com), which supports community organizations, youth groups and charities working with young people in the outdoors, or by giving it to the Continuum Project, which accepts outdoor clothing (outer layers, insulation layers, mid layers, base layer tops, as well as wetsuits) that it gives to people who need them, from homeless people to outdoor education establishments.

Winter green

Online trading company EcoSki vets winter gear for how it is manufactured and how suppliers are treated to help customers choose more ethical brands and products, limit unnecessary purchases (and waste) and keep all that hard-wearing kit in circulation for longer. In particular, they select kit that has non-toxic durable waterproof repellents and utilizes post-consumer waste, as part of four criteria: Repair, Rent, Preowned, or New 'kit with a conscience' that aims 'to provide a more positive step towards a circular solution' (ecoski.co.uk).

Ecolabels

Checking whether a business has been awarded an accredited certification scheme is one of the mechanisms that can help you figure out if it is walking the talk on its green initiatives. The most reliable schemes send a trained professional technician out to the business to assess its environmental performance, both in front of house and behind the scenes. Some focus on particular technical aspects, while others grade the business based on a whole gamut of environmental and social responsibility, including waste management, biodiversity conservation and human rights of workers' conditions. Here are some well-established schemes you're most likely to come across when looking for a green holiday.

United Kingdom

BREEAM (Building Research Establishment Environmental Assessment Method) evaluates all aspects of a building's sustainability, from the initial siting and design, to how they are used in the context of local environmental, social and economic issues. It can be applied to individual buildings, such as the Gibson Hotel in the centre of Dublin, to multi-use developments, such as Kings Place on the Regents Canal in London, and to whole neighbourhoods, such as Tivoli GreenCity in Belgium (breeam.com).

David Bellamy Blooming Marvellous Pledge for Nature builds on the David Bellamy Conservation Award (set up in 1997 by the British Holiday & Home Parks Association and the late botanist, presenter and environmental campaigner David Bellamy, which certified holiday parks in Britain) that requires parks to pledge to protect wildlife and to commit to starting at least one of five projects to help nature, from protecting at-risk species to boosting the wildlife value of their ponds and other fresh-water habitats (ukparks.com/bellamy-awards).

Greener Camping Club is a symbol for low impact campsites. The scheme was started by four campsite owners who wanted to bring together a resource for campsites that 'share a common theme of high quality, environment-friendly camping, in truly beautiful settings.' They started the scheme in Pembrokeshire but are now expanding throughout Wales and England. There are now over 75 campsites, most are in West Wales but the number of sites in England is growing all the time (greenercamping.org).

Green Tourism (green-tourism.com) is a sustainability grading scheme for the travel and hospitality industry that awards businesses bronze, silver and gold grades based on how green they perform in its audits. It also offers businesses practical technical advice on how to be greener. Examples of gold businesses are Fenham Farm – a B&B in Northumberland (fenhamfarm.co.uk), and the self-catering River Cabin at Trericket Mill in the Brecon Beacons (rivercabin.co.uk).

Guardians of Grub is a certification scheme for businesses that track, measure, save and report on wasted food (guardiansofgrub.com). It's run by the UK charity WRAP, which promotes and encourages sustainable resource use through product design, waste minimization, reuse, recycling and reprocessing of waste materials (wrap.org.uk).

The Environmental Quality Mark is a grading scheme focused on businesses in the Peak District and Staffordshire (eqm.org.uk).

Global Sustainable Tourism Council

The Global Sustainable Tourism Council (GSTC) is an independent accreditation scheme that has established international standards for sustainable tourism certification whose criteria are designed to be adapted to fit the context of local conditions and activities (gstcouncil.org).

Europe

Alpine Pearls is a network of 19 alpine villages in Austria, Germany, Italy, Slovenia, and Switzerland, that promote sustainable transport combined with eco-friendly outdoor adventure (alpine-pearls.com).

Bio Hotels certifies hotels for their commitment to sustainability (energy efficiency, recycling and plastic reduction), organic cuisine and 'natural body care' (biohotels.info).

Blue Swallow (you may see it in German: 'Blaue Schwalbe') is awarded by a German sustainability agency Fairkehr (fairkehr means 'fair return'). Since 1990, it has been singling out eco-friendly accommodation (many are family-run businesses) that provides wholefood, organic and regional fresh food (wirsindanderswo.de).

EU Ecolabel is a European-wide environmental label managed by the EU Commission for a range of industries, from manufacturing to hospitality, including hotels and campsites. An example of a business with the EU Ecolabel is the Bamboo Eco Hostel in Turin, Italy (ec.europa.eu).

Nature's Best is a Swedish certification scheme for eco-minded tour operators. It assesses how the operators minimize their impact on the environment, support local economies and protect wildlife across the range of eco adventure activities in Sweden, from dog sledding and driving a reindeer sleigh with Sami herdsmen, to sea kayaking, white-water rafting, timber rafting, horse riding and wolf tracking (naturesbestsweden.com).

Sustainable Travel Ireland (previously known as Ecotourism Ireland) is a certification scheme for accommodation and activity providers in Ireland (sustainabletravelireland.ie).

TourCert is a corporate social responsibility system for hotels to increase their energy and environmental efficiency (tourcert.org).

France

Écogîte is managed by the well-established Gîtes de France, which manages over 70,000 owner-run B&Bs and self-catering cottages (gîtes). The Écogîte label is given to about 400 owners who have demonstrated that part of their 'way of life' is based on preserving natural resources, using renewable energies and using natural, local and recyclable material with no harmful effects on health (gites-de-france.com).

Flocon Vert has been awarded to mountain destinations, such as The Chamonix Mont-Blanc Valley and La Pierre Saint Martin, that have demonstrated their commitment to 20 sustainable criteria, including a year-round strategy for tourism, reduction in greenhouse gases, supporting local economies and protecting natural resources and ecology (flocon-vert.org).

Gîtes Panda is a scheme set up by the World Wide Fund for Nature (WWF) for about 170 environmentally friendly gîtes that are near walking routes in protected areas, such as National Parks and Reserves. All are run by owners who care for the environment, provide binoculars, maps, guidebooks and educational nature guides to help visitors identify, protect and respect local plants and wildlife (gites-de-france.com/en/our-holidays/panda-wwf).

Italy

Fattorie del Panda is the Italian equivalent of Gîtes Panda and is awarded to small farmstays located in or near protected areas (wwf.it).

Legambiente Turismo assesses accommodation, from hotels to B&Bs and agritourism establishments, on a range of criteria, including waste and energy resource management, sustainable transport, accessibility, provenance of food, enhancement of cultural heritage and environmental issues, as well as communication (legambienteturismo.it).

Worldwide

B Corp is a legally bound certification scheme for businesses in general (not just the travel industry) that vets companies for their social and environmental performance, public transparency and legal accountability to balance profit and purpose. The outdoors adventure company, TYF Adventure was the founding UK member of B Corp. Since then, the small group adventure operator Intrepid has gained B Corp membership, so too have accommodation specialists Sawday's, Lovat Holiday Parks in southern England, adventure travel specialists Flooglebinder and Joro Experiences, and Pura Aventura, which organizes holidays in Spain, Portugal and Latin America. All have collaborated to form Travel by BCorp to share best practice (travelbybcorp.co.uk).

Earth Check is an Australian-based worldwide certification scheme for the travel and tourism industry, benchmarking sustainability for businesses, from hotels, such as the boutique Memmo Alfama, Lisbon, to communities and destinations, such as the Snæfellsnes Peninsula in western Iceland (earthcheck.org).

Green Globe is based in the USA but has local partners worldwide. It has a standard 'certified member' award and two further awards based on length of certification – gold is for those that have been certified for five years and platinum for those certified for ten years (greenglobe.com).

Green Key is an international environmental ecolabel whose global office is run by the Foundation for Environmental Education (FEE) Copenhagen, Demark with nearly 3,000 members in over 55 countries, from boutique hotels to B&Bs, campsites and visitor attractions. Green Key is managed in Wales by the environmental charity Keep Wales Tidy. An example of a business with the Green Key Award is the Larkhill Yurt and Tipis in Carmarthenshire whose owners have been using wind, solar and water power to create electricity for 25 years. (greenkey.global).

Green Leaders is Tripadvisor's badge that showcases the eco-friendly initiatives of B&Bs and hotels. It's not an accredited scheme, but the idea is that businesses can list their green practices so you can see what they are doing (or at least claim they are doing), such as recycling, cooking with local and organic food and electric car charging. Those that have the Platinum badge are deemed to be the greenest. (tripadvisor.co.uk).

ISO numbers are international standards for environmental reporting organized by an independent NGO that was established in 1947. Examples are ISO 14001 – a voluntary technical

Blue flag beaches

Blue Flag is a 30-year-old environmental certification scheme awarded to beaches, marinas and (more recently) boat operators in Europe, Africa, New Zealand, Canada and the Caribbean, which meet a series of stringent environmental, educational, safety and accessibility criteria. Spain has the most awarded sites, followed by France, Turkey, Greece, Italy and Portugal. Beaches in the UK that have been awarded Blue Flag status include New Quay Harbour in Cardigan and Whitby West Cliff in Yorkshire. Examples of European boat operators that have the Blue Flag are Cabrera Sea Fun, Majorca, and Scorpion Yachting in Greece (**blueflag.global**).

tool to help businesses reduce the environmental impact of their business, and ISO 21401 – for environmental management systems (iso.org).

Travelife is operated by the UK Travel Association (ABTA) and operates in over 50 countries certifying hotels in the mainstream travel industry, so you're most likely to see its logo in the travel brochures of the large tour operators, such as TUI, SAGA and Travelbag. In order to be certified, a hotel will have been evaluated by an independent auditor based on an on-site assessment of a series of criteria, from energy efficiency and conservation to human rights, cultural impacts and animal welfare. Top performing properties are awarded Travelife Gold Certification, which is valid for two years (travelife.info).

Let's go!

Guides for the green traveller

Car-free travel

Leave the traffic jams behind and explore the best of Britain on foot, by bike or on public transport.

Car-free walks

Travelling by train from London to the Scottish Highlands is a long, slow, meander to the mountainous fresh and wild. Leaving Euston on a Thursday evening, I ate a late dinner of neeps and tatties washed down with a beer in the train's dining carriage, and then had a decent night's sleep as the train trundled across up through the north of England and across the border. The next morning I tucked into a simple breakfast of Scottish Porridge and tea at 8am, before getting off the train just before 9am at Corrour, an isolated station a few stops short of Fort William in the western Scottish Highlands. From the station, it was a 10-minute walk along a track to Loch Ossian, a small, off-grid youth hostel among a small clump of birch and rowan trees at the edge of the narrow 3-mile (5-km) long Loch Ossian, surrounded by boggy moorland and sparsely covered mountains. There was nothing else in sight: no pylons, no street lights, no roads.

After jettisoning my sleeping bag and spare clothes in one of the hostel dorms, I spent the day walking on Rannoch Moor, catching sight of several ptarmigan on the low ground and dozens of deer upwind. I climbed a Munro, sucked in the clean air of this remote area of wilderness, and swam in the loch. That evening, I ate a hearty stew in the small station restaurant at Corrour, then walked back to the hostel to see the moon lighting up the loch. It's remarkable – and immensely satisfying – that just 24 hours earlier I had been in London, and reached this special place not via a nose-to-tail, long-distance motorway journey, but by train – all the way.

The good news is that you're never really far from a footpath in Britain – there are about 150,000 miles (over 240,000km) of public rights of way in England, Scotland and Wales, and many of them can be reached by public transport. Walking to catch a bus, boat or train is a great way to begin a walk – the adventure starts as soon as you leave your house – whether you're going on a day walk out of a city centre, or a long-distance walk across areas of great natural beauty. Many train, bus and boat operators are keen for walkers to use their services, especially at weekends, and provide multi-modal ranger tickets that you can use across their networks. Here are a few examples of car-free itineraries. Lace up your boots and away you go.

Rail to trail

This is a series of 12 self-guided walks from stations along the Bentham Line, totalling 68 miles (109km) from Heysham Port to Skipton across Yorkshire and Lancashire. The train travels through the lovely valleys of Aire, Ribble, Wenning and Lune, passing the hills of the Yorkshire Dales National Park, before reaching the huge estuary of Morecambe Bay. Four of the stations along the route, Wennington, Bentham, Clapham and Giggleswick, are handy gateways to the Forest of Bowland. The shortest walk is just 2½ miles (4km) from Morecambe station to Bare Lane station, while the longest is the 11⅓ miles (18.2km) from Wennington station to Carnforth – the station that famously featured in the classic 1945 film *Brief Encounter* directed by David Lean (communityraillancashire.co.uk).

People power:

Find hundreds of car-free walks in the UK at carfreewalks.org and a network of walking routes that connect Britain's towns and villages at slowways.org. Keep an eye out too for the 'Walkers are Welcome' logo given to over 100 towns and villages that are particularly welcoming to walkers.

England's Coast Path

England's Coast Path is a new National Trail (nationaltrail.co.uk), which runs all the way around the country's seashore – when complete it will be around 2,800-mile (4,500-km) long and will be the longest continuous coastal path in the world. There are any number of railways and bus connections along the route. One of the most fascinating stretches is the 11-mile (17.7km) walk along the Durham Heritage Coast from Seaham railway station to Crimdon (you can get the train back at Hartlepool railway station), where you travel through the region's industrial heritage, passing wonderful wildflower meadows and via some beautiful beaches. Keep an eye out at sea for basking sharks, they're frequently sighted off the Durham Heritage Coast during the summer (durhamheritagecoast.org).

Walks from railway stations

Several rail operators provide information on walking routes from their stations:

- Scotrail.co.uk/scotland-by-rail/things-do/walking-routes-train
- northernrailway.co.uk/great-days-out/days-out/
- midcheshirerail.org.uk
- northstaffsrail.org.uk/rails-to-trails-station-walks
- settle-carlisle.co.uk/walks
- southeasternrailway.co.uk/destinations-and-offers/local-escapes/
- eastsuffolklines.co.uk/walks
- west-somerset-railway.co.uk/walking-and-running-beside-the-west-somerset-railway
- greatscenicrailways.co.uk/great-days-out/walks

One of the idyllic coves along the Pembrokeshire Coast Path

Heart of Wales Line Trail

This trail is linked to the many of the stations along the rural Heart of Wales railway that runs between Swansea and Shrewsbury, passing through remote uplands of the Shropshire Hills Area of Outstanding Natural Beauty, the Radnorshire Forest and Brecon Beacons, the woodland and salt marshes of the Loughor valley and on to the Millennium Coastal Park in Llanelli. The entire route is 143 miles (230km), but you can easily do it in car-free stages, accessing it at the various railway stations along the way. The trail also links up with several other long-distance paths such as the Shropshire Way at Craven Arms; Offa's Dyke Path and Glyndwr's Way at Knighton/Llangynllo; the Wye Valley walk at Newbridge-on-Wye/Builth Wells; and the Wales Coast Path at Loughor, near to Llanelli (heart-of-wales.co.uk).

Pembrokeshire Coast Path

The 186-mile (299-km) Pembrokeshire Coast Path, from St Dogmaels in the north to Amroth in the south, is connected by five coastal bus services – the Puffin Shuttle, Poppit Rocket, Strumble Shuttle, Celtic Coaster and Coastal Cruiser – operating seven days a week from May to September, and two days a week in winter. They all operate on a Hail and Ride basis in rural areas, so you have to flag down the driver to stop and so you can be picked up or set down at any point along the bus route, providing it is safe to do so. The buses go to many of the crucial stages along the coastal path, such as St Brides Bay, Marloes and Bosherston. The main gateway railway station for the coastal path is at Carmarthen, and there are bus services from Haverfordwest where the Puffin Shuttle connects with St Davids and Milford Haven. (pembrokeshire.gov.uk).

Car-free days out

As you emerge into the open air from a pitch-black tunnel, the small steam train trundles along a narrow-gauge railway over a small bridge, skirts past a floating pontoon by a wildlife pond and then continues through an exquisite garden, resplendent with tall grasses and flowing ribbons of hardy herbaceous plants, trees and shrubs.

The Rhododendron Line is a 90-seater steam railway that departs from a small replica Victorian station, Exbury Central, for 1½ miles (2.4km) around the north-east corner of Exbury Gardens in the New Forest. It's a wonderful way to see some of the hidden highlights of this fabulous 200-acre (81-ha) woodland garden (the Summer Lane Garden is inaccessible by foot and can only be seen from the train). The world-famous rhododendrons and azaleas are the big draw, but in early spring magnolias and camellias burst into flower, in mid-May swathes of primroses and bluebells carpet the woodland, in summer vibrant dahlias display their vibrant red and white flowers, while in the autumn maples, deciduous azaleas and dogwoods provide a riot of colour by the Beaulieu River.

Exbury Gardens is just one of the wonderful attractions along the route of the car-free New Forest Tour, a hop-on, hop-off bus service that runs on three circular routes around the ancient forest and to the coast at Barton-on-Sea and Milford-on-Sea. From the top deck of the open-top bus, there are grandstand views of the wild ponies grazing and the many historic villages of the New Forest, en route to places such as the Beaulieu National Motor Museum, Ringwood Brewery and Hythe Ferry, home to the world's oldest pier train where

Plan a good journey

Find how to travel car-free to many of the UK's best visitor attractions with discounts when you arrive by train, bus, bike or on foot at goodjourney.org.uk

you can take the short return ferry ride over to Southampton. The flexible hop-on, hop-off tickets mean you can stop off and spend some time at one of the attractions along the way and rejoin the bus later in the day. The tour calls at Brockenhurst railway station, which has frequent trains from London, so it's an effortless, car-free day out from the capital as well as from cities along the south coast, such as Southampton, Bournemouth and Salisbury (thenewforesttour.info).

Travelling on trains and buses makes the journey all part of the day out. On the way you can read the paper, play cards, take time to switch off. Without being tied to where you've parked the car, you can do linear walks and bike rides, and of course you can enjoy a drink before returning home. Most major cities have excellent rail and bus networks, so you can travel across town without the hassle of parking, or head out to the countryside to many wonderful visitor attractions that often give discounts if you arrive by public transport. On p76 are a few examples of car-free days out: leave the car and the congestion behind, and away you go.

Campsites reachable by public transport

Campsites and glampsites are often in fairly remote, rural locations, but if you want to travel traffic-free, there are lots that can be reached by train or bus followed by a short walk for the final leg of the journey. Ready-pitched glampsites are particularly convenient as you don't have to lug your tent and equipment with you on public transport. Some sites even offer discounts if you arrive car-free. Here's a selection of campsites and glampsites that are either less than a mile (1.6km) from a railway station or bus stop, or, if a little further, the owners provide a transfer.

1 Guilden Gate Smallholding, Hertfordshire
Less than an hour on the train from London (and just 15 minutes from Cambridge), there are just two sites in this glorious smallholding: choose between the yurt and renovated camper van in the native 2-acre (0.8ha) Coppice Woodland or the hobbit hole in the Secret Garden. The owners run their own seasonal veggie box scheme, with asparagus and rhubarb in May, sprouts and leeks in December, along with fruit, herbs, mushrooms, honey and eggs. Take the train to Royston then the 17 bus to Park View, from where it's a 5-minute walk to the Guilden Gate Smallholding (guildengate.co.uk).

2 Ivy Grange Farm, Suffolk
There's a £10 discount if you arrive car-free to this lovely 3-acre (1.2-ha) meadow with four yurts and a shepherd's hut, each with their own wood burner, campfire pit and BBQ. It's just 2½ miles (4km) from Brampton Station, on the London Liverpool Street to Lowestoft line, from where the owners can collect you (trains run every hour, connecting at Ipswich). It's also on the Sustrans National Cycle Route 1 and there's a village store nearby for provisions (ivygrangefarm.co.uk).

3 Tom's Ecolodge, Isle of Wight
Take the ferry from Lymington to Yarmouth, then catch the Southern Vectis 27 bus to the farm, home to safari tents, wood cabins, eco pods, and mudulogs (log-built pods for groups of up to six), as well as a farm shop, restaurant and a slip-n-slide aqua park (tapnellfarm.com).

4 Ty Du Farm, Llanelli

A car-free campsite on a small wildlife-friendly farm with just 5 pitches and a large 7m imperial bell tent (sleeps up to 8) where the owners encourage children to explore the woodlands and collect firewood. Walks and cycle rides on smooth tracks lead to Furnace Pond, Swiss Valley Reservoir and local beaches. The L2 or 128 bus travels from Llanelli to Felinfoel in just 12 minutes, from where it's a 20-minute walk to the campsite (glampingcampingtydufarm.co.uk).

5 Allibella Shepherd's Hut, Barmouth, Gynedd

A lovely little retreat (for two adults and two children) overlooking the sea, just 100 yards (90m) from the railway station at Llanaber, on the scenic Cambrian Coast line along the west coast of Wales. The sandy beach is just over the road and it's about a 10-minute walk to the popular Norbar restaurant (airbnb.co.uk).

6 Lee Valley Almost Wild Campsite, Broxbourne, Hertfordshire

A 17-pitch rural site, remarkably less than five miles from the M25, is among the green spaces of the 10,000 acre (4,000 Ha) Lee Valley Park on the border of Essex and Hertfordshire. Choose between 12 riverside or five woodland pitches with basic amenities, including a compost toilet, cold water tap and solar-powered lights. Take the train to Broxbourne railway station from where it's a 10 minute walk to the campsite, or a 15-mile (24-km) cycle along the River Lee Navigation towpath (or canoe along the river) from Stratford or Hackney (visitleevalley.org.uk).

7 Le Vaugrat Campsite, Guernsey

A spacious traditional campsite on the grounds of an eighteenth-century Guernsey farmhouse with just a 5-minute walk to Port Grat Bay, one of the island's best beaches. The campsite has plenty of facilities, including two separate toilet blocks, washing machines and Wi-Fi. Take the ferry to Guernsey from Poole or Portsmouth, and hop on the 31 or 32 bus to Les Vardes bus stop from where it's a few minutes' walk to the campsite (vaugratcampsite.com).

8 The Olive Branch B&B, Andalucia, Spain

Popular with rock climbers and potholers visiting the immense Gorge of the Gaitanes (one of the best-known climbing areas in Spain), but also great for hikers and mountain bikers. There's traditional camping among olive and fruit trees, or you can bed down in one of the ready-pitched tents, in a smart, modern bunkhouse or one of five small en suite rooms. Take the train from Malaga to El Chorro, from where it's about a mile (1.6km) to the campsite (olivebranchelchorro.com).

9 Arolla, Valais, Switzerland

Reputedly the highest altitude campsite in Europe, this stunning location 6,400ft (1,950m) up in the Swiss Alps has superb views of the north face of Mont Collon and the Pigne d'Arolla. I came across it while hiking along the Haute Route – the 12-day trek from Chamonix to Zermatt – but you can reach it easily by public transport by taking the train or bus to Sion then changing to the bus to Arolla (direction 'les Haudères') and asking the driver to drop you off at the campsite (camping-arolla.com).

10 North Koster, West Sweden

A stunning family site by the sea on the car-free island of North Koster. Guided kayaking, paddleboarding, seal-safari and snorkelling tours, walks and cycle paths, plus several great places to eat, including a lovely café in the grounds of a permaculture garden. It's a wonderful journey up the west Coast of Sweden from Gothenburg to Strömstad (by train or bus) then 45-minute ferry across to Vettnet on the east of North Koster from where it's 880 yards (800m) to the campsite (reservatet.nu).

Centre for Alternative Technology (CAT), Machynlleth, Wales

Learn all about modern sustainable living at the epicentre for all things green in the UK. CAT was established by a group of environmental scientists and engineers in 1973 on the site of a disused slate quarry, initially to reinvent green technologies, but it then evolved into a demonstration and teaching centre for practical solutions for a decarbonizing world. Despite its name, it now provides hands-on learning for all aspects of sustainability (not just alternative energy), including environmentally friendly building techniques, woodland management, organic gardening, ecology and conservation of biodiversity. The large outdoor centre has lots of fun wildlife activities for children to connect with nature and the environment. You can also stay overnight at CAT in one of several eco cabins (each sleeps up to 18) or in the Wales Institute for Sustainable Education (WISE) building, which has 24 twin and double rooms. From the railway station in Machynlleth, take Bus 34 or T2 to CAT. At the ticket office, it's a 10-minute walk up the steep steps to the site's entrance, but from Easter to October you can take a water-powered cliff railway up to the top (cat.org.uk).

Scottish Seabird Centre, North Berwick, Scotland

Learn about Scottish marine life – deep sea corals, kelp forests, marine mammals and the 5 million seabirds that breed around the Scottish coast each year – at this innovative interactive discovery centre. There are live cameras to zoom in on the local wildlife but if you want to get closer to the action, there are several boat trips out to the Firth of Forth, including a 1-hour cruise around the island of Craigleith and the Bass Rock, home to the world's largest colony of northern gannets – if you're lucky you may also spot a dolphin. The centre is a 15-minute walk from North Berwick railway station, which is about 30 minutes by train from Edinburgh Waverley (seabird.org).

Weekend first

For a small fee, many UK train operators allow you to upgrade to first class at the weekend and on Bank Holidays. Prices vary depending on the operator and the length of your journey, but they all allow you access to the larger, more comfortable seats with extra legroom, plus facilities such as enhanced Wi-Fi and hot and cold drinks served at your seat in the usually quieter first-class carriages (nationalrail.co.uk).

Whinlatter Forest Park, Keswick, Cumbria

England's only true mountain forest, Whinlatter Forest provides views across Bassenthwaite Lake, Derwentwater and Keswick and is home to the longest purpose-built mountain bike trails in the Lake District. You can hire bikes and head off on one of the bike trails (Altura, Gorse and Quercus) to reach the viewpoints with speedy descents or take part in mountain bike orienteering along a combination of forest roads and parts of the Quercus trail. There's also horse riding through the forest, guided walks with alpacas, or you could spend a few hours on the high-ropes course at the onsite activity centre. During the summer, you can reach Whinlatter on the hourly 77/77A bus from Keswick, a wonderful route that's also known as the Honister Rambler – one of Britain's most scenic bus routes. Route dates and times may vary so do check the Stagecoach timetable before you travel (stagecoachbus.com). You get free admission if you arrive by bus or by bike (forestryengland.uk).

St Mawes Castle, Truro, Cornwall

The English Heritage St Mawes Castle is one of the most elaborately decorated and best-preserved of Henry VIII's coastal artillery fortresses built to defend the anchorage of Carrick Roads by the Fal estuary on the south coast of Cornwall. The best way to approach the castle is by sea on the foot ferry from Falmouth, which runs almost every day of the year. The ferry departs from the Prince of Wales Pier, just a short walk from Falmouth Town railway station. After a morning at the castle, you can spend the afternoon at Gyllyngvase Beach, a wide, arching Blue Flag sandy beach from where it's just a 10-minute walk back to the station for the journey home (english-heritage.org.uk).

Cycle rides by train

Cycling out of the market town of Devizes on the towpath of the Kennet and Avon Canal just north of Salisbury Plain, you pass over a small bridge and come to the lovely Caen Hill Café in an old lock-keeper's cottage perched at the top of a hill.

It is here you first get your first glimpse of the remarkable Caen Hill Locks, the UK's longest continuous flight of locks, descending 237ft (72m) feet over 2 miles (3.2km), west from the Vale of Pewsey to the Avon Valley. This remarkable aquatic stairway is one of the most impressive feats of engineering in Georgian Britain. Built by John Rennie at the turn of the nineteenth century to allow canal boats to climb the steep stretch of land up to Devizes, Caen Hill Locks was the last section to be completed of the 87-mile (140-km) route of the Kennet and Avon Canal between Bristol and Reading. This towpath now forms part of Route 4 of the National Cycle Network – miles of relatively flat, easy cycling, mostly on light gravel or compact earth, and with railway stations conveniently dotted long the route, it's great for a long weekend's cycling by train.

By train from London, it's just 25 minutes to Reading railway station from where it's a short cycle to the towpath at the point where the River Thames flows into the canal. Cycling west from here, you pass by lots of lovely canalside pubs, via Newbury and Hungerford, the Pewsey White Horse, limestone aquaducts, Claverton Pumping Station and then on to Bradford-on-Avon with its medieval cottages and converted cloth mills. You could stay the night in any of these historic market towns or continue for a few miles to the Georgian splendour of Bath, spend an hour or two soaking in the city's renowned spa and eat at one of the many gourmet restaurants. The following day, it's a relatively gentle 15-mile (24-km) ride along a flat, traffic-free former railway line all the way to Bristol, or you could do the Bath Two Tunnels Circuit – a 13-mile (20-km) loop from Bath to Bristol through two long tunnels (the Combe Down Tunnel is the UK's longest cycling tunnel), over the Tucking Mill Viaduct and past the Dundas Aqueduct back to Bath where you can put your bike on the train home (greatwestway.co.uk).

Below is a selection of bike rides reachable by train. At many railway stations there are bike hire facilities so if you do a loop, you can return the bike afterwards before catching the train home. If you bring your own bike, you can cycle as far as you want then jump on the train home.

Cotswolds Line

This beautiful route follows the Cotswold Line railway from Oxford to Worcester, via some of the prettiest villages in the Cotswolds, including Charlbury, Moreton-in-Marsh, Chipping Campden and Evesham. Experienced cyclists can do the route in a single day, but it's a great for a weekend's ride, especially coming by train from London or Birmingham, which have regular trains to both Oxford and Worcester (cycle.travel).

Mawddach Estuary, Snowdonia

Take the train to Barmouth then choose any number of one-day cycling trails around the area, such as the Mawddach Trail, an easy cycle along a disused railway track on the southern edge of the beautiful Mawddach estuary – a Site of Special Scientific Interest with salt marshes and peat habitats rich in birdlife. The trail continues to Dolgellau with

stunning views of the Rhinog mountains. A more challenging ride is to extend the cycle on quiet roads back to Barmouth via the beautiful Cregennan lakes (mawddachestuary.co.uk/cycling).

Carlisle to Newcastle, Tyneside

A great ride for a short break that follows much of the route of Hadrian's Wall via market towns such as Brampton and Haltwistle. You'll cross the North Pennines but it's a much easier alternative to the steep hills of the popular coast-to-coast route from the Lake District to Newcastle (cycle.travel). Before catching the train home in Newcastle, head to The Cycle Hub on the quayside, a buzzing café and repair shop for all things cycling (thecyclehub.org).

Dundee to Aberdeen, Scotland

This 92-mile (148-km) ride via the Capel Mounth Heritage Path and the Deeside Way is a challenging day ride or great for a two-day adventure. There's a steep climb out of Glen Clova, but at the top there are wonderful views across Loch Muick, the Lochnagar Massif and the Cairngorms National Park. If you decide to do this ride over two days, you can end with the exhilarating descent at Ballater, where you can stay overnight (sustrans.org.uk).

PlusBike

Look for the PlusBike icon on the website and app for National Rail when you search for a particular train journey. It's a handy guide that tells you the onboard cycle carriage and reservation rules for taking bikes on the trains relevant to your journey, and also includes information on bike facilities at the railway stations en route, such as the type of storage, its location, and number of available cycle parking spaces (nationalrail.co.uk/PlusBike).

West Kernow Way, Cornwall

There are plenty of long-distance cycle rides in the UK, where you can start and end the journey at railway stations and stay at bike-friendly accommodation along the way, including coast-to-coast routes, such as Oban to Inverness, Ilfracombe to Plymouth, and the Trans Pennine Trail from Southport to Hornsea. The West Kernow Way is a 150-mile (240-km), off-road loop of west Cornwall that takes 3–4 days to complete, and starts and ends in Penzance, which is on the Cornish main line from Plymouth and can be reached on the overnight sleeper from London. The route passes the Botallack tin mines, the Bronze Age monument Mên-an-Tol, Land's End, St Michael's Mount and Lizard Point (cyclinguk.org).

Train Loire à Vélo, France

The long-distance scenic cycle route Loire à Vélo follows the Loire river from its mouth at Saint-Brevin-les-Pins on the Atlantic coast of France to Cuffy (near Nevers), along flat cycleways with very little traffic, via medieval cathedral cities, riverside villages and lots of châteaux. Throughout the summer, a dedicated bike train service, Train Loire à Vélo, transports cyclists between a number of railway stations along the route, including Blois, Tours, Angers, Nantes, Saint-Nazaire and Le Croisic. It's a convenient way to cycle sections of the route if you don't want to do the entire 560 miles (900km). The train has special carriages to accommodate bikes of all sizes (there's an assistant to help board and unload bikes), the trains can carry up to 83 bikes and the service runs round trips several times a day. The route's website has details of eco-friendly accommodation you can book for one night or more (loirebybike.co.uk).

The Hungry Cyclist Lodge, Burgundy

Explore the quiet country roads and villages of the wine region of Burgundy by bike, then rest your limbs at this smart cyclist-friendly, country-style lodge in the village of Auxey-Duresses, 6 miles (10km) from Beaune. Owner Tom Kevill-Davies organizes tailor-made cycling holidays for all abilities, incorporating the most appropriate routes and the best restaurants and vineyards, else organize your own itinerary on either a B&B basis or by renting the entire lodge - there's room for up to 10 in five double ensuite rooms (thehungrycyclist.com).

Railway cycle paths

About one-third of Britain's rail network closed in the 1960s, but since then there has been a concerted country-wide effort to repurpose hundreds of these disused railway lines into walking and cycle paths. They're usually fairly flat, safe, well-maintained and often run along the banks of beautiful rivers and provide a convenient link between towns and villages. Tunnels add to the sense of adventure and bridges can give wonderful, elevated views of the countryside. Some of these green corridors are just a few miles long and take only an hour or two to complete, some are great for a whole day out, while others stretch over great distances and can be cycled as part of a multi-day itinerary. In Europe they're often known as 'greenways' (Vias Verdes in Spanish, Voies Vertes in French, Ecopistas in Portuguese). Here are ten examples where you can enjoy fabulous scenery, lots of fresh air and sociable exercise from the comfort of a saddle, traffic-free.

1 Tarka Trail, North Devon and Exmoor
The longest, continuous, off-road cycle path in the UK. It's actually two loops centred in Barnstaple, passing through villages and wooded valleys, alongside rivers and beautiful beaches, and over moorland with wonderful views of Exmoor and Dartmoor. There are several excellent places to eat along both loops, including Yarde Orchard Café, an upcycled 1930s sailor's dormitory from Plymouth docks (with charging for electric bikes), and the Puffing Billy Trading Co. café, which sells home-cooked food at the old Victoria railway station (tarkatrail.org.uk).

2 Camel Trail, Cornwall
This 18-mile (29-km) jaunt around North Cornwall starts at Wenford Bridge at the edge of Bodmin Moor and runs along the bank of the River Camel into Wadebridge before heading along the estuary to the foodie town of Padstow. It's one of the best-known greenways, so if you're planning to hire a bike (there's cycle hire in Bodmin, Wenford Bridge, Wadebridge and Padstow), it's worth booking well ahead (cameltrail.org.uk).

3 Collier's Way, Somerset
A 23-mile (37-km) path along the former railway line of the Somerset Coal Canal between Great Elm and Radstock and on to Limpley Stoke Valley. Here you can either carry on to the Dundas Aqueduct or link with the Two Tunnels cycleway that connects Bath with the Midford Valley. En route, it's just a mile's detour to the village of Mells, where you can eat at the stylish Talbot Inn, Walled Garden or village café (sustrans.org.uk).

4 The Down's Link, Surrey/West Sussex
Following the line from St Martha's Hill near Guildford to Shoreham-by-Sea, this 37-mile (60-km) route joins the North Downs in Surrey with the South Downs in West Sussex and is great for a full day's cycling to the sea. If you want to cycle it in shorter sections, there are plenty of access points at Bramber, Steyning, West Grinstead, Southwater and Rudgwick as well as railway stations at Chilworth, Shalford, Christs Hospital, Horsham and Rudgwick (cyclinguk.org).

5 Dava Way, Highlands of Scotland
A great day's cycling in the Highlands, from the town of Forres near the Moray coast to Grantown-on-Spey in the Cairngorms National Park following the 24-mile (39-km) route of the dismantled Highland Railway. At Forres the Dava Way links up with the North Sea Cycle Route and also The Moray Way (morayways.org. uk) – a 95-mile (153-km) circular route that combines the Dava Way with the Moray Coast Trail and the Speyside Way. (davaway.org.uk).

6 Scarborough to Whitby, Yorkshire
A 21-mile (34-km) cycle along the North Yorkshire coast between the two mainline railway stations at Scarborough and Whitby. Pass by Scarborough Castle, Robin Hood's Bay, Ravenscar, and Whitby Abbey, and en route, stop off at quiet bays such as Crook Ness, Cloughton Wyke or Stoupe Beck Sands. The final leg passes over the spectacular Larpool Viaduct before you continue into Whitby. The trail is part of the Moor to Sea Cycle Route from the heart of the North York Moors to the coast (northyorkmoors.org.uk).

Finding railway cycle paths

On OS Explorer maps, look for a green dashed line or green triangles that show the footpath or bridleway marked on cuttings and embankments – among these will be orange dots that show they are designated as a traffic-free cycle route (getoutside.ordnancesurvey.co.uk).

7 Great Western Greenway, Ireland
A 26-mile (42-km) trail that follows the route of the old Westport to Achill railway along stunning coastline. Heading north out of Westport, the trail passes through to Newport then hugs the coast of Clew Bay to Mulranny on the isthmus between Blacksod Bay and Clew Bay, then winds round Tonragee to Achill, the gateway to Achill Island (greenway.ie).

8 Véloroute du Lin, Normandy, France
Many of France's greenways pass by the banks of rivers and over spectacular viaducts (such as the ride from Thury-Harcourt to Pont d'Ouilly in Normandy). One of the most accessible is the Véloroute du Lin between Pourville-sur-Mer and Fécamp – there are plenty of hilly rides along the coast here, such as La Vélomaritime (EuroVelo 4), but this 50-mile (80-km) route is an easier alternative and there are railway stations at either end – at Dieppe and Fécamp. Other favourites are La Dolce Via in the Ardèche, and Via Fluvia between the Loire and Rhône, between stations at Lavoûte-sur-Loire and Oumey (francevelotourisme.com).

9 Pista Ciclabile del Ponente Ligure, Italy
A beautiful stretch along the Ligurian coast that hugs the Mediterranean between Ospedaletti and San Lorenzo – known as the Riviera dei Fiori. The route heads east along the seafront via San Remo, Arma di Taggia, and Santo Stefano al Mare. It's only 15 miles (24km) long, but there are plenty of diversions off the trail to some wonderful old villages, including Bussana Vecchia, Cipressa and Costarainera (pistaciclabile.com).

10 Val de Zafán, Catalonia, Spain
Spain has over a hundred greenways covering over 1,500 miles (2,400km). Taking the train to Barcelona, there are several options to reach Catalonia's green corridors, such as the path from the mountains to the sea between Arnes and Tortosa. The trail loops 30 miles (49km) around the rock outcrops of Els Ports Natural Park, through several long tunnels, and past historic towns and villages, such as Horta de Sant Joan, where Picasso spent some years. It then follows the Ebro Nature Trail, ending in the Ebro Delta Natural Park on the coast (viasverdes.com).

On the water

Kayaking, canoeing and paddle-boarding can take you to otherwise inaccessible places, while surfing is the ultimate low-impact exhilaration sport. Here's how to enjoy the waterways the sustainable way.

Kayaking

After a dreich start to the day, we continued to paddle across the protected waters of the Summer Isles archipelago in north-west Scotland and found the conditions began to improve: the sea was calm, the sun began to shine, and the sky cleared to blue.

We'd already spent a few hours kayaking along the shoreline from Achiltibuie, passing any number of empty beaches, sea-cliffs and wildflower-strewn sea stacks, and ahead were enormous sandstone mountains providing an epic age-old backdrop to the glittering water. It was ridiculously beautiful.

This pitch and paddle trip was organized by Wilderness Scotland, which also runs kayaking trips to the Isle of Mull, Sound of Arisaig, and the Outer Hebrides, as well as other outdoor adventure holidays in the wilderness areas of Scotland (wildernessscotland.com). Each day, we paddled 7–10 miles (11–16km), picking our way through channels and inlets between the uninhabited islands, stopping off to swim in shallow turquoise bays and drying off on near-perfect sandy beaches. At night we wild camped under Scotland's famously clear skies. We crossed to Tanera Mor, passed the sandstone cliffs of Eilean Flada Mor, the distinctive peaks of Assynt and Coigach, the island of Eilean Mullagrach, the wildlife reserve of Isle Ristol, and the sea-cliffs to the north of Riff.

Our kayaking guide was Myles Farnbank, an experienced kayaker who also holds the Master Educator qualification from the Leave No Trace centre for outdoor ethics, and there was a strong emphasis on making sure we left each campsite exactly as we found it. Protected from the Atlantic Ocean by the Outer Hebrides, the Summer Isles are part of the Wester Ross Marine Protected Area, home to white-tailed eagles, seal colonies, porpoises, dolphins and even whales.

One of the joys of kayaking is that it can be the only way to reach remote places like the Summer Isles. With just the soft splashes of your paddle propelling your kayak through the water, you're also more likely to see and hear birdlife and see other marine life without disturbing them. Here is a selection of places to go paddling in remote, beautiful locations.

North Coast Sea Kayak Trail, Northern Ireland

A 70-mile (113-km) route around Ireland's northeast corner from west to east from Magilligan Point in County Londonderry to Torr Head in County Antrim, then south to Waterfoot at the mouth of Glenariff, Queen of the Glens of Antrim, including a challenging circumnavigation of Rathlin Island. Along the way there are sea caves, a wealth of marine life and some wonderful places to visit, such as Carrick-a-Rede Rope Bridge near Ballintoy and the Giant's Causeway. There are six sections and a range of access points, including small fishing piers, beaches and harbours and several iconic places to stay overnight, such as the Port Moon Bothy and Ballycastle Harbour. The trail is more suitable for experienced kayakers though there are several operators who run guided trips (canoeni.com).

Weather Islands, West Sweden

The Weather Islands are half an hour by boat from Fjällbacka, which is about 4 hours by train from Gothenburg on the west coast of Sweden. The windblown island we stayed on had just a clutch of little red cottages that clung tightly to the rocks. You can spend days here going on blustery walks among the rocks and swimming in the clear waters, holing up in the guesthouse's hot tub or sauna and tucking into a beer and a plate of fresh shrimp. One morning, with the odd heron for company, we paddled out into velvety, clear water around the island of Bassholmen. Slipping between smooth granite boulders, forested islands, sheltered bays and remote fishing villages, it was a brilliantly unobtrusive way to see the local wildlife – and to get a welcome glimpse into the local culture, later that day, as we pulled up the kayaks and sat drinking coffee and eating cinnamon buns on a deserted jetty (upplevelsebolaget.com).

Kardamili, Southern Peloponnese, Greece

The Mani Peninsula has one of the prettiest coastlines in the Peloponnese, between the blue waters of the Messinian Gulf and Mount Taygetos. Setting off from Kardamili old harbour, you're never far from the shore as you pass by sea caves, rock gardens, and rock pyramids en route to Stoupa. Don't miss stopping off at the Blue Cave, a spectacular natural phenomenon where sunlight filters through a crack in the rocks and bounces off the sea floor to illuminate the brilliant aquamarine water. Moor up for lunch at an idyllic forest-backed sandy beach, feast on fresh tomatoes, feta cheese, olives and home-baked bread, then slowly kayak back along the rocky coastline back to Kardamili in the shade of the afternoon. Alternatively, you can carry on paddling for days, exploring for 60 miles (97km) the entire Mani coastline to Cape Tenaron, the southernmost top of the European mainland, stopping off at small fishing villages, Byzantine chapels and many small coves and beaches. It's paddling perfection (exploremessinia.com).

Surfing

Surfing is commonly perceived as a low-impact pursuit; all you need to enjoy the laid-back sport is a board and a bit of courage to enjoy the thrill of the waves. Yet as the sport has grown in popularity, so too has the amount of environmentally damaging kit that is being mass-produced. The core of modern boards is often made from polystyrene or polyurethane; wetsuits are fashioned from non-biodegradable neoprene; and resins are made out of harmful toxins. Thankfully, there's been a concerted effort among the surfing community to raise awareness of the issues and a great deal of progress has been made in greening the industry. Initiatives such as the #2MinuteBeachClean and #PlasticFreeCommunities have helped, so too has an ongoing commitment from ethical suppliers to instil better practices throughout the manufacturing process. There are now boards made with renewable materials, wetsuits fabricated from natural rubber, and resins that are petroleum-free. Some companies will recycle your old wetsuit in exchange for a discount on your next one, and there are any number of bio-based sunscreens. There has also been a movement to encourage surfing closer to home to reduce the carbon emissions of travelling.

Five places to go surfing by public transport

The UK and Ireland have just about every kind of beach and reef set-up, so there's always somewhere to go, whatever the weather. North Cornwall and Ireland are reputed to have the most consistent conditions, although the waters off the south-west of Wales and the swells of the North Sea along the north-east coast of England are

becoming increasingly popular. It's not possible to take a surfboard on coaches or trains as they exceed the maximum luggage size allowed (although GWR does allow boards on its overnight sleeper service to Penzance), but the increase in popularity of surfing has seen a host of board hire and surf schools become established at many of the go-to surfing locations. Here are five surfing hot spots that can be reached by bus or train, where you can hire boards either on the beach or from a nearby surf school or hire shop.

PEMBROKESHIRE, WALES

There are about a dozen established surfing beaches along the Pembrokeshire Coast and thanks to the region's interconnected summer coastal bus services you can get to most of them straight off the bus (for timetables see pembrokeshire.gov.uk), such as Broad Haven (there's a YHA hostel opposite the beach), the huge 2-mile (3.2-km) beach at Newgale and the dune-backed Manorbier. My favourites are Marloes Sands, which can be great for beginners (though there is quite a long walk down to it), the Blue Flag beach at Whitesands Bay (Ma Simes surf school based in St Davids has been running surf lessons at

Whitesands for over 30 years), and the gently shelving, south-west-facing beach at Freshwater West, where you can hire boards and have lessons at Outer Reef School, who also have outlets at Manorbier, Broad Haven and Newgale (outerreefsurfschool.com). For the perfect post-surf bite to eat, head to Café Môr – a solar-powered pop-up beach shack, which parks up just opposite the main entrance to the beach where the bus stops. It sells a range of excellent local food, including crab sourced from just up the road at Little Haven, smothered in Welsh Sea Black Butter and a squeeze of fresh lemon, and a delicious veggie burger made with caramelized red onion, garlic, Captain Cat's Môr Seasoning, kelp, laver and dulse seaweed served with homemade pickles.

GOWER PENINSULA, WALES

The Gower Area of Outstanding Natural Beauty is home to a handful of excellent surfing locations that are all reachable by bus from Swansea. The most accessible is at Caswell Bay, where the bus drops you off adjacent to the beach. Each location has operators providing year-round surf hire (and/or surfing lessons): Gower Surfing (gowersurfing.com) and Surf GSD (surfgsd.com) at Caswell Bay (and

Rhossili in summer); Llangennith Surf Lessons (llangennithsurflessons.co.uk) and PJ's Surf Shop (facebook.com/pjs.s.shop) at Llangennith beach; Hot Dog Surf Shop (hotdogsurf.com) at Kittle, and Oxwich Watersports (oxwichwatersports.co.uk) at Oxwich Bay. For timetables and routes of all the bus services in the Gower, as well as information on the Gower Day Rider all-day bus ticket: swanseabaywithoutacar.co.uk

SOUTH WEST ENGLAND

Newquay is the mecca for Cornwall surfing, not just for the pros but for anyone wanting to try their hand at surfing in the clear Atlantic waters of this popular surfing location, which lives and breathes the waves. There are two main surfing spots, the closest to the railway station is Towan Beach (also known as Newquay Town Beach), while Fistral Beach is a little further to walk but is the heart and soul of the Newquay surfing scene and probably the best-known beach in the UK. The north of the beach (North Fistral) is popular with the locals and more experienced surfers, while the middle and southern end are where the beginners tend to go. En route to both beaches there are numerous places to hire kit and book surfing lessons, for all abilities, such as Fistral Beach Surf School (fistralbeachsurfschool.co.uk) and Newquay Activity Centre (newquayactivitycentre.co.uk). Newquay railway station is just a short train ride on the Atlantic Coastal branch line from Par, which is on the mainline from Bristol and London.

If you're looking for somewhere away from the razzamatazz of Newquay, there are over 60 other surfing beaches in Devon and Cornwall. The railway line runs along the south coast, so the beaches here are the easier ones to reach by train, such as Falmouth (Gyllyngvase Beach is just a few minutes' walk from Falmouth Town railway station), but there are some wonderful surfing beaches on the north coast that be reached by bus, such as Woolacombe, which is served by several

buses from Barnstaple (13 miles/21km away), including routes 300, 303, 308, 31, and 31a.

EAST COAST OF SCOTLAND

There are about 20 established surfing locations along the east coast of Scotland, from Coldingham Bay just south of St Abbs in the Scottish Borders, up to Brora Beach near Dornoch on the Far North Line from Inverness (the 1-mile/1.6-km long sandy beach is just a few minutes' walk from Brora railway station). One of the most popular is Belhaven Beach in Dunbar, home to the Coast to Coast Surf School (c2csurfschool.com), which has lessons on the beach and hires out surfboards, skateboards, stand-up paddle boards, wetsuits and other accessories. Take the X7 bus from Edinburgh to the Old Police Station bus stop, from where it's a few minutes' walk to the beach; or go by train to Dunbar railway station, which is 1½ miles (2.4km) from the beach.

NORTH EAST ENGLAND

Thanks to the East Coast Main Line, which hugs the coast all the way from Newcastle to North Berwick and interconnecting rail and bus services, there are

Surfers Against Sewage (SAS)

Founder by a group of Cornish surfers in 1990, SAS is a grassroots marine conservation charity that has long championed the protection of the UK's coastlines, and has grown into one of the country's most active and successful environmental charities. It campaigns on a range of issues, including water quality, plastic pollution and recovery of the oceans. Its website has a handy map where you can check the water quality of beaches at over 350 locations around the UK coast, and its Safer Seas Service app includes live surf and tide conditions as well as real-time water quality alerts for beaches. SAS also organizes bi-annual beach cleans that have been responsible for removing hundreds of tons of packaging across the UK, and organizes the Million Mile Clean, inspiring volunteers to walk 10 miles (16km) and clean up the places they love: 100,000 volunteers x 10 miles each = 1 million miles (sas.org.uk).

many surfing locations along the North East coast of England that are reachable by train and bus, from the Blue Flag beach at Whitby (home to Whitby Surf School: whitbysurf.co.uk) up to the 2-mile (3.2-km) stretch of sandy beach at Seaton Carew. On the Tees Valley Line, which runs between Bishop Auckland and Saltburn, via Darlington, there are several surf schools based out of Saltburn-by-the-Sea, east of Middlesbrough, including Drift Surf Shop (driftsurfshop.co.uk), Saltburn Surf Hire (saltburn-surf.co.uk), and Flow Surf School (flowsurfcoaching.com). From the railway station, it's just few minutes' walk to a funicular railway that takes you down to the excellent north-facing surf beach – probably the most well-known in the North East, with beach breaks either side of a pier that are good for beginners and intermediates, while to the south is where there are more powerful breaks for the more experienced.

Check out the surf

Watch live feeds from surfing beaches in the UK, Ireland and continental Europe, as well as read the latest surf reports and surfing weather forecasts at **magicseaweed.com**

Artificial wave pools

Several inland watersports centres produce consistent, man-made waves for everyone from beginners to pros to hone the art of surfing. The first to open in the UK was Surf Snowdonia in North Wales (**adventureparcsnowdonia.com**), followed by The Wave in Bristol (**thewave.com**) where the shaped lagoon produces up to 1,000 waves each hour for all levels. A third wave pool is now under construction in Scotland (**wavegarden.scot**). Further afield, there are wave pools at Langenfeld in Germany (**surf-langenfeld.de**), Alaïa Bay in Sion, Switzerland (**alaiabay.ch**), and at Siam Park, Tenerife (**siampark.net**).

West coast of Ireland

There is a thriving surfing culture throughout the west coast of Ireland with many excellent surfing beaches, thanks to the Atlantic Ocean providing plenty of powerful swells, especially between September and May. Travelling to Ireland flight-free is made more convenient with the Sail & Rail ticket provided by both Stena Line and Irish Ferries, which allows you to book both the rail and ferry legs of your journey in one go, at a price that is much lower than if you booked the two services separately. This combined train and ferry ticket can be used for journeys from anywhere on the UK mainland to anywhere in Northern Ireland and Republic of Ireland via the UK ferry ports of Holyhead, Fishguard or Cairnryan.

Within Ireland, the intercity rail network (irishrail.ie) spans out from Dublin to Sligo, Westport, Galway, Tralee and Cork, from where you can reach many of the surfing beaches via local bus networks (buseireann.ie). There are several surf schools dotted along the coast, often in clusters around surfing hotspots, such as at Lahinch in County Clare, where there are three surf schools: Lahinch Surf School (lahinchsurfschool.com); Bens Surf Clinic (benssurfclinic.com); and Lahinch Surf Experience (lahinchsurfexperience.com). There's a bus to Lahinch that leaves Ennis and Galway five times a day, every day of the week (route 350). Achill Island has 3 miles (5km) of sandy beach and is great spot for beginners, while Donegal is one of the best surfing locations in Ireland – it is quite a journey to get there but it's worth it for the magnificent beaches that are often deserted, and the surf can be spectacular, from surf spots such as Rossnowlagh in the south of Donegal (just north of Bundoran), which has hosted the Irish Inter Counties Surfing Championships for over 40 years and is home to Rossnowlagh Surf School (rossnowlaghsurfschool.com) up to Fanad in the north of Donegal, home to the Adventure One Surf School (adventureone.net) and a handful of wonderful surf locations throughout Inishowen, such as Tullagh Bay and Pollan Bay. There are several bus services to Donegal from Dublin: Route 30 and X30 goes to Donegal Town, while Route 32 goes to Letterkenny. If you're looking to travel from Scotland, there are two operators that run return bus trips from Glasgow: Feda O'Donnell (busfeda. ie) and John McGinley (johnmcginley.com), which also runs coach trips from Dublin to Inishowen (Route 933). For a list of surf schools in Ireland, see: irishsurfing.ie.

Surf schools in France, Spain and Portugal

The western edge of Europe's continental shelf combined with the powerful swells of the Atlantic Ocean create wonderful conditions for surfing along the west coasts of France, Spain and Portugal.

FRANCE

Brittany is the quickest surfing hotspot to reach by ferry (via Roscoff from Plymouth or Cork or St Malo from Portsmouth), and has many family-friendly and intermediate-level surfing beaches and several surf schools, such as Heol Surf School based at the Tronoën beach in Saint-Jean-Trolimon just west of Bénodet (heolsurfschool.fr) and the École de Surf de Bretagne on the Quiberon Peninsula (esb-penhors. com). Further south along the Atlantic coast is Europe's surfing mecca – Hossegor, just north of Biarritz on the Côte d'Argent, which is host to the

The powerful swells of the Atlantic Ocean create wonderful conditions for surfing along the west coasts of France, Spain and Portugal

World Surf League's Quiksilver Pro France at the end of September. You can reach Hossegor by train or bus from Santander (Brittany Ferries runs ferries from Portsmouth and Plymouth to Santander) or by train from Paris to Saint Vincent-de-Tyrosse or Labenne Capbreton from where it's about 7 miles (11.3km) to Hossegor, or by bus from Paris (Bercy Seine) to Seignosse-Bourg Gambetta. While Hossegor attracts the pros, it is also great for intermediate surfers at places such as Les Bourdaines, Les Estagnots, and La Sud, further south towards Capbreton, home of Second World War bunkers and huge sand dunes. There are about a dozen surf schools in and around Hossegor, including Surftrip Surfschool (surftrip.fr) and Yosurf-School (hossegor-surf.fr).

SPAIN

In Spain, there's a huge variety of reefs, points, river mouths and beach breaks in the Basque Country, and places such as La Zurriola in San Sebastian and Zarautz Beach are great for honing your surfing skills, while further west there's Somo Beach, just west of Santander and Razo Beach near A Coruña in Galicia. From the ferry ports at Santander and Bilbao there are buses that go all along the north coast of Green Spain to Galicia (alsa.es).

PORTUGAL

Portugal is best known for being home to the biggest surfable waves in the world at Nazaré (Praia do Norte or North Beach), but with over 1,000 miles (1,600km) of shoreline, there are plenty of other locations where there's excellent surf for all levels of experience. The most popular are around Lisbon – at Ericeira and Peniche – and the Algarve where the water is warmer and the waves are usually gentler. Ericeira and Peniche are easily reached by bus from Lisbon (Compo Grande) – the journey takes 75–90 minutes and buses to both run throughout the day.

There are any number of surf schools, including Surf Riders Ericeira (surfriders.pt) and 3Surfers (3surfers.com) in Ericeira, and Peniche Surf Camp (penichesurfcamp.com) and Baleal Surf Camp (balealsurfcamp.com) in Peniche. In the Algarve, there are several surf schools in the surf town of Sagres on the extreme southwestern tip that are reachable by bus from Lisbon: Wavy Surf Camp (wavysurfcamp.com) and the Algarve Surf School, which has been running surf lessons since 1996 (algarvesurfschool.com), while further east there's the Future Eco Surf School in Portimão (future-ecosurf.com). By train, it takes just under 3 hours from Lisbon (Estação do Oriente) to Tunes for connections to the west of the Algarve (such as Lagos and Portimão) and just over 4 hours by train from Lisbon to Faro in the Algarve for connections to the east of the Algarve (such as Tavira, Monte Gordo and Olhão). For train times: cp.pt. By bus, it's about 4 hours from Lisbon to Sagres and just over 3 hours from Lisbon to Portimão. For bus times: rede-expressos.pt.

Paddleboarding by public transport

One of the advantages of paddleboarding over some of the other kit-heavy watersports is that you can use inflatable paddle boards that can be packed away into a small bag and carried on public transport to reach some wonderful locations.

Many waterways in England and Wales require a licence to paddle. You can buy an annual licence as part of membership of the British Canoeing (britishcanoeing.org.uk) or you can buy a specific licence for the waterways managed by the Canal and River Trust (canalrivertrust.org.uk), the Environment Agency (gov.uk), and the Broads Authority (for paddling in the Norfolk Broads: broads-authority.gov.uk). In Scotland, there is the 'right to roam' so you don't require a licence, but joining the Scottish Canoe Association will give you lots of information about routes, access, courses and clubs. Here are six great locations for paddleboarding that can easily be reached by public transport.

1 The coastline of Swansea Bay and the Gower Peninsula is blessed with a wonderful range of rivers, estuaries, streams, points, reefs and beaches that are easily reached by bus from Swansea (swanseabaywithoutacar.co.uk). Stand Up Paddle Gower hires out boards and runs lessons for all levels at over 20 locations throughout the Gower as well as a night-time Glow Paddle in the more sheltered area at Mumbles (supgower.com).

2 The River Trent in the Midlands is the third longest river in the UK (after the Thames and Severn) and is great for a day out or longer paddle-touring multi-day adventure. The river was once a transport highway during the nineteenth century, rising in the Staffordshire moors and

meandering through large industrial cities, including Stoke-on-Trent and Nottingham before joining the River Ouse and entering the North Sea via the Humber estuary. Along the way, it passes under the medieval bridge at Swarkestone, by Newark Castle and some wonderful sprawling countryside. Calm Yoga SUP School runs a wide range of beginner and improver courses and sessions as well as SUP Yoga from its base in Burton upon Trent. (calm.online).

3 **Frenchmen's Creek** is a peaceful picturesque inlet off the Helford River just south of Falmouth. Koru Kayaking runs guided paddleboarding tours from Helford Passage across to *Frenchman's Creek*, the inspiration for Daphne du Maurier's novel Frenchman's Creek, along banks of ancient oaks. Beginners go to the sheltered Port Navas Creek with beautiful river fronted houses and magical wooded smaller creeks while more experienced paddlers can go to several secluded beaches and cave near Durgan, depending on wind direction and tides (korukayaking.co.uk). The Line 35 bus runs from Falmouth to Helford Passage (firstbus.co.uk).

4 **Lulworth Cove** is a beautiful shell-shaped oasis on the Jurassic Coast in West Dorset from where you can paddle along the World Heritage coast to the natural arch of Durdle Door – out on the open sea you're far from the masses that can crowd this famous natural attraction, and it's a wonderful paddle along the coast, with views of the spectacular white limestone cliffs and golden shingle beaches. Lulworth Activities is based at a hotel built in the 1650s on the shores of Lulworth Cove hires out boards by the hour or for a full day (lulworth-activities.co.uk). The X54 Weymouth-Poole bus runs via Lulworth Cove and the Durdle Door park entrance (firstbus.co.uk).

5 **The River Arun** has one of the strongest tides in the UK and is a wonderful paddle from Littlehampton inland to Arundel with views of spectacular eleventh-century Arundel Castle and the South Downs, while the upper stretch travels through the Arundel Wetland Centre to end at the Riverside Tea Rooms in Amberley (riversidesouthdowns.com). You can also hire stand-up paddle boards from here. There are several operators that run paddleboarding trips along the Arun, including Moxie Unleashed (moxieunleashed.com) and TJ Boardhire (tjboardhire.co.uk). There's a railway station in Arundel with rail connections from London, and it is also the bus stop for several local bus services from throughout West Sussex and beyond.

6 **The River Dee** runs through beautiful Royal Deeside from its source high in the Cairngorm mountains for 88 miles (142km) passing mountains, moorland, pine forest, birchwood and farmland, as well as several small towns and villages, on its way to the sea at Aberdeen harbour. Stonehaven Paddleboarding runs guided trips for 3 hours up to a full day along the Dee from Stonehaven, where there's a railway station with rail connections from Aberdeen and Edinburgh (shpb.co.uk).

Travel on an electric boat

Just as kayaking can allow you to reach places you wouldn't otherwise be able to reach, electric boats can provide a means of low-impact transport to remote places. They're virtually soundless, so there's little disturbance to the local wildlife and they produce less pollution than traditional diesel-powered motor cruisers. Thanks to the recent advances in lithium battery technologies, there are now a variety of options for electric boating; some are even charged by solar panels on the journey. You can cruise along the Thames with The Electric Boat Company (electricboatcompany. co.uk); potter along the river from the Quay at St Ives, Cambridgeshire with St Ives Electric River Boat Co. (electricriverboat.co.uk); discover Chichester Harbour on Solar Heritage (conservancy.co.uk); or explore the Broads in Norfolk on the solar-powered boat Ra, which takes up to 11 passengers from Hoveton Riverside Park towards Coltishall and into Bridge Broad (broads-authority.gov.uk). There are also plenty of places where you can hire electric boats in France, such as from Nort-sur-Erdre, just north of Nantes (atlantic-loire-valley.com) and on the Cote d'Azur between Nice and Monaco or between Antibes and Juan-les-Pins with seaZen (seazen.fr). You can also cruise the Norwegian fjords on the

Go paddling

A nationwide initiative from British Canoeing Go Paddling encourages people to go canoeing, kayaking and stand-up paddleboarding. Its website lists hundreds of paddle points and slipways throughout the UK in rivers, lakes and canals, and provides links to paddle operators, kit hire, centres and clubs: **gopaddling.info**

The solar-powered Algarve Sun Boat setting off along the Arade River, Portugal

battery-powered Rygerelektra (rodne.no) or for a more sedate option, explore the protected waters of Copenhagen's harbour on board the solar-powered GoBoat (goboat.dk). One of my favourite trips on an electric boat was on the solar-powered Algarve Sun Boat, which runs trips from the marina at Portimão along the Arade River to the medieval city of Silves. In just over two hours gently maneuvering along the river, we saw a host of birds including common sandpiper, egret, spoonbill, grey heron, black-headed gull, sandwich tern, greenshank, whimbrel, and marsh harrier (algarvesunboat.com).

In the latter part of the twentieth century, the invention of neoprene turned surfing into big business, and thanks to recent technological advances in equipment, we're now seeing a similar revolution in alternative watersports, from kitesurfing, wing surfing and hydro-foiling to back-to-basic marine activities, such as paddleboarding and free diving. To cater for the surge in demand, watersport centres, surf schools and camps are popping up all over Europe and there are plenty of great places to stay either on site or nearby that cater for eco-minded visitors. Here are five great surfing locations where you can ride the waves then kick back in a cocoon of eco-chic comfort.

1 Embruns d'herbe, Finistère, Brittany

Choose between a cosy two-person Finnish-inspired nest, a six-person straw house or a seven-person hemp eco lodge among permaculture at this fabulous earthy place that calls itself a 'slow camp' near to the surf at Trépassés Bay between Pointe du Raz and Pointe du Van on the west coast of Finistère, Brittany (embrunsdherbe.com).

2 Surf Camp Moliets, France

The complete surf package of lessons, yoga, food and lodgings in private bell tents in the town of Moliets in south-west France, just a short walk from the huge sandy beach backed by pine forest (starsurfcamps.com).

Watersports centres, surf schools and camps for eco-minded visitors are popping up all over Europe

3 Eco Surf House Bilbao, Spain

There are four excellent surf spots within walking distance of this state-of-the-art eco-architectural wooden building in the quiet village of Sopelana in the north of Spain, from where it's just 5 minutes to the local train station for a 20-minute ride into Bilbao, the capital of the Basque Country. The accommodation is eco minimalist: dorms for 8–10 people, with vegetarian and vegan options for all meals, and there's yoga seven days a week on the roof terrace or in the large garden, as well as an on-site sauna. The camp is part of the Pure Camp portfolio that run surf camps in classic surfing locations all over the world, including France, The Canaries, Portugal and Morocco – great for year-round waves (puresurfcamps.com).

4 Lanzarote Retreats

A quirky collection of family-run holiday villas, luxury Mongolian yurts, stylish stone cottages spread across a solar- and wind-powered, low-rise eco village just over 300 yards from the sandy beach at Finca de Arrieta in the north of the laid-back, surf-obsessed Canary island of Lanzarote. Couples or small families will love the Eco Surf Shack studio in the heart of the village, with a split-level, open-plan living room, Balinese pebbled shower and private terrace (lanzaroteretreats.com).

5 Bukubaki, Peniche, Portugal

Canadian-inspired treehouses and large, safari-style tents are on offer at this eco surf resort in the renowned surfing area of Peniche, in Portugal, a small fishing town just 1 hour from Lisbon. You can rent surf equipment, bikes and skateboards, and there are plenty of activities on site, such as yoga and surf balance exercises. For a post-surf soak there's a Finnish sauna and massage rooms, while children will love using the Skate Bowl (en.bukubaki.com).

10 of the best

Beaches worth the walk

There's nothing quite like having a beach all to yourself: the soothing sound of the waves breaking just for you over undisturbed golden sand. The kind of ambience you enjoy when you're the first there in the morning before the rest of the world arrives. Here is a selection of lovely beaches, bays and coves reachable by foot, mostly in dramatic locations, where the long walk in or scramble down puts most people off. You may not have these off-the-beaten-track gems all to yourself, but it's unlikely there'll be too many people to share the bliss. Just don't forget to pack enough food and water for the day.

1 Tramore, Dunfanaghy, Donegal, Ireland
There are any number of superb beaches along Donegal's wild Atlantic coast that are reachable only on foot, but the pick of them is the 30-minute walk from the edge of the sea inlet west of Dunfanaghy to Tramore. Beginning in the woods of the Lurgabrack Nature Reserve the route is a somewhat rollercoaster trek up and over large rolling sand dunes to this wonderfully remote and wild 2-mile (3.2-km) long sweep of sand.

2 La Grande Grève, Sark, Channel Islands
A beautiful sandy beach on the historic, car-free island of Sark that's reached via a 330-ft (100-m) climb down rocky steps (built by volunteers) from the narrow isthmus known as La Coupée, which connects the island to Little Sark.

3 Aberforest Beach, Newport, Wales
A horseshoe-shaped, mostly shingle beach a few miles along the coast from Newport in north Pembrokeshire along a largely undeveloped stretch of the Wales Coast Path. Flanked on either wide by headland, it's great for a protected swim at high tide. There's also a pretty streamside walk in from inland, passing by a waterfall in an ancient forest valley.

4 Riserva dello Zingaro, Sicily, Italy

You pay a small entrance fee to access this stunning protected area in north-west Sicily. There are several stunning beaches along the 4½-mile (7.2-km) stretch of wildflower-lined coastline and they all require a short but steep walk down from the main track. The reserve is also great for birding, there are nearly forty species that breed and nest here.

5 Plage de Saleccia, Corsica

A long sweep of soft sand with an impressive backdrop of high dunes in the unlikely setting of the Désert des Agriates, a remote, 20 sq. mile (52 sq. km) protected area of dense scrubland east of L'Île-Rousse. There are pleasure boats that travel here, but you can walk in along a 25-mile (40-km) trek along the desert's rugged coastal path, and if you want to have this idyll to yourself (once the day-trippers have gone), you can pitch a tent in the shade of trees behind Saleccia's dunes at Camping U Paradisu.

6 Prussia Cove, Cornwall

One of the gems along the South West Coast Path in the Cornwall Area of Outstanding Natural Beauty, this collection of four small sandy coves, the site of eighteenth-century smuggling, is tucked away on the coast of Mount's Bay to the east of Cudden Point, a 2½-mile (4-km) coastal walk from Perranuthnoe to the west or Praa Sands to the east.

7 Hayburn Wyke, North Yorkshire

A small cliffside pebble beach with two lovely waterfalls that cascade onto the rocks just north of Scarborough, reached through a wooded valley and a scramble down from the Cleveland Way. It can also be accessed via the Cinder Track, a disused railway walking and cycling track that runs between Scarborough and Whitby.

8 Inverie Bay, Knoydart, Inverness

The only way to reach this remote beach on the Knoydart peninsula is by taking the train up to Mallaig and then the ferry across Loch Nevis or by walking in along a rough 16-mile (26-km) trek from the end of the road at Kinloch Hourn. A short walk from the bay is the Old Forge, the most remote pub in mainland Britain where you can find a range of seafood sustainably caught from within a 7-mile (11-km) radius of Knoydart, such as hand-dived Loch Nevis scallops, Glenuig smoked salmon and Loch Nevis langoustines.

9 Porthdinllaen, Morfa Nefyn, Gwynedd

Residents of the beautiful fishing village of Porthdinllaen in North Wales can drive here, but visitors have a short walk in to reach this lovely, sheltered sweeping sandy beach at the tip of this scenic peninsula in the Llŷn Area of Outstanding Natural Beauty. Don't miss the nautical-themed real ale Ty Coch Inn at the far end of the beach looking out to the Irish Sea (access is restricted when the tide is high).

10 Sandwood Bay, Kinlochbervie, Sutherland

A wild and spectacular beach flanked by cliffs in Kinlochbervie backed by huge sand dunes and a loch that's only reached by a 4-mile (6.4-km) fairly flat path from the hamlet of Blairmore. The bay is part of an estate run by the John Muir Trust, a conservation charity dedicated to protecting and enhancing wild places in the UK.

In the

Breathe and relax. The joy of outdoor swimming at a range of locations, from lidos, ponds and converted quarries to lakes, rivers and sea pools.

Day three of a five-day wild swimming trip in the Scottish Inner Hebrides was the one we'd all been anticipating: crossing the Gulf of Corryvreckan between the islands of Jura and Scarba. I'd read about the Corryvreckan in Roger Deakin's iconic swimming book *Waterlog: A Swimmer's Journey Through Britain*. It is home to the third largest whirlpool in the world, but it's possible to swim across it during slack water, when the whirlpool is dormant. We wild camped the night before on Jura and walked over to have a look at the whirlpool at its height; it looked unswimmable – a mass of white froth and swirling water. In the morning as we travelled over to the Corryvreckan by boat, our swimming guide said that last year he'd seen a humpback whale in these waters, which didn't help

to calm our nerves! But as we approached the site, it soon became obvious how calm the waters had become, and in fact the crossing was one of the easiest of the week. There were a few little eddies (no whales), and the occasional slight sideways pull of water that at first was a little unsettling, but soon became just a distraction. It took about 30 minutes to swim across to the other side of the gulf, finishing beneath the huge 400-ft (122-m) slate cliffs of Scarba with an enormous sense of relief and achievement.

My trip had been organized by SwimTrek (swimtrek.com), one of the first operators to run swimming holidays in the UK. Although there have been river swimming clubs since the 1930s, as the technology became available for heating

Safe swimming

The Royal National Lifeboat Association (**rnli.org**) provides information and advice on cold water swimming, rip tides, lifeguarded beaches, buoyancy aids and lifejackets. The Outdoor Swimming Society has compiled an Outdoor Swimmer's Code to guide swimmers on a range of issues, including respecting and protecting the environment, being considerate of other water users and local communities; and being safe swimmers (**outdoorswimmingsociety.com**).

indoor pools, many of these clubs closed down. Today, only the one remaining is the Farleigh and District Swimming Club in Somerset, which was founded in 1933. However, the publication of Deakin's book in 1999 signalled a resurgence in the popularity of outdoor swimming. SwimTrek was founded in 2003, and the company now runs a range of guided swimming holidays all over the world, including trips along the coast of Donegal and among the Isles of the Scilly (both based on a tall ship), as well as weekend trips to the Lake District, and week-long swimming holidays in the warm waters of the Mediterranean in Greece, Spain and Turkey. There are also several other operators that run swimming holidays, such as SwimQuest (**swimquest.uk.com**), which runs luxury swimming holidays worldwide, and operators that organize swimming breaks in specific parts of the country, such as Swim the Lakes in the Lake District (**swimthelakes.co.uk**), Sea Swim Cornwall (**seaswimcornwall.co.uk**) in Cornwall, and The Big Blue Swim in Greece (**thebigblueswim.com**).

In 2006, the Outdoor Swimming Society (**outdoorswimmingsociety.com**) was created for swimmers to share their favourite swimming spots in rivers, lakes, lido and seas, and now has over 100,000 members. It runs long distance swimming events such as the Dart 10K in Totnes, Devon and the Hurly Burly in North Wales. My favourite is the Bantham Swoosh, a 6K swim down the estuary of the River Avon in Devon in clear, shallow water, so you can swim along and see the sandy bed most of the way. In the final stretch, there's a 'swoosh' as the ebbing tide is funnelled through a narrow section of river, speeding you along over the river-bed at several times your usual swimming speed. The National Open Water Coaching Association (**nowca.org**) was founded in 2010 to help improve safety standards at open water swimming venues around Great Britain and its website lists over 40 swimming lakes and venues around the country that are operated under the supervision of qualified coaching staff.

Places to swim

1 Open water swimming in lakes and rivers
The River and Lake Swimming Association provides of list of places to go swimming and bathing in lakes and rivers in the UK (riverandlakeswimming.org.uk). The Lake District is probably the best-known location for lake swimming, where you're spoilt for choice for places to go; among the most popular are Derwentwater, Rydal Water, Buttermere, Wastwater, Crummock Water and Windermere. Susanna Swims organizes guided swims predominantly in the north/west Lakes (suzannaswims.co.uk).

2 Waterfalls and gorges
Some of the most memorable walks are when you come across a waterfall or gorge to have a refreshing dip, such as Lady Falls in Powys, Wales, Falls of Falloch in Crianlarich, Scotland, and Galleny Force, Stonethwaite, in England's Lake District. There are many others in the UK – just be mindful of the conditions when water levels are high, it's always best to read up on them before you head off.

3 Sea pools
There are about 30 tidal sea pools in the UK, formed where the ocean meets land in the inter-tidal zone, such as the Clevedon Marine Lake in North Somerset that gets filled with seawater from the Bristol Channel every spring tide (clevedonmarinelake.co.uk), Shoalstone Pool, Brixham, Devon (shoalstonepool.com), Dun Ara Bathing Pool near Glengorm Castle on the Isle of Mull, and Walpole Bay Tidal Pool, Cliftonville, Margate (facebook.com/walpolebaybathing). One of the most accessible is the 1930s Summerleaze 300-ft (91-m) sea pool (budeseapool.org) a few minutes' walk from the centre of Bude in north Cornwall. Bude is just less than 2 hours by bus 6 or 6a from Exeter St Davids railway station.

4 Converted quarries
Several quarries in the UK have been converted into controlled swimming areas; they are usually very popular and require joining as a member before you can swim there. I go to Vobster Quay (vobster.com), Somerset, a former limestone quarry that is fed by a natural spring so the water is very

clear. It is also a national diving centre, so swimmers share the water with scuba divers, as well as free divers and stand-up paddle boarders. There's an on-site café selling hot meals and a shop selling a range of swimming and diving equipment. Another limestone quarry converted into a swimming spot is Henleaze (henleazeswimmingclub.org), Bristol, which has a high diving board and is surrounded by lawns and trees. There's also outdoor swimming at Dosthill Quarry, Tamworth near Birmingham, (dosthillquarry.com) and Gildenburgh Water, Whittlesey, near Peterborough (gildenburgh.com), both of which are also scuba diving centres.

5 Ponds

Perhaps the best-known swimming ponds are on Hampstead Health, London, where there's a ladies' pond, mens' pond and a mixed pond (cityoflondon.gov.uk). I love the discreet pond at One Cat Farm near Lampeter (onecatfarm.com); the large wildlife-friendly pond at Wheatland Farm in Devon (wheatlandfarm.co.uk); and the views of the valleys of Mynydd Epynt from the hillside pond high up at Pantechnicon Powys (welshlavender.com).

6 Lidos

The golden age of outdoor swimming pools, known as lidos, was during the Art Deco era of the 1930s when there were over 300 across the country, and although many have since closed there's been a revival in recent years with several being refurbished or reopened, including Tinside Lido in Plymouth, Ilkley Lido in West Yorkshire, Lido Ponty in Pontypridd, Wales, Jubilee Pool in Penzance, and Saltdean Lido in Brighton.

Clevedon Pools in Bath is Britain's oldest lido, built in 1815, while the country's longest lido is the 295-ft (90-m) Tooting Bec Lido, home to the South London Swimming Club and a state-of-the-art Finnish sauna (slsc.org.uk). Probably the largest lido in Europe is the 492-ft (150-m) Piscine Nakache Été at Parc des Sports in Toulouse, where there's an adjacent Olympic-sized, 50m swimming pool – great for a decent swim followed by a few hours chilling at the water's edge of the enormous, but shallow, main lido (toulouse.fr). Perhaps the most elaborate is Piscine Molitor in Paris, once a magnet for the fashion conscious during the two world wars (it was where the bikini was launched), it is now part of a luxury spa hotel (mgallery.accor.com).

Hotels with natural swimming pools

What can be more welcome on a hot summer's day than a plunge into the crystal-clear waters of an outdoor natural swimming pool? Designs vary, but the basic premise of these chemical-free pools are that a retaining wall partitions the swimming area away from a 'regeneration zone', where aquatic plants and sand act as a natural filter for oxygenizing and cleaning the water and provide a natural habitat for wildlife and insects. When you're reclining on the poolside lounger, don't be surprised if you see dragonflies and butterflies flittering across the water. Without the expense of added chemicals, or the regular wholesale change of water like many conventional chlorinated pools, it's no wonder hoteliers are installing these eco-friendly alternatives. Here are some examples in beautiful locations. Jump in – the water's lovely!

1 The Scarlet Hotel, Cornwall
It's the setting of this natural pool (with a wood-fired hot tub) that sets it apart – on the clifftops overlooking the golden sands of Mawgan Porth on the north Cornish coast. After a rejuvenating swim, be pampered in the Ayurvedic spa and feast on delicious fresh shellfish and sea herbs with a glass of Camel Valley Cornwall fizz at this stylish, trend-setting, small luxury hotel (scarlethotel.co.uk).

2 Orion B&B, St Paul de Vence, France
One of the pioneering natural pools in France set among a collection of four smart treehouses opposite the stunning medieval fortified village of St Paul de Vence, inland from the French Riviera. There's early morning outdoor yoga followed by breakfast served on the terrace by the pool, complete with barrel sauna and massage therapy (orionbb.com).

3 Il Paluffo, Tuscany, Italy
A collection of luxurious small villas and B&Bs in a restored fifteenth-century historic building powered by solar energy and other renewable sources, and surrounded by classic rolling Chianti Hills, not far from Florence and Siena (paluffo.com).

4 Chaumarty, Pyrenees, France
Irises, waterlilies, and papyrus line the water's edge of the gorgeous natural pool-with-a-view at this ecogîte south of Toulouse, facing the Pyrenees. There's a diving board and a smaller pool for children, while adjacent to the pools is a large terrace where you can lay your towels and admire the mountain panorama all day long (chaumarty.com).

5 Le Mas de Saribou, Avergne, France
The splendid natural pool at this four-room, self-catering ecogîte is just one of the many environmental features amid the rambling gardens of a 400-year-old farmhouse in the Ardèche. Solar panels for electricity, wood from old trees in the orchards for the fuel for heating, and a grass roof and thick walls keep you snug inside. There's also an organic garden for you to plunder your own veg, fruit, fresh herbs and flowers (masdesaribou.fr).

6 Le Camp, Varen, France
A luxury seven-pitch camp in an oak woodland overlooking the green valley of the Aveyron in south-west France. Every pitch – on a raised wooden platform – has been carefully chosen for its views, privacy and mood. There are large handmade beds, soft solar lighting, individually crafted tables and chairs, and an outdoor woodland spa shower house, but pride of place is the glorious 66-ft (20-m) natural pool. The owners can help plan your journey by train and offer a free transfer to and from the local train stations; they also provide bikes, including trailers and tagalongs for children (lecamp.co.uk).

7 Muxima, Algarve, Portugal
A single-storey farmstead that Jorge and his wife, Sofia, have turned into a splendid rural guesthouse north-west of Faro. There's early morning yoga by the natural pool followed by a vegetarian breakfast feast with mostly organic, local, homegrown and homemade produce, and a 70-acre (28-ha) forest to explore (muxima-montesferreiros.com).

8 Mas Ardèvol, Falset, Catalonia, Spain
The natural pool is a welcome oasis in the heat of the summer at this idyllic rural house in the green hills above Porrera. Dine here too, for the owners specialize in preparing traditional Priorat food, including fresh, seasonal produce from their own vegetable garden – asparagus in spring, fabulous fruit salads in summer, and mushrooms and almonds in autumn (masardevol.net).

9 Agroturismo Can Martí, Ibiza
A beautiful, authentic and organic farmhouse in a quiet and idyllic spot in the unspoilt north of the island. This has long been a favourite of mine, a wonderfully peacefully part of the island, far from the crowds of Ibiza Town and near some great beaches. Even better, it has recently installed a hammam (Turkish-style bath) and a wonderful natural swimming pool (canmarti.com).

10 La Jument Verte, Aix-les-Bains, France
Relax by the stunning natural pool at this B&B, guesthouse and country inn on a seventeenth-century farm above the spa town of Aix-les-Bains and the beautiful Lac du Bourget in the Bauges Natural Regional Park of the in the heart of the Savoy (la-jument-verte.com).

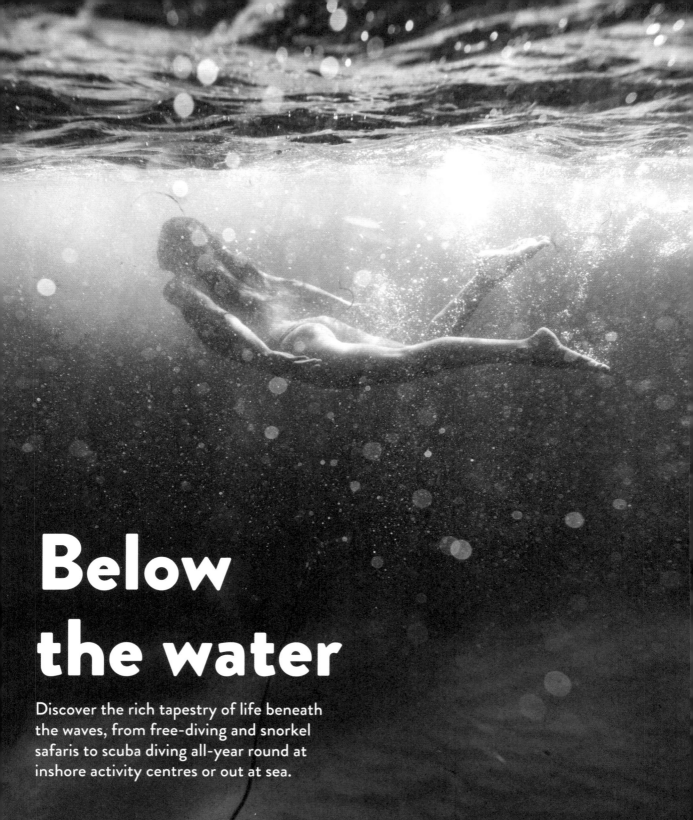

Below the water

Discover the rich tapestry of life beneath the waves, from free-diving and snorkel safaris to scuba diving all-year round at inshore activity centres or out at sea.

Scuba diving

As we descended beneath the warm blue waters off the west coast of Galicia in Northern Spain, our breath bubbling up to the surface like blobs of liquid mercury, the diffracted light turned the water turquoise, and we had our first opportunity to see that the visibility on this dive was going to be good. The dive leader pointed the way ahead, and after 5 minutes or so he beckoned me to fin down slowly to a clump of brightly coloured coral among swathes of tall seaweed. He moved away so I could see more clearly, and it wasn't long before I was rewarded with my first ever glimpse of a seahorse swaying back and forth with the current, camouflaged against the light brown sea fans.

No matter how many wildlife documentaries you see, nothing really compares to seeing creatures like this in their natural habitat. I was transfixed for several minutes, captivated by its nonchalance. Later in the dive we came across an octopus, a host of colourful sea fans and nudibranchs, and the remains of the wreck of the *Bayonnaise*, a three-masted French corvette with a wooden hull lined in copper that was scuttled in November 1803.

I'd been taken on this dive by Buceo Finisterre, one of several diving operators that run trips in the treacherous waters off the north-western coast of Galicia that are notorious for shipwrecks – the region we were diving in is known as the Costa da Morte, where there are plenty of other wrecks to dive, such as the *Solway* (1843), a nineteenth-century steam vessel which lies at a depth of 89ft (27m) and the Aegean Sea, which at the shallower depth of 59ft (18m) right beneath the iconic Tower of Hercules – the only Roman lighthouse in the world that is still functioning. The remains of the wrecks are home to a variety of marine species, such as breams, large basses, pintos, wrasses, octopus, cuttlefish, lobsters, crabs and eels. The region is also home to Cape Finisterre, which was believed by the Romans to be the most westerly point of the known world, facing out towards the Atlantic Ocean, and is the final destination for many walkers on the pilgrim route Camino de Santiago.

The variety of diving off the coast of Galicia is typical of many locations along the eastern flank of the Atlantic Ocean, to the south along the Portuguese coast at Sesimbra, Cascais and Portimão, and also north to Cornwall and to Donegal in the far north-west of Ireland – locations that have many world-class diveable shipwrecks but also have a similar geology of reefs, caves and rugged underwater mountains, seasoned with amazing kelp forests, gorgonian corals and any number of colourful marine invertebrates. These locations also share a common Atlantic heritage that relates to their maritime history and culture, and many of the best eco-minded diving operators, such as Buceo Finisterre, in these regions have joined together to create the Wildsea Atlantic Ocean Heritage Route, a programme of WILDSEA Europe (wildsea.eu), an EU-funded initiative that aims to showcase the best marine ecotourism experiences in Europe.

The temperature of the waters around the UK coast may not be as warm as the balmy western and southern shores of Spain and Portugal, but the diving can be just as good – there's a rich heritage of wrecks, huge tidal ranges and drift dives and a wide range of marine life, from tiny seahorses to huge basking sharks. You can find hundreds of dive clubs and centres in the UK that organize local dives, and lots of advice and support for dive training, planning and how you can conserve and safeguard marine life, on the websites of the two main diving organisations – the British Sub Aqua Club (bsac.com) and PADI (padi.com).

Diving in the UK

Here are a few scuba diving locations in the UK that you can reach by public transport, with suggestions on where you can hire tanks and weights on arrival.

ST ABBS, BERWICKSHIRE

St Abb's Head on the east coast of the Scottish Borders has some of the best sub-30m diving in the UK, partly because the waters here are unusually clear and also because the area of St Abbs and Eyemouth is a voluntary marine reserve, the oldest in the UK. In the shallow water there are spectacular kelp forests, sea urchins, sea slugs and territorial fish, and as you descend the reefs are carpeted with soft corals that are home to velvet swimming crabs, butterfish and anemones. Take the train to Berwick-upon-Tweed, and it is then a 35-minute ride on bus number 235 to St Abbs.

Dive operators that run dives at St Abbs include Dive Stay (divestay.co.uk), Dive St Abbs (divestabbs.com), Deep Blue Pirates (deepbluepirates.net) and there are dives organized at St Abbs from the Diving Centre based further south at East Boldon thedivingcentre.com. Don't miss the wonderful Ebbcarrs Café on the harbour front that has fresh local seafood, home baking and local ales.

OBAN, ARGYLLSHIRE

Oban is the gateway to the wild coat of Argyll and the tremendous dive sites in the Firth of Lorn Special Area of Conservation and Marine Protected Area, which includes Corryvreckan Whirlpool and the offshore Garvellachs Islands, whose deep channels provides a great variety of dive sites as well as the sheltered channels of inshore sea-lochs such as Cuan, the Sound of Luing and the Grey Dogs. The railway station in the centre of Oban is the final stop of one of the branches of the scenic West Highland Line from Glasgow Queen Street (Oban is just 2 hours on the train from Glasgow). Puffin Dive Centre is 1½ miles (2.4km) from the station and runs scuba diving training courses as well as taster dives and drysuit diving for the more experienced. Dives in this area can also be done with one of the most established dive operators in Scotland; Dive Scotland (divescotland.com) is run by First Class Diver David Ainsley who has operated a dive charter boat for 30 years and has racked up over 4,000 dives.

FARNE ISLANDS, NORTHUMBERLAND

The Farne Islands are a group of 20 small islands and rocky outcrops lying a few miles off the Northumberland coast, known for their colonies of seabirds and grey seals, with hundreds of places to go diving, including several wrecks. There are a number of dive operators that run dive charters out to the islands, including Billy Shiel's Boat Trips out of the harbour at Seahouses (reachable by the X18 bus from Newcastle to Berwick) and Farne Islands Diving Charters (farne-islands-diving.co.uk), which run trips out to the Farne Islands on its RIB boat from Beadnell Village (buses 418 and X18 stop in the village).

FALMOUTH, CORNWALL

Falmouth Bay is home to some easily accessible shore dives from beaches such as Castle Beach and Silver Steps, and wreck diving at the Manacles Reef where the SS *Mohegan* sank in 1898 and is now adorned with rock stacks covered in jewelled anemones and home to dogfish and anglerfish. Falmouth has a railway station from where it's just a few minutes' walk to Falmouth Bay and also to the Cornwall Dive Centre where you can go on shore dives and take a refresher course (cornishdiving.co.uk). A more recent wreck is HMS *Scylla* that was sunk in 2004 by the National Marine Aquarium in Whitsand Bay to create an artificial reef that is now rich in biodiversity, with more than 270 marine species. The waters around the rocky islands of Quies off Trevose Head, north of Newquay, are also rich with starfish, spider crabs, dahlia anemones and sea squirts, while on night dives you can see lobster, crabs and octopus.

Inshore places to dive

Dosthill Quarry, Staffordshire. Bus 15, 6/6A, X16 Tamworth to Dosthill from where it's a 5-minute walk (dosthillquarry.com).
Gildenburgh Water, Cambridgeshire. Bus 33 from Whitmore Street to Coronation Avenue from where it's a 13-minute walk (gildenburgh.com).
National Diving and Activity Centre, Gloucestershire. Bus from Chepstow to Bishton Lane, from where it's a 6-minute walk (ndac.co.uk).
Stoney Cove, Leicestershire. Bus X55 from Hinkley to South Drive, from where it's a 5-minute walk (stoneycove.com).
Vivian Quarry, Gwynedd. Bus 85/86 to Llanberis Lake Railway (duttonsdivers.com/vivian-quarry).
Vobster Quay, Somerset. Bus 184 from Frome to the Bus Shelter, from where it's a 7-minute walk (vobster.com).
Wraysbury, Berkshire. Train to Wrasbury from where it's a 10-minute walk (wraysbury.ws).

Make every dive a survey dive

You can help turn your dive into part of several mass citizen science conservation projects by collecting data on underwater marine debris you come across on your dive and logging it on a global database.

Dive Against Debris is run by the PADI AWARE Foundation to collect data that can be used for conservation, particularly supporting the development and implementation of policies around the world to improve solid waste management (padiaware.org).

Tips for responsible diving

● **Be careful with your buoyancy** so that you don't touch or step on marine wildlife, especially coral, which can take decades to regrow.
● **Keep your distance from marine wildlife**, let the animals decide the nature of the encounter.
● **Keep visits to underwater caves to as short as possible** as the air bubbles you create can remain in pockets usually colonized by marine organisms that are unable to move and can be killed.
● **Don't ever collect dead or living marine wildlife**. Certain species are protected in different countries, and you could be heavily fined.
● **Do pick up plastic or other types of rubbish** if it's safe to do so, and properly dispose or recycle it.
● **Cover up as much as possible** to reduce the amount of your exposed skin and then choose a mineral-based sunscreen that forms an actual block on your exposed skin, for example one that uses zinc oxide or titanium dioxide, rather than one that contains chemicals, such as oxybenzone and octinoxate (or any form of microplastic), which can harm coral reefs.
● **Choose a sustainably minded tour operator**, one that supports marine conservation and has a responsible tourism policy regarding their boating, mooring and diving operations. Ask if they partner with environmental organizations and whether they educate their diving guests about local marine flora and fauna. If so, they are more likely to be aware of ecological practices.

Global Dive Log is run by earthdive in partnership with the UN Environment Programme World Conservation Monitoring Centre and marine biologists from all over the world to help build a worldwide database of key indicator species and a snapshot of the world's oceans. It's mantra is: 'See it, log it, map it' (earthdive.com).
Seasearch is a volunteering project run by the Marine Conservation Society for scuba divers and snorkellers to help map the seabed found in the near-shore zone around Britain and Ireland. Volunteers attend a short course on marine recording and then join one of the organized dive or snorkelling events that are planned throughout the year by local coordinators (seasearch.org.uk).

Seashores & snorkelling

There are hundreds of places along the coastline of the UK where you can get to know more about the marine wildlife and how to conserve it. Local Wildlife Trusts (wildlifetrusts.org) often have information on local events, such as snorkelling trips and seashore safaris. Here are a few ideas:

Join the Dorset Wildlife Trust on an underwater snorkel trail in a marine conservation zone at The Fine Foundation Wild Seas Centre in Kimmeridge Bay, Dorset. You'll see peacock's tail seaweed, Connemara clingfish and Montagu's blennies, and in the shallow water, there are large wrasse and shoals of small fish against the colours of rainbow wrack and coralline seaweed. If you're lucky you may also see some of the large marine mammals that visit the zone, such as seals and dolphins (dorsetwildlifetrust.org.uk).

Go on a snorkel safari on Lundy Island off the north coast of Devon. Managed by the Landmark Trust, Lundy was the first Marine Nature Reserve, Marine Conservation Zone and No Take Zone, and an experienced guide will take you to explore the shallow waters of the Landing Bay, home to spider crabs, ballan wrasse and scarlet and gold star corals, as well as beautiful cup corals and magnificent kelp forests. You may even encounter one of the island's resident playful grey seals (landmarktrust.org.uk).

Go snorkelling off the coast of Cornwall in the Looe Voluntary Marine Conservation Area that's teaming with biodiversity. You can head into the water from the seashore at three locations: Hannafore, West Looe; Second Beach, East Looe; and Portnadler Bay – a 15-minute walk west of Hannafore via the coastal path. Among the eelgrass beds, kelp forests, and reefs are ballan and corkwing wrasse, bass, pollack, cuttlefish, flatfish, dogfish, sand gobies, tompot blennies, sea cucumbers, edible crab, velvet swimming crab, spider crabs, hermit crabs, sea anemones, sponges and many species of snails (looemarineconservation.org).

Explore the underwater boulders of Loch Long near Helensburgh in the west of Scotland – a sea loch that's famous for its clear waters, where visibility can be greater than 33ft (10m). Some of the underwater pinnacles are less than 3¼ft (1m) below the surface so it is incredibly easy to see the marine life from the surface with a snorkel, including shoals of pollack and saithe (similar to cod), and mussels and starfish clinging to tree roots just under the water (wildaboutargyll.co.uk).

Learn about marine life

The British Sub Aqua Club (BSAC) runs a one-day marine life appreciation course to help divers understand more about marine wildlife and the underwater environment and what you can do to conserve it (bsac.com).

The Professional Association of Diving Instructors (PADI) runs a Project AWARE Specialty classroom-based course introducing the work of the Project AWARE global movement. It includes a range of modules from open oceans to freshwater lakes, where you'll explore issues such as overfishing, pollution, coral bleaching and debris, and the everyday actions you can take to protect the environment (padi.com).

Mulberry Divers, based in Selsey, West Sussex, runs a series of marine ecology courses to help you better understand and protect the marine environment. Courses include coral and fish identification, manta and ray ecology, and sea turtle ecology (mulberry-me.co.uk).

10
of the best

Cafés and seafood shacks

The sustainable seafood scene is sizzling. Across the land, sea-to-plate dishes are commonplace on the menus of some of the best restaurants, gastro pubs and gourmet supper clubs, but there's also been a quiet revolution of ethical eateries at seaside cafés and beach shacks. They come in all shapes and sizes, from upcycled shipping containers to converted fishing boats, but what they all have in common is that they strengthen the connection between the local catch and the provision of fresh seafood, with daily menus that change depending on what's been caught, conveniently serving them up in beautiful locations.

1 DRIFT, North Berwick
A unique farm diversification project has led to this wonderful coffee house and café in an upcycled shipping container on the clifftop at Quarrel Sands, a few miles east of North Berwick, with views across the Firth of Forth, Bass Rock and Fife. Just half a mile from Tantallon Castle, it serves simple brunches and light lunches from seasonal Scottish produce prepared fresh every day, such as Harris gin-cured salmon with pickled cucumber and a Scottish smorgasbord of cheeses, charcuterie, pickles, whipped Crowdie, smoked nuts, figs and apple cider chutney. It has recently added a take-away service from a trailer for those wanting a quick bite to eat (driftalong.co.uk).

2 The Hidden Hut, Cornwall
I first came across this gem of a place when it was little more than a snack shack, but it has since grown into one of Cornwall's foodie hotspots, garnering plaudits from food critics and celebrities alike, including Rick Stein and Dawn French. Despite the notoriety, it has retained its secluded salty-sea charm, tucked away on the coast path above Porthcurnick Beach on the Roseland Peninsula (between Porthbean and Portscatho beaches). Expect soups, chowders and spiced dhals in the spring and autumn, big beach salads and grilled seafood in the summer, all with fresh and seasonal ingredients. On selected summer nights, it transforms into an open-air, one-dish, bring-your-own-plate (and alcohol) celebration of the best local produce, such as 'Lobster & Chips' and 'Mackerel Grill', all cooked over a wood fire or local charcoal (hiddenhut.co.uk).

3 Killybegs Seafood Shack, Co. Donegal
An extremely popular fish and chip take-away on the pier of Ireland's largest fishing port, selling a range of freshly cooked seafood, including haddock, cod, scampi, prawns and calamari (facebook.com/killybegseafoodshack).

4 Off Grid Gourmet, Hay-on-Wye
A solar-wood and charcoal-powered supper club for up to 20 guests prepared by chef Hugh Sawyer in an elegant dining shed at the Walkers Cottage campsite in the Wye Valley (offgridgourmet.co.uk).

5 The Seafood Shack, Ullapool
An award-winning takeaway run by two local women, Kirsty and Fenella, on the main street in Ullapool – the gateway to the Summer Isles and the ferry to Stornaway. They provide the names of the boats and fishermen that have landed the catch, such as: Bon Ami, 'skippered by Josh with his crewman Dave' for the langoustines, lobster, spineys and crab; Gary who skippers on one of the scallop boats for Hand Dived Highland Shellfish; and Joe who owns Ockran oysters in Ullapool. Being made aware of the provenance of these local delicacies makes them taste that much better (seafoodshack.co.uk).

6 Gylly Beach Café, Falmouth
A smart, stylish café on Falmouth's Gyllyngvase Beach with a menu packed with dishes made from local ingredients, such as fish from St Ives, eggs from St Ewe and meat from Launceston, that you can wash down with beer from St Austell or wine from the Camel Valley (gyllybeach.com).

7 Oban Seafood Hut, Oban, Argyll
Also known as the Green Shack, this popular informal hut sells fresh seafood, including lobster, scallops and crab from its position on the town's railway pier, conveniently next to the ferry port that's the gateway to the isles of the Inner Hebrides and a popular scuba diving hub (facebook.com/obanseafood.hut.9).

8 The Company Shed, West Mersea, Essex
Run by the Haward family for 30 years alongside their fishmonger business, this highly successful, no-frills seafood restaurant among the salt marshes and boatyards of West Mersea operates on a bring-your-own-bottle-and-bread policy, selling platters of shellfish and other fresh seafood landed by locals (thecompanyshed.co).

9 The Crab Hut, Brancaster Staithe, Norfolk
A popular small harbourside hut that sells fresh baguettes filled with a range of seafood caught locally, including cockles, mussels and whelks, as well as crab and lobsters caught by the owner's own boat from the harbour, and salmon from their smokehouse (letzersseafood.co.uk).

10 Café Môr, Freshwater West, Pembrokeshire
A solar-powered, portable shack selling seafood caught by Pembrokeshire fishermen from the car park overlooking the fabulous beach at Freshwater West. The crab and lobster rolls are delicious, served with Welsh Sea black butter and a dash of lemon, so too are the imaginative veggie and vegan burgers, such as the homemade black bean burger with kelp, laver and seaweed (beachfood.co.uk).

Into the woods

Make the most of the sights and sounds
of the forest while helping to support
these vital green lungs.

At 3pm, bang on cue, dozens of red-brown kites came swirling in to pick up off-cuts of meat, they would settle for a moment, gnawing at the scraps, then fly off hastily to eat their spoils on the wing. Standing in front of a lakeside forest in the late summer sun, it was a thrilling sight to see so many of these once rare birds, distinguished by their mewing calls, deeply forked tails and angled wings with a span of nearly 6½ft (2m).

Two decades ago, the red kite – the national bird of Wales – was one of only three globally threatened species in the UK, but its successful reintroduction throughout the country has seen numbers recover dramatically. There are now more than 400 pairs in Wales alone, and more than 10,000 across the UK – it is one of the country's most successful conservation stories. As a result, there are any number of places across Mid Wales where you can see these magnificent birds of prey. One of the most scenic is where I'd come to, at Bwlch Nant yr Arian Forest Visitor Centre at the head of the Melindwr Valley, about 10 miles (16km) east of Aberystwyth. You can watch the birds feeding from a hide to the east of the lake, adjacent to where the food is scattered, from a viewing area on the opposite shore, or from inside or outside the café at the visitor centre. The red kites are the main attraction, but this eco-friendly centre is also a hive of activity for a range of low-impact outdoor pursuits, with multiple waymarked trails for walkers, runners, horse-riders and mountain bikers heading out into the Cambrian Mountains on a variety of wilderness rides, from mountain climbs to river crossings and technical rocky descents.

Bwlch Nant yr Arian is one of 14 sites that are part of the new National Forest of Wales, which is aiming to link existing forests with new woodland, creating green corridors for wildlife as well as a carbon sink. Other sites include Coed-y-Brenin, Dyfi Forest and Wye Valley woodlands.

Conservation in action

Numbers of red kite have increased dramatically thanks to sites like Bwlch Nant y Arian Forest Visitor Centre in West Wales. With walking, cycling, horse-riding, and an onsite café, it's a great day out for all the family.

These activity centres represent a new kind of regenerative travel experience, where your low-impact visit funds biodiversity conservation and tree planting, helping to regulate ecosystems, protect biodiversity and play an integral part in the carbon cycle. There are thousands of forest locations around the UK and in the Europe. Here are some examples where you can make the most of the woodland environment while helping to support these vital green areas.

Waterfall walks

Late spring is the best time of year to visit waterfalls, when the rivers are high and the forests come alive with new growth. It is even better if it's been raining beforehand as the waterfalls are likely to be in full flow. Two of my favourite waterfall walks are in France – the Cascades des Anglais in the pine forest of Vizzavona in the mountainous central Corsica, a short walk up from Vizzavona railway station. I first came across it on a 6-mile (9.7km) loop trail while hiking the GR20 and have been back twice since to walk in the forest and swim in its pools. The other is the Grande Cascade de Gavarnie in the Pyrenees, one of the biggest in Europe, which you can reach on the GR10. I recommend spending some time at Refuge Wallon-Marcadau, either in the hostel or camping, and exploring the scenic area of the Cirque de Gavarnie – it is one of the most spectacular locations in the whole of France. Switzerland is also home to some of the most impressive waterfalls in Europe, including the spectacular Staubbach Falls, which plunges almost 1,000ft (300m) down the vertical cliff face above the village of Lauterbrunnen in the Bernese Alps (you can see it on the right-

hand side of the train as it leaves the village station); the glacier-fed Trümmelbach Falls in the caves of the Lauterbrunnen Valley, which are Europe's largest subterranean waterfalls; Rhine Falls, Schaffhausen, which is the most powerful waterfall in Europe; and the thunderous Giessbach Falls, which you can reach by a short ferry boat from Interlaken across Lake Brienz then a ride up Europe's oldest funicular to the secluded Grand Hotel Giessbach, a magnificent fin-de-siècle hotel from where, over lunch in the gardens, you have a full view of the falls.

There are hundreds of waterfall walks in the UK, a favourite of mine is the Four Falls Trail in the Waterfall Country of the Brecon Beacons National Park. You can walk to the trail from the bus stop in Glynneath (buses stop here from Swansea, Neath and Merthyr Tydfil) or a little closer in is Pontneddfechan (although fewer buses stop here). The walk through woodland is along steep-sided gorges to the four picturesque waterfalls; at Sgwd yr Eira you can walk on a rocky path behind the cascade of tumbling water. A gentler stroll that's great for families is Ninesprings walk, conveniently at the edge of the centre of Yeovil, just 5 minutes' walk from Pen Mill railway station. It's a lovely

The waterfall walk to Pontneddfechan in the Brecon Beacons

woodland walk within the 20-acre (8ha) Yeovil Country Park, along a network of paths, bridges and multiple mini waterfalls. There's an outdoor play area for children and an excellent café for an end-of-walk cup of hot chocolate.

For more ideas of great waterfall walks in the UK, there's an excellent Facebook group where members share photos and their favourite waterfall locations: facebook.com/groups/925413064237658. In Europe, there are hundreds of waterfalls listed on the websites europeanwaterfalls.com and world-of-waterfalls.com.

Forest cycling

Forestry England is the nation's largest land manager; it is the largest supplier of Forest Stewardship Council (FSC) certified timber in England but also runs over 270 woodland centres open to the general public with activities ranging from walks and horse-riding to Segway and mountain bike trails. Natural Resource Wales and Forestry and Land Scotland fulfil a similar role. These forests are great days out for families, many have discovery trails and are home to Go Ape outdoor high ropes adventure playgrounds. Some of the best mountain bike trails in the UK are in these forests, where you can hire bikes or take your own, and enjoy hundreds of miles of single-track woodland trails. One of the most famous is Coed-y-Brenin in North Wales, but there are many other centres throughout the UK, including Whinlatter in the Lake District, see p77, (take the 77 bus – known as the Honister Rambler – from Keswick), Cannop Cycle Centre in the Forest of Dean, Gloucestershire, on the site of an old colliery (take the 30 bus from Coleford, then it's a 14-minute walk), and Comrie Croft in Perthshire (there are 17 buses a day from Perth to Comrie Croft on Stagecoach route 15).

The National Forest

Spanning 200 sq. miles (518 sq. km) of mixed habitat forest across parts of Derbyshire, Leicestershire and Staffordshire, the National Forest is a regeneration success story, turning denuded land with a history of coal mining and heavy industry into rolling forest and new planted woodlands – over 9 million trees have been planted since it was established in 1995. Over 80 per cent of the forest has public access and there's a wealth of things to do, from woodland walks and cycling to woodland crafts and wildlife spotting. Pride of place is Conkers, a 120-acre (48.5ha) adventure playground (nationalforest.org).

Forest bathing

Forest bathing is an ancient Japanese practice of seeking solace in woodland. The idea is that while you stay calm and quiet, breathing deeply and taking the time to observe nature in a natural setting, you help to nurture your wellbeing. While it's possible to go forest bathing in any woodland setting, there are special trips organized to help you make the most of your time in the forest, such as Forest Bathing Isle of Wight (forestbathingisleofwight.co.uk) and at Cabilla in Cornwall (cabillacornwall.com).

The Natural Navigator

Tristan Gooley's UK-based courses on natural navigation teach you how to find your way using only natural clues, such as the sun, moon, stars, land, sea, weather, plants and animals. It's a fascinating and handy way to understand your location before you automatically reach for a map, compass or GPS (naturalnavigator.com).

10
of the best

Treehouse holidays

Treehouses have come a long way from makeshift wooden shacks with flimsy rope ladders at the bottom of the garden: the modern constructions are carefully crafted, cosy, highly insulated, state-of-the-art structures. They're often in beautiful, secluded woodland locations, cocooned but with plenty of creature comforts, including double beds, wood-burning stoves, running water, fully equipped kitchens and spring-water showers. Breakfast may served via a pulley to haul up a hamper of fresh bread and homemade jam; some treehouse abodes even have rope bridges to children's rooms or require a harness to reach them. All enable you to live the high life in the lofty boughs of a tree: lie back, count the stars and listen to the owls.

1 The Living Room, Powys
Six state-of-the-art architectural wonders in wood, high up in the tree canopy in a dense woodland in the heart of Wales with double beds, fold-down bunk beds, and wood-burning stoves that heat spring-water showers (living-room.co).

2 The Enchanted Fareway Tree, Kent
A picturebook treehouse pod with glass-domed ceiling, wood-fired hot tub, fire pit and outdoor hot water showers amid a secluded garden. Located in the village of Blean, from where it's a short walk to the ancient Blean Woodlands (kent-cottage-holidays.co.uk).

3 Hudnalls Hideout, Gloucestershire
Indulgence for couples only at this large, carefully crafted luxury treehouse in the Wye Valley. Sited in ancient woodland with access to a wildflower meadow for picnics. Massages, reflexology treatments and yoga can be arranged (hudnallshideout.co.uk).

4 Bensfield Treehouse, East Sussex
Pick up a hamper full of local goodies then walk along a 79-ft (24-m) rope bridge over a pond to this cosy retreat for two built around a mature oak in the heart of the beautiful East Sussex countryside near the village of Wadhurst (bensfieldtreehouse.co.uk).

5 Into the Woods, Isle of Wight
Two beautifully hand-built larch treehouses in Wootton, on the other side of the creek to where the ferries arrive from Portsmouth. The Roost sleeps up to six, while The Nest is a cute hideaway for couples (isleofwighttreehouse.com).

6 The Treehouse, Argyll
An eight-sided eco build with triangular dormer windows, underfloor heating and a traditional slated roof. There's just a double bed, but an oak staircase spirals around the central oak tree up to a mezzanine level where the kids can stay. This unique eco-friendly abode is in an eighteenth-century orchard by a woodland on the historic Kinlochlaich House estate, halfway between the railway stations of Oban and Fort William in the west of Scotland (treehousescotland.co.uk).

7 Rufus's Roost, York
Walk across a raised boardwalk through the forest to this wonderfully secluded large treehouse in a private woodland on the Baxby Manor estate. It sleeps up to six in three treetop rooms, and between two turrets there's a large veranda with a log-fired pizza oven and a hot tub. The kids will be in den heaven when they discover the hidden doorway under the stairs that opens up a wooden slide down to a secret room with bean bags and comfy cushions. Magical (baxbymanor.co.uk).

Alnwick Gardens Treehouse Restaurant

Seasonal local produce is the focus of the menu at the wonderful treehouse restaurant at Alnwick Gardens in Northumberland. It's a great place to go after a tour of Alnwick Castle, which starred in the Harry Potter films as the magical Hogwarts School of Witchcraft and Wizardry (alnwickgarden.com).

8 Les Cabanes de Labrousse, Ardèche, France
Choose between nine perched huts in a glorious Douglas pine and chestnut tree forest in the Monts d'Ardèche Regional Natural Park. Some are on stilts and accessed by clambering up a stairway, including the Beaver Hut for a family of four, while others are for adults who have a head for heights – reached via a high-ropes adventure course, including the 6-metre high Owl Hut, 8-metre high Fox Hut and 10-metre high Squirrel Hut, where you're given a harness to climp up a rope ladder (cabanesardeche.com).

9 Perché dans le Perche, Normandy, France
A perfectly formed abode (sleeps up to six) in an old sweet chestnut tree, with a large terrace and summer kitchen. It sits in splendid isolation among a naturalist garden within 25 acres (10ha) of sustainably managed countryside in the Le Perche Regional Nature Park. Hiking trails lead to La Renardière and through sunken lanes to the Bellou-le-Trichard valley (perchedansleperche.com).

10 Treehouse Hotel, Falköping, Sweden
Hoist up your organic breakfast every morning to your wooden cabin, 21ft (6.5m) high in a cluster of oak trees in tranquil setting near Falköping in western Sweden. There are two cabins: Respite and the statelier Seventh Heaven. Both have double beds and were built sustainably; natural colour pigments were whipped together with linseed oil and eggs from the neighbour's hens; organic textiles adorn the interiors; and you'll drift off to sleep on double organic mattresses listening to the rustling of the leaves in this very special arboreal abode (islanna.com).

Rewilding

See rewilding in action, enjoy the great outdoors and the natural world while contributing to much-needed regeneration of the land.

On the short walk down to the off-grid boathouse, I count over a dozen marbled white butterflies criss-crossing the path, fluttering in the gentle summer breeze. There are other butterflies too: Essex skippers, meadow browns, and ringlets. At one point, by the settling pond of an enormous reed water purification system, I spot a clump of ragworts with orange and black striped cinnabar moth caterpillars clinging to their stems. There are bees buzzing all around in the warm summer sun, birds chirping – the place has the feel of a nature reserve. As I walk round the corner of an ancient oak and ash forest, I come to the exquisite hexagonal boathouse set in splendid isolation in front of a pontoon leading down to a long lake that stretches as far as the eye can see. It's a wild swimmer's dream.

It is the summer of 2021 and I've come to Sheepdrove Farm (sheepdrove.com), a 2,000-acre (810-ha) organic farm in the North Wessex Area of Outstanding Natural Beauty. The boathouse is a basic hideaway for two, with a double room, a small kitchen, shower, plenty of natural light and large bifold doors through which you can gaze out over the lake. It is heated by an air source heat pump; all the energy it draws on is generated on-site through two wind turbines and solar panels (there are 900 across the farm), and all wastewater is treated through the reedbed water filtration system. The eco credentials of the boathouse are impressive, but it's the scale and diversity of environmentally sustainable projects throughout the farm that creates the feeling you're staying somewhere special. There's an eco conference centre, a natural burial wood, a wedding venue and a former farm building that sleeps up to 18. While I was there, the staff were getting busy for a photo shoot to launch a new electric car.

For over 25 years, Sheepdrove has been at the forefront of sustainable, regenerative and organic farming across its green pastures, wildflower meadows, ancient woodland and fields of heritage grains on chalk downland. It is now one of an increasing number of farms and rural estates that are using the income and profile of nature-based tourism to help fund and publicize rewilding projects, restoring large-scale ecosystems to help repair damaged habitats, regenerate degraded landscapes and promote more biodiversity. It is otherwise known as 're-naturing' as they are re-engineering the land as nature intended. Governments, too, are putting in place measures to encourage rewilding as a means to combat climate change, on land and at sea, through the storing of carbon in soil, bogs, scrub and trees, and the restoration of seagrass meadows and kelp forests. Examples include rewetting of peat bogs, restoration of watercourses, creation of wetlands, removal of intensive grazing, reintroduction of key flora and fauna, allowance of natural regeneration and planting forests. Here are some examples of places, like Sheepdrove, where you can see rewilding in action while contributing to much-needed regeneration of the land.

Fritton Lake, Norfolk

A family-run outdoor holiday club among a 1,000-acre (405-ha) rewilding project near the Broads, and part of the Somerleyton Estate. Stay in the smart clubhouse rooms, in designer woodland cabins or in traditional estate farm cottages. There's a wonderful 2-mile (3.2-km) long lake where you can swim, paddleboard, kayak or just soak up the sounds of nature from a floating sauna. The rewilding project here is part of the Wild East initiative, which is aiming to return over 600,000 acres (250,000ha) of East Anglia to nature. At Fritton, they are restoring one-fifth of the land, reintroducing deer, water buffalo and ponies, as well as lots of bird and plant life (frittonlake.co.uk).

Knepp Castle Estate, West Sussex

Camp in a meadow or stay in one of the glampsites (treehouses, tents, yurts, shepherd's huts), and go on safari around one of the largest and best-known rewilding estates in lowland Britain, where you will see herds of wild ponies, cattle, deer and pigs as they roam 3,500 acres (1,400ha) of Sussex, driving the forces of habitat regeneration. The co-owner, Isabella Tree, is the author of the seminal book on the subject that charts how she and her husband transformed their loss-making farm in lowland Britain into a ground-breaking rewilding project: *Wilding: The Return of Nature to a British Farm* (kneppsafaris.co.uk). Keep up to date with this evolving project by watching Kneppflix – snapshot videos of the latest happenings (knepp.co.uk).

Rewilding Britain

Rewilding Britain was founded in 2015 to restore ecosystems across Britain. Its manifesto is to see 'a mosaic of species-rich habitats restored and connected across at least 30 per cent of Britain's land and sea by 2030', which it hopes to achieve by the creation of core rewilding areas across at least 5 per cent of Britain, and the establishment of nature-enhancing land and marine uses across at least 25 per cent of Britain (rewildingbritain.org.uk).

Rewilding Europe

Rewilding Europe is based in The Netherlands and has been working since 2011 to create rewilded landscapes in over ten regions across Europe, including the Greater Côa Valley in Portugal, The Danube Delta in Ukraine, Romania and Moldova, the Rhodope Mountains in Bulgaria and the Oder Delta in Germany and Poland (rewildingeurope.com).

Kingsdale Head, North Yorkshire

A 1,500-acre (600-ha) upland farm near the village of Ingleton, just below Whernside, the highest peak in the Yorkshire Dales. The owners are working to restore the natural hydrology of the wet heathland and grassland habitats, enabling it to hold more water and store more carbon by using a small herd of cattle to change the impact of grazing, while reintroducing more native shrubs and trees. You can see it all while staying in a cottage next to the main farmhouse – explore the farm's sheltered woodland and waterfalls, and venture further to the Forest of Bowland (kingsdalehead.com).

Ken Hill Estate, Norfolk

One of the filming locations for BBC's *Springwatch* programme, this estate's rewilding project is as much about regenerative agriculture as it is about nature recovery, demonstrating that land can be used to tackle climate change as well as improve air and water quality. Join guided tours of the farm and the extensive rewilding area and learn about vital grazing of the Exmoor ponies, Tamworth pigs and Red Poll cattle, as well as the variety of wildlife, including beavers (wildkenhill.co.uk).

Dundreggan Rewilding Centre, Inverness

Based at its own 10,000-acre (4,000-ha) estate at Dundreggan in the Scottish Highlands, Trees for Life is working to restore ancient Caledonia Forest from the last remains of this original wild forest, especially around Glen Affric and Glenmoriston. Visit the centre for the day or stay at the estate as a conservation volunteer, or at its bothy in the nature reserve of Glen Affric (treesforlife.org.uk).

Alladale Wilderness Reserve, Sutherland

Owner Paul Lister has for many years been one of the most vocal advocates of rewilding. His 23,000-acre (9,300-ha) reserve includes extensive native tree planting, peatland restoration, outdoor learning for teenagers and multiple wildlife conservation projects. Stay in fully catered lodges (for groups of up to 30) or go self-catering 7 miles (11.3km) away at the off-grid Deanich Lodge, which sleeps ten (alladale.com). The income from your stay will contribute to The European Nature Trust (below).

The European Nature Trust

Discover some of the last remaining wild corners of Europe in Italy, Romania and Spain on a week-long conservation holiday where you'll be guided by local experts and meet with ecologists working to save habitats and species. A portion of the cost of your holiday includes a donation to the foundations and charities you meet. The European Nature Trust (TENT) was founded by Alladale's Paul Lister, and the trips are organized by the Gloucester-based outdoor conservation holiday specialist tour operator Steppes Travel (theeuropeannaturetrust.com).

European Safari Company

Support wild nature and the reintroduction of species in Europe by joining one of 40 safari holidays in Bulgaria, Croatia, Germany, Italy, The Netherlands, Portugal, Romania, Poland, Slovenia and Sweden. Holidays including wolf tracking in Italy's Apennines and bison tracking in the Tarcu Mountains of Romania. Five per cent of your booking goes directly to the local Rewilding Europe organization, funding projects such as bear corridors in the Central Apennines, the reintroduction of bison in the Southern Carpathians and developing wildlife reserves in Croatia's Velebit Mountains (europeansafaricompany.com).

Off-grid Deanich Lodge in the Alladale Wilderness Reserve

Other places to see rewilding in action

Broughton Sanctuary, Yorkshire: Stay in a range of self-catering holiday homes on this 3,000-acre (1,200-ha) estate, home to the Broughton Sanctuary Nature Recovery Programme (**broughtonhall.co.uk**).
Rewilding Escapes, Scotland: Join a week-long, organized holiday for small groups in some of the wilder areas of Scotland, including the Highlands and the Knoydart Peninsula (**scotlandbigpicture.com**).
Coombeshead, Devon: Camp in a small meadow or stay in one of several shepherd's huts at the edge of a 150-acre (61-ha) rewilding project close to Dartmoor (**rewildingcoombeshead.co.uk**).

Off-grid places to stay

In the strictest sense, off-grid means you're not connected to any public utilities, such as the electricity grid, gas supply or mains water, where these are supplied by alternative means, if at all. It can also refer to places that have no television, Wi-Fi or mobile phone signal (do check before you go). The opportunity provided by these boltholes – sanctuaries from the electronic demands of modern life – is to switch off, recharge, and enjoy the simple things: butterflies, birdsong and the night sky, where the only air conditioning is likely to be the sea breeze or the wind in the trees.

1 The Bothy at Nether Glenny, Port of Menteith

Found in the splendid isolation of The Trossachs on an 84-acre (34-ha) hillside farm in the Menteith Hills overlooking the gorgeous Lake of Menteith, The Bothy is billed as a retreat just for two. There's no TV or Wi-Fi, just wonderful views from a wood-fired hot tub on the front decking. The pine-clad interior has one double room, kitchen, electric shower, and a cosy mezzanine bedroom reached via a wooden ladder (netherglenny.com).

2 Laggan, Ardnish

A gorgeous whitewashed cottage by the sea on the Ardnish peninsula in the north-west of Scotland that's about as remote as it gets in the UK – there's no road access, and the only way in is a 3-hour walk or a 10-minute private boat trip. Lest you feel a little trapped, there's a boat (with outboard engine) provided, so you can discover the marine wildlife and explore the wild coastline on foot or by sea before returning to the tranquil idyll (ardnish.org).

3 Birch Cottage, Co. Antrim

A solar- and wind-powered cottage in birch woods on an organic smallholding among the rolling drumlin hills of the Mourne Mountains, one of the most beautiful places in Northern Ireland. The owners of this pioneering project, Steve and Claire, have aimed to meet its energy, food, waste and water requirements themselves. They've become so adept at it, the farm has become a centre for practical sustainability and they now supply off-grid equipment across Ireland. (lackancottage.co.uk).

4 Bulworthy Cabin, Devon

A lovely little cabin for two in its own private glade that's part of a DIY woodland management enterprise known as the Bulworthy Project, transforming the woodland into a nature reserve. Solar power provides the electricity and the water is heated by a wood-burning stove. The owners plant a native or fruit tree for every night booked, under guidance from the Devon Wildlife Trust. The site is within the North Devon Biosphere Reserve, designated by UNESCO as an area of special environmental importance, so biodiversity abounds (bulworthy.uk).

5 Cosy Under Canvas, Powys

A well-established glampsite in the Brecon Beacons close to Hay-on-Wye. The roomy geodesic domes are dotted throughout the woods out of sight of one another. Lanterns are rechargeable electric, water comes from a spring, plus there's a wood-fired hot tub, woodland shower, and an outdoor, upcycled Chiminea woodstove with a fire pit. Founded in 2009, Emma and Dan have accumulated a vast experience of running a glampsite, kitting out the kitchens with everything you could possibly need, including a Rayburn oven – great for slow cooking stews (cosyundercanvas.co.uk).

6 Devon Dens, Devon

Two sustainable timber cabins (sleep up to four and six) in woodland close to Dartmoor and beaches, north and south Devon and Cornwall. Solar energy provides power, toilets are dry with natural water filtration systems, all waste is composted and there are lots of initiatives to encourage biodiversity, including Freedom beehives and a wildlife pond (devondens.co.uk).

7 Blackthorn Cottage, Crickhowell

A beautiful stone-roofed cottage on the slopes of the Black Mountains in the Brecon Beacons National Park close to the Georgian town of Crickhowell and Abergavenny, where there's a railway station on the Welsh Marshes Line from Newport to Hereford. There's just one room but there are day beds in the living room for extra people (sugarandloaf.com).

8 Eco Retreats, Powys

This was one of the first yurt camps in the UK, on a working organic farm just outside Machynlleth, close to the Centre for Alternative Technology (see p76). Soak in the finest remote forest bathing – there are just five yurt camps (each with their own wood-fired baths) spread over 50 acres (20ha) in the Dyfi Forest (ecoretreats.co.uk).

9 Chaffinch Cottage, Northumberland

One of several holiday cottages converted from old stone houses 1,400ft (427m) above sea level in the hills of the upper Coquet Valley in the Northumberland National Park. Electricity for the estate is provided by solar panels and wind turbines, water comes from bore holes and wood burners use wood from the owners' own wind-felled trees (kidlandlee.co.uk).

10 Hinterlandes, Cumbria

Three places to stay that are moved to a new location every 28 days to ensure the lightest environmental footprint. Inspired by the tiny house movement in the USA, owners Hannah and John Graham have converted an American school bus and built a portable 'hidden hut' and contemporary larch cabin that they move to selected remote hideouts somewhere in the Lake District (hinterlandes.com).

Wildlife watching

You don't need to fly halfway round the world to witness marvels of nature, there are jaw-dropping wildlife spectacles much closer to home where your visit can help protect the local biodiversity.

Hundreds of us lined up on the bank of the marshes on a cold Sunday in the middle of January waiting to see the famous starling murmuration at Somerset's Shapwick Heath National Nature Reserve in the heart of Somerset's Avalon Marshes.

We waited patiently, repeatedly looking out over the water as the sun dropped lower in the sky and the evening drew closer. Had we missed it? Had they moved to another location? You can never guarantee anything when wildlife is involved. Then a young girl tugged at her father's coat and said,

'Over there, Daddy, above the trees'. We all turned in unison to see thousands of starlings gathering into a cloud and swirling around, like shoals of fish turning together simultaneously against the pink-red sky. It was mesmerizing.

Witnessing the age-old roosting behaviour of thousands of starlings felt pretty special, yet epic wildlife displays like this are commonplace in the UK. Television series such as *Spring Watch* and *Autumn Watch* have helped raise the profile of local wildlife, capturing the imagination of young and old, and thanks to organizations such as the Wildlife Trusts, Natural England and the RSPB, British wildlife is now more accessible than ever. Here are a few examples of where to watch wildlife and how your visit can help contribute to habitat protection and nature conservation:

Starling murmuration near Glastonbury Tor, Somerset

Skomer Island, Pembrokeshire

Skomer Island and neighbouring Skokholm Island are home to the world's largest concentration of Manx shearwater (related to albatrosses), as well as the largest breeding puffin colony in southern Britain. Some 8,000 breeding pairs of puffins are there from May to early July, while vast numbers of Manx shearwaters fly to the islands at night throughout the summer. A great way to see Manx shearwaters is on an evening boat cruise from Martin's Haven (pembrokeshire-islands.co.uk). The waters around the islands are also rich in marine life and have been designated as the first Marine Nature Reserve in Wales, with a huge population of Atlantic grey seals, porpoises, dolphins and whales.

How to get there: There are bus services throughout Pembrokeshire to Marloes village from where the Puffin Shuttle travels out to Martin's Haven where the boats depart for Skomer.

Where to stay: Wave goodbye to the last visitor boat of the day and stay in the centre of Skomer at a self-catering farmhouse that sleeps up to 16 in private rooms. Complete the bird log with your day's sightings then put your feet up by the cosy wood burner and hear all about the latest conservation efforts from the island's staff and researchers (welshwildlife.org).

Donna Nook National Nature Reserve, Lincolnshire

Every November and December, grey seals visit the Donna Nook coastline off the east coast of England (between Grainthorpe Haven and Saltfleet) to give birth to their pups near the sand dunes. They arrive in their thousands and it's a spectacle that is quite hard to believe occurs every year in the UK. The marked-out viewing area, staffed by volunteers from the Lincolnshire Wildlife Trust, is usually open from late October to December (depending on seal numbers) and is at the foot of the sand dunes to reduce disturbance to the seals and ensure the safety of visitors. Britain has about 40 per cent of the world population of grey seals so Donna Nook is becoming an increasingly important habitat (lincstrust.org.uk).

How to get there: Bus 51N travels from Louth to Donna Nook.

Where to stay: There's self-catering at Brackenborough Hall Coach House just outside Louth that is powered by solar panels and a biomass boiler (brackenboroughhall.com), while further south is the wonderfully restored fishermen's cottage Twentysix in Anderby Creek, tucked away behind the dunes (26anderbycreek.com).

The Aigas Field Centre, Scotland

Explore the wildlife, habitats and landscapes of the Scottish Highlands at the Aigas Field Centre (home of naturalist and author Sir John Lister-Kaye) where you can stay in one of several lodges on a B&B basis and use it as a base to foray into the wildlife-rich outdoors. There are lots of wildlife hides and a network of nature trails around lochs and moorland where you can see red squirrels, field voles, red and roe deers, slow worms and a variety of birds, including several birds of prey. For 30 years, this wonderful nature centre has trained over 180 young rangers who have gone on to full time career posts in wildlife management, nature conservation and environmental education (aigas.co.uk).

Eco coasteering

Take coasteering one step further and learn about the coastal marine life on an informative 'eco coasteering' trip:

Newquay Activity Centre in Cornwall has teamed up with Cornwall Wildlife Trust to run an ecology-focused coasteering adventure at low tide along the Gazzle (newquayactivitycentre.co.uk).
Coasteering Wales runs a half-day eco coasteering adventure around parts of the normally inaccessible coastline of Anglesey. You will learn about the geology and marine life living in the rockpools and caves (coasteering-wales.co.uk).
Coasteering Northern Ireland runs a 2½-hour trip that combines the thrill of scrambling over rocks, swimming through pools, and jumping off cliffs with a guided instruction on the wildlife and geology of the coastline of Ballintoy, County Antrim (coasteeringni.co.uk).

Moose and beaver safari in West Sweden

Based at Kolarbyn Ecolodge in the wilds of central Sweden, learn bushcraft and foraging for berries, mushrooms and edible plants, then head off by boat in search of beavers or trek deep into the forest to track elusive moose, all the while keeping an eye out for a host of other birds and wildlife, including roe deer, hares, boars, badgers, herons, cranes and owls (if you're lucky you may also see lynx). You'll stay in a basic charcoal burner's hut (billed as 'Sweden's most primitive hotel') that's all part of the get-back-to-nature experience at this wonderful off-grid eco camp (there's no electricity nor showers). After a day's safari, swim in the idyllic lake then relax in the floating sauna. My favourite memory of Kolarbyn is returning from a moose safari late one evening and hearing the howling of wolves in the forest (wildsweden.com).
How to get there: Train from Stockholm to Köping, then take the bus 550 to Skinnskatteberg.
Where to stay: Stay onsite in the mud grass huts camouflaged in the forest (kolarbyn.se).

Whale watching, Cork

The waters off the west coast of Ireland are home to many wonderful large marine creatures, including minke, fin and humpback whales, common dolphins, harbour porpoises, seals, turtles and basking sharks. Of course there's never any guarantee that you'll see any of them on one trip, but the chances are pretty high, especially out of Cork where there are two experienced operators that have been running whale and dolphin watching trips for over 25 years. Whale Watch West Cork (whalewatchwestcork.com) is run by Nic Slocum

(his on board commentaries are legendary), and Cork Whale Watch (corkwhalewatch.com) is run by Colin Barnes, a former commercial fisherman who started working in ecotourism in 2001, and has since worked closely with the Irish Whale and Dolphin Group, contributing records to their sightings database and making his vessel available as a research platform for research trips.

How to get there: Bus 237 from Cork to Skibbereen (1½ hours), then change for bus 237 or 251 to Baltimore (20 minutes).

Where to stay: The characterful Bushes Bar overlooks Baltimore Harbour where the boats depart (bushesbar.com), or further out of town uphill is the beautiful two-room Cedar Boathouse that sleeps up to seven people (airbnb.ie).

The Earth Project

Listen to recordings of birdsong taken from all over the world, from the suburbs of Melbourne, Australia to the rainforest of South America, on the website of The Earth Project. You can also record and upload your own local birdsong for others to enjoy (theearthproject.world)

Birdwatching on the Ebro, Spain

Admire the colourful and charismatic species that throng the banks of the Ebro – Spain's longest river, flowing 565 miles (910km) south from the Cantabrian Mountains to the Mediterranean at the shimmering delta south-west of Tarragona, Catalonia. A kayak along a peaceful stretch of the river between Garcia and Móra d'Ebre with a guide from En Blau – a small, family-run outfit – may reward you with sightings of dazzling blue-plumed kingfishers and house martins swooping around the Garcia bridge. We saw lots of moorhens and coots lurking in the reeds alongside the bank and several species of egret and herons, including the delicately pink squacco heron with milk-white underwings (enblau.cat).

How to get there: Train from Barcelona to Móra la Nova, then bus L0520 to Móra d'Ebre (total journey is 3½ hours); or bus direct from Barcelona to Móra d'Ebre (just over 2½ hours).

Where to stay: Hotel L'Algadir del Delta is a beautiful family-run hotel in the Delta de l'Ebre Natural Park with an excellent restaurant serving delicious local cuisine. It was the first hotel in Catalonia to gain the EU's Ecolabel certification (hotelalgadirdelta.com).

Keep an eye out for the flash of a Kingfisher on the River Ebro, Catalonia

Britain's big five

Keep an eye out for these five examples of wildlife that signal how healthy their ecosystems are. Environments where these biological indicators are struggling are where many other plants, insects and animals are also likely to be in trouble. The more that they and their habitats are celebrated and protected, the more that biodiversity is likely to thrive.

1 **Seagrass** grows around the coast of Britain – it is the only flowering plant able to live in seawater yet is highly sensitive to environmental stress, so is an early warning sign of coastal pollution. It also has an excellent capacity to store carbon.

2 **Beavers** build dams, dig canals and restore dead wood, creating water habitats that enable other wildlife to flourish.

3 **Mayflies** are highly sensitive to pollution, so they are a valuable indicator of the health of aquatic ecosytems.

4 **Common Blue Butterflies** live in meadow grasslands rich in wildflowers that enable other important species, such as orchids and horseshoe bats, to thrive.

5 **Dormice** live in woodland and hedgerows but a decline in their numbers can signal habitat destruction – often by deer.

Responsible wildlife watching

In any interaction with nature, there's a balance between marvelling at wildlife and not disturbing it. Here are a few tips on ensuring the experience is good for you and for nature:

Before you go learn as much as you can about what flora and fauna you might see and understand the best way to act around it. This will also help you improve your chances of seeing it.

Observe from a distance: take a pair of binoculars if you can.

If you're at a reserve, keep to designated viewing areas.

Avoid getting near mothers with their young.

Wear clothes that have colours appropriate to the habitat – dark green or brown for woodlands or seashore, white or light grey for snowy hillsides.

Avoid wearing strong smelling fragrances – many animals and birds depend on a keen sense of smell and may run (or fly) a mile if they come across unusual scents.

Leave no trace – take away any litter.

If you are booking a wildlife watching experience with an activity provider or operator, choose one that can demonstrate its commitment to sustainable wildlife watching. In Scotland, all tour operator members of Wild Scotland (wild-scotland.org.uk) have signed up to its code of conduct on how to watch wildlife sustainably. If you're going to see marine life, choose an operator that has undergone training through the Wise Scheme for minimizing disturbance to marine wildlife, or is certified by Marine Life (marine-life.org.uk) or the Seawatch Foundation (seawatchfoundation.org.uk).

You can never guarantee seeing wildlife, but you can optimize your chances by acting responsibly

The Wildlife Trusts

The Wildlife Trusts are a federation of 46 independent wildlife conservation charities covering the whole of the UK, looking after more than 2,300 nature reserves and operating more than 100 visitor and education centres. Every Wildlife Trust is an independent charity and organizes a range of ways you can get involved in local conservation efforts, from volunteering to fundraising (wildlifetrusts.org).

UK Glampsites

In less than a decade, the UK has become a world leader in glamping (a combination of the words 'glamorous' and 'camping') – outdoor accommodation that includes self-catering facilities considered more comfortable than traditional camping. Glampsites vary greatly from hard-wearing canvas structures, such as yurts, tipis, geodesic domes, bell tents and safari tents, to more solid constructions, such as eco pods, treehouses, cabins, lodges, shepherd's huts, Gypsy caravans, train carriages and upcycled shipping containers. For traditional campers, nothing can replace the convenience (and low cost) of pitching your own tent, but for those who want a little more luxury but still have a close connection to the great outdoors, there are now hundreds of options across the UK. Here's a selection of some of the greenest, where you can switch off, run wild and stargaze, in relative comfort.

1 Mallinson's Woodland Retreat, Dorset
Yurts, tipis, bell tents, a shepherd's hut (made of wood, on wheels) and three remarkable treehouses that are the stuff of dreams, lovingly crafted by the owner Guy Mallinson and his team of skilled woodsmen: Dazzle is a camouflage design inspired by patterns used to conceal First World War ships; Pinwheel is in a clearing between a ring of mature oak trees in a corner of a bluebell wood; and Woodman's is a stylish, secluded haven for two, senstively perched in the bows of an ancient oak (mallinson.co.uk).

2 Inshriach House, Aviemore
Four quirky off-grid sites (each sleep two) spread out over 20 acres (8ha) alongside the river Spey on a large estate in the Cairngorms National Park: choose between a yurt, shepherd's hut, converted 1950s fire lorry, and the innovative 'Bothy Project' – partly funded by the Royal Scottish Academy, it doubles for half the year as an artists' residency and the other half as an isolated retreat for those looking for a self-sufficient, back-to-nature experience in the great Scottish outdoors (inshriachhouse.com).

3 Loveland Farm, Devon
A mile (1.6km) from the dramatic rocky outcrop of Hartland Point (part of the North Devon UNESCO Biosphere) and close to popular surfing beaches, this collection of six smart modern geodesic domes come with private showers, compost loos and a kitchen. Heating for the indoor swimming pool is from a biomass boiler fed by the farm's recycled wood chip, and electricity is powered by solar panels (loveland.farm).

4 Wild Northumberland, Hexham
A family- and dog-friendly place to stay in the Northumberland National Park. Choose from four Mongolian yurts, two shepherd's huts (one handcrafted, the other an antique original) or a unique treehouse yurt, in secluded sites among wildflower meadows and woodland with views of the fells and dark skies of the Tarset Valley (wildnorthumbrian.co.uk).

5 One Cat Farm, Ceredigion
Among 4 acres (1.6ha) of wildflower meadow, the cosy grass-roofed cabins are the heartfelt work of owners Jessie and Lyndon. Expect a homely vibe: there's an honesty shop, a blackboard in the communal kitchen with local tips, freshly baked bread, and a small boat to row around the large pond. Hire bikes and ride the 20-minute route for fresh fish and seafood from Cardigan Bay on the Wales Coast Path (onecatfarm.com).

6 Fforest Farm, Cardigan
Owners James and Sian instigated the magic in 2004, and have since extrapolated their unique blend of heart and soul in and around Cardigan. The hub is by the Teifi Gorge where there's an assortment of options (kata tents, geodesic domes, crog lofts and 'shacs'), and a 200-year old cosy stone pub; further up the coast is 'Manorafon' with domes, cabins and a cedar barrel sauna; while in the heart of Cardigan, boutique apartment granary lofts overlook Fforest's woodfired pizza restaurant and events venue, the Pizzatipi. Nearby are sandy beaches (Mwnt is my favourite) and lots of outdoor activities in this special corner of Wales (coldatnight.co.uk).

7 Brook House Woods, Herefordshire
A beautiful collection of home-crafted cabins, a hobbit house and a treehouse fashioned by the owner Will from coppiced woodlands in the heart of Herefordshire. A woodland cinema is the latest addition, there's yoga, reiki, and massages on site plus a range of courses on woodwork, foraging for gin infusions, and raw chocolate. Order breakfast hampers and pizza packages to cook in the wood-fired oven (brookhousewoods.com).

8 Penhein, Chepstow
Come here for woodland seclusion 850ft (260m) high on a 450-acre (182-ha) farm in the heart of the Monmouthshire hills – on a clear day you can see both Severn bridges. There are just a handful of persian high-domed tents each with their own kitchen, wood-burning stove and shower, and there's sustainable ethos throughout, from the local crafting of the tents to the spring-fed filtered water. If you have unopened tins of food at the end of your stay, they can quarantine them for 72 hours and then donate them to a local food bank. Exemplary (penhein.co.uk).

9 Glen Dye, Strachan
A collection of cabins and cottages that are part of an ongoing 25-year ambitious, hands-on regeneration project on a large private estate among wilderness forest and moorland on the banks of the River Dye. There's a refurbished 1950s Airstream Safari caravan, a showman's caravan, bothy, hay loft and several smart holiday cottages, each with outdoor wood-fired hot tubs. The owners are happy to collect from Stonehaven or Aberdeen railway stations (glendyecabinsandcottages.com).

10 Craig Wen, Snowdonia
Overlooking the beautiful Mawddach Estuary, a cluster of three handcrafted yurts and a shepherd's hut in a glade of silver birch and oak trees, plus a yurt and bell tent each in their own field, and a dozen or so tent pitches. Walk from Graig Wen to the summit of Cader Idris; it's popular with cyclists who come here to cycle the Mawddach Trail as it's a short ride from Morfa Mawddach railway station on the scenic Cambrian Line between Machynlleth and Pwllheli (graigwen.co.uk).

Active winter

Choosing alternative low-impact winter
activities, such as snowshoeing, ski-touring
and cross-country skiing, means your impact
on the mountains will be only snow deep.

Few winter holidays can beat the exhilaration of skiing through fresh powdered snow in the clean mountain air, surrounded by spectacular mountain views, followed by feasting on a fondue with friends in a cosy, fireside chalet at the end of a muscle-aching day. Historically, the infrastructure that's been put in place to cater for the downhill winter sports industry has put a great strain on mountain ecosystems, including the levelling of wildlife-friendly pine forests in order to make way for long, flat pistes, while local water supplies have been drained in order to provide billions of gallons of water for artificial snow-making machines at purpose-built resorts.

In recent years, many ski areas have sought to lessen their environmental impact, using renewable energy to operate chairlifts and power accommodation, and improving their public transport network to reduce the need for cars. However, in terms of carbon emissions, the single biggest environmental impact of a ski holiday is likely to be the carbon pollution emitted from just travelling to and from the ski area, especially if you fly. Reducing the distance you travel, and choosing lower emission alternatives to flying, will make a huge difference to your carbon footprint, and switching to lower impact activities, such as snowshoeing, ski-touring and cross-country skiing, will reduce your impact on the mountains.

Skiing in the UK

There are five main ski areas in Scotland, and if the conditions are good, the skiing and scenery can be as good as anywhere in the world. Glenshee in the Cairngorms is the largest Scottish ski area, though in the west the Glencoe ski area has higher snowfalls. Scotland's newest ski area, Nevis Range, is reached by the UK's only mountain gondola, which is a 10-minute bus ride away from the railway station in Fort William (trains run from Glasgow direct to Fort William, plus there's an overnight sleeper train from London to Fort William). The front of the mountain is good for beginners and intermediates, but the area is best known for its lift-served gullies, bowls and cornice drops in the Back Corries for advanced off-piste skiers.

Snow trekking

The gentlest way to enjoy the power and pine is to go snow-trekking, which involves attaching specialized outer footwear ('snow shoes') to your shoes or boots that distribute your weight over a larger area to prevent your feet from sinking into the snow. Think of it as simply a winter walk made easier. Kitting up with just the usual ski clothing, gloves and poles is all you need to head into the wintry landscape, where you're far more likely to see mountain wildlife and appreciate the beauty of the mountain environment than you would hurtling down a manicured slope on skis.

The Swiss Alps and the Italian Dolomites are popular locations for snow trekking (or 'snow-shoeing') though one of the best places is the Pyrenees. Spanning 270 miles (435km) across the south-west of France, northern Spain and Andorra, the region lacks the scale and crowds of the Alps but it's no less rewarding.

Ski touring

Ski touring (in France it's known as ski de randonnée) involves attaching synthetic 'skins' to the underside of your skis to give you traction to walk uphill, then, once you're gained some height, you then detach and pack away the skins and start your descent, enjoying the exhilaration of skiing down deserted untracked snow. Going off-piste can be dangerous and should only be done once you have attained an appropriate level of skill, fitness and familiarity with navigating in the mountains, including the ability to read weather systems and the variable snow conditions.

There are many organizations that offer courses in ski touring where you'll learn how to skin and kick-turn efficiently, how to avoid avalanche terrain and use essential safety equipment. Once you're proficient in ski touring, it opens up a whole new dimension to skiing where you can stay overnight in mountain huts and continue touring day after day in the glorious wild hinterland.

In Scotland, there are lots of ski touring routes that traverse many of the Munros (mountains over 3,000ft/914m high), such as the 6¼-mile (10-km) traverse of the Pass of Drumochter, the main mountain route between the northern and southern central Scottish Highlands, and the 10-mile (16-km) traverse of Ben Macdui in the Cairngorms, where you can take the longer tour of the five 4,000-ft (1,219-m) peaks that takes in Cairn Gorm, Ben Macdui, Angel's Peak, Cairn Toul and Braeriach.

In Europe, one of the most popular ski touring routes is the Haute Route – a seven-day 75-mile (120km) tour traversing sections of two of the highest Alpine ranges between Zermatt and Chamonix. But there are many other equally rewarding ski tours in Europe, including the Silvretta Traverse in the Austrian Alps, south of the ski resort of Saint Anton, which is a great tour for those just starting out ski touring as the summits are lower than in the West Alps; the Bernese Oberland Traverse in central Switzerland, with superb views of the Jungfrau, Mönch and Eiger; the Dolomites Circuit, which passes through remote valleys, dominated by the iconic towering limestone cliffs and pinnacles; and the Gran Paradiso Traverse, which includes a strenuous trek up to the summit of the Paradiso itself (13,323ft/4,061m), followed by a thrilling descent of over 6,500ft (2,000m).

Specialist adventure holiday operator Tracks and Trails runs a range of snow-trekking and cross-country skiing holidays in the mountains of Europe, including snow-trekking in the Swiss Chablais mountain range and cross-country skiing across the Finnish Russian frontier (**tracks-and-trails.com**).

Cross-country skiing

Cross-country skiing involves using skis that are thinner, lighter and longer than downhill skies, and have a free-heel binding system that you use with lightweight boots; they have scales on the underside to help stop you slipping backwards so that you can push and glide quickly and smoothly across the snow. The technique involves sliding one foot directly forwards followed by the other foot, using poles alternately. It's a great way to travel quickly across long distances on the flat. As with all forms of skiing, while fitness is important, balance and co-ordination are crucial if you're to enjoy this strenuous form of exercise.

Many popular ski resorts have groomed pistes for cross-country skiers, so it is widely available across the Alps (particularly in Switzerland and the Dolomites), but there are also excellent tracks in other areas, such as Poland and Slovakia. Norway and Finland are the best-known locations for cross-country skiing, where it's a national sport.

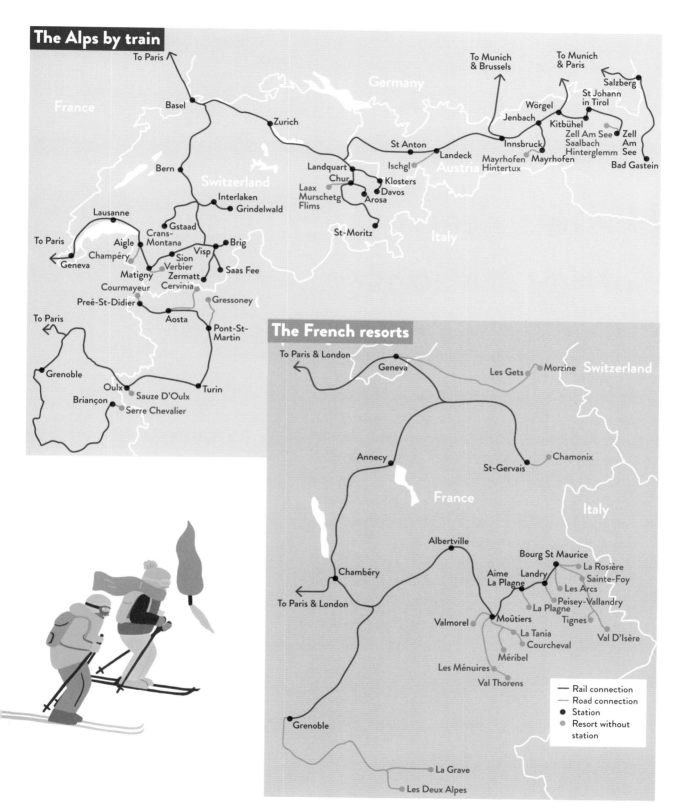

The Alps by train

To Paris

France

Basel

Zurich

Germany

To Munich & Brussels

To Munich & Paris

Salzberg

Wörgel

St Johann in Tirol

Jenbach

Kitbühel

Zell Am See Saalbach Hinterglemm

Zell Am See

Bern

Switzerland

St Anton

Landeck

Innsbruck

Ischgl

Austria

Mayrhofen Hintertux

Mayrhofen

Bad Gastein

Interlaken

Grindelwald

Landquart

Chur

Klosters

Davos

Laax Murschetg Flims

Arosa

Italy

Lausanne

Gstaad

Crans-Montana

Brig

To Paris

Aigle

Champéry

Sion

Verbier

Visp

Geneva

Matigny

Zermatt

Cervinia

Saas Fee

St-Moritz

Courmayeur

Gressoney

Preé-St-Didier

Aosta

To Paris

Pont-St-Martin

Grenoble

Oulx

Sauze D'Oulx

Turin

Briançon

Serre Chevalier

The French resorts

To Paris & London

Geneva

Les Gets

Morzine

Switzerland

Annecy

St-Gervais

Chamonix

France

Italy

Albertville

Bourg St Maurice

Aime La Plagne

Landry

La Rosière

Sainte-Foy

Chambéry

Les Arcs

Peisey-Vallandry

La Plagne

To Paris & London

Valmorel

Moûtiers

Tignes

La Tania

Val D'Isère

Les Ménuires

Méribel

Courcheval

Val Thorens

—— Rail connection
—— Road connection
● Station
● Resort without station

Grenoble

La Grave

Les Deux Alpes

Hostels near railway stations

Historically, hostels were designed to encourage the nation's growing urban population to spend time out of the city and enjoy fresh air and the great outdoors on foot or by bike at minimal cost. Many are therefore designed to be near transport hubs so that they can be easily accessible. Here's a selection of rural hostels that are conveniently close to railway stations, from where it's just a short cycle or walk off the train for a car-free adventure in wild and beautiful areas of open countryside – in National Parks, Biosphere Reserves and Areas of Outstanding Natural Beauty.

1 YHA South Downs, East Sussex
Southease railway station (25 minutes from Brighton) is literally on the hostel's doorstep, so too is the fabulous South Downs Way. There's storage space for cycles and the rooms are either dorms or private rooms – some are en suite – plus a campground for your own pitch, but if you want to go up a notch, there are camping pods, land pods and bell tents that are great for families. The hostel building is in a pretty, former farm courtyard and the dining room opens out onto an enclosed field so, when you've finished breakfast, you can sit out with a free top-up of coffee while the kids run around letting off steam (yha.org.uk).

2 YHA Berwick, Northumberland
Right on the quayside by the River Tweed in the centre of Berwick, a 10-minute walk from the railway station. There are 55 beds across 13 rooms, all en suite, some are private and family rooms. The hostel's granary bistro has open mic nights, comedy clubs and live music, plus there's an art gallery featuring local as well as international artists (yha.org.uk).

3 Ludlow Mascall Centre, Shropshire
It's 5 minutes' walk from Ludlow Railway Station and 5 minutes' walk to the centre of the beautiful market town of Ludlow from where there are wonderful walks in the Shropshire Hills and Mortimer Forest. This independent hostel has storage for bikes, twin rooms, a family room, and a room for those with limited mobility; there's a small café downstairs, plus you can order a locally sourced breakfast and a packed lunch (ludlowmascallcentre.co.uk).

4 Loch Ossian Hostel, Rannoch Moor
A small, off-grid hostel in splendid isolation among a clump of birch and rowan trees at the edge of Loch Ossian in the western Scottish Highlands (see also p71). There's a male and female dorm each with 8 beds, a small kitchen and common room, racks for drying clothes, boot stands by the fire, and a bike store. Though remote, it's just a 20-minute walk along a track from Corrour railway station (the highest mainline railway station in the UK), a few stops short of Fort William on the train from Glasgow (hostellingscotland.org.uk).

5 YHA Hathersage, Yorkshire
Half a mile (0.8km) from the railway station, there are 17 beds in the main house and 25 in an annex. It's a great base for exploring the Peak District: you're in the heart of Charlotte Brontë country – follow the literature trail that includes North Lees Manor featured in *Jane Eyre*; climbers can tackle the challenging Stanage Edge, while walkers and cyclists exploring outside of Hathersage can easily reach the Derwent Reservoir and caves (yha.org.uk).

6 Wayfarers Independent Hostel, Penrith, Cumbria
Penrith is on the west coast mainline that runs between London and Glasgow, with branches to Birmingham, Liverpool, Manchester and Edinburgh. The hostel is just 8 minutes' walk from the railway station and is 100m from the Sea to Sea (C2C) cycle route, so it's geared up for cyclists (there's secure bike storage, drying room as well as bike cleaning and maintenance facilities) with twin rooms and dorms (wayfarershostel.com).

7 YHA Penzance, Cornwall
A large 100-bed hostel in a Georgian mansion, just over a mile (1.6km) from the railway station and harbour, so handy for the ferry to and from the Isles of Scilly. There are dorms and private rooms, a campsite with views across Mount's Bay to the Lizard Peninsula, as well as six bell tents for up to five people (yha.org.uk).

8 Oban Youth Hostel, Argyll and Bute
Less than a mile (1.6km) along the seafront from Oban railway station, this hostel is a great base if you're using Oban as a gateway to the Inner Hebrides, including Colonsay, Craignure and Castlebay. There's a mix of shared and private en suite rooms, and a lounge with views over the Firth of Lorne (hostellingscotland.org.uk).

9 YHA Beverley Friary, Yorkshire
A few minutes' walk from the railway station in the heart of the pretty market town of Beverley, this hostel was home to Dominican friars 600 years ago. It's recently undergone a £340,000 refurbishment and has a large kitchen dining room and a beautiful lounge with an exposed beam ceiling and stone fireplace (yha.org.uk).

10 Toad Hall Hostel, Machynlleth
A small three-room independent hostel above the owner's family home beside the River Dovey, close to Snowdonia National Park. There's a mix of family, double and twin rooms, a small self-catering kitchen and a single shower room. It's just 2 minutes' walk from the railway station and a great base for cycling the National Cycle Route 8 and walking the wonderful Glyndŵr's Way National Trail (independenthostels.co.uk).

Holidays in history

Relive times past at castles, forts, towers, museums and cottages where your stay will help contribute to the preservation of national heritage.

Just 10 nautical miles (18.5km) off the north coast of Devon, Lundy Island feels like another world. The journey there, from either Bideford or Ilfracombe, takes less than 2 hours on a refurbished German ferry boat, the MS *Oldenburg*, but once you've disembarked with your luggage, and you turn to see the boat disappear out of sight, you feel properly cut off from the mainland. It's a terrific place to go for a long weekend's mini adventure.

The island is only 3 miles (4.8km) long and half a mile (0.8km) wide, but there are plenty of things to do, including birdwatching, climbing, fishing, snorkelling and diving – Lundy's Marine Protected Area is one of the UK's prime diving sites with clear waters, a huge diversity of marine life and 10 shipwreck dive sites. You can choose from an eclectic mix of accommodation, including a simple fisherman's cottage, a thirteenth-century castle, a late Georgian villa, a lighthouse, the isolated coastguard's off-grid watchhouse, and a traditional campsite (numbers are limited to 40 people). There is locally brewed beer at the island's pub, the Marisco Tavern, which also provides fireside meals with everything cooked in-house.

Lundy Island is looked after by the Landmark Trust (landmarktrust.org.uk), which protects historic buildings and other places of historical interest. By staying in their properties, you can help contribute

The heritage of Lundy Island is managed by the Landmark Trust

to their upkeep and preservation. The Landmark Trust has about 200 properties elsewhere to rent, including a collection of fishermen's dwellings built in the 1840s in Caithness in the north of Scotland and Coed y Bleiddiau – a small railway cottage at a remote private halt on the restored Ffestiniog & West Highland Railway. Here are some examples of other historic buildings where you can either stay overnight or visit for the day, knowing that your trip will help conserve these special places:

Champing

Champing (church camping) is essentially glamping in a church, with camp beds under a beautifully timeworn vaulted roof and surrounded by ancient stone pillars. Run by the Churches Conservation Trust, a charity which maintains over 350 historic churches in the UK as a way of funding its conservation work, the scheme has been such a success that it now operates at over 15 locations. Each participating church sleeps between four and 16 guests. Locations range from the chalky Dunstable Downs in Buckinghamshire to the wild heights of Dartmoor, the wide plains of East Anglia, the Ribble Valley in Lancashire that's handy for the Forest of Bowland Area of Outstanding Natural

Beauty, and as far north as St Peter's Kirk on Orkney. At each church you're provided with chairs, tables, basic tea- and coffee-making facilities and exclusive use of your chosen church between 6pm and 10am. If you don't want to pack a sleeping bag you can pay extra to have the beds made up with duvets, blankets and hot-water bottles before you arrive. The churches come with a water supply and basic toilets though heating is rare – so the champing season is usually limited to stays between late March and the end of September (champing.co.uk).

Castell Henllys, Pembrokeshire

This is a unique Iron Age village recreated by the Pembrokeshire National Park Authority using replica roundhouses, standing in the exact same place that the structures originally stood around 2,400 years ago. It is surrounded by woodland and river meadows, and has a visitor centre, sculpture trails and excellent exhibitions. You'll get to explore the roundhouses, grind flour and make bread just like the Celts used to, while your entrance fee will contribute to maintaining this important archaeological site (castellhenllys.com).

Grimsby Fishing Heritage Centre

Get a flavour of what it was like to be a Grimsby trawlerman in the 1950s – one of the most dangerous peacetime occupations in the UK. This fascinating museum will transport you back in time to when the town was one of the world's premier fishing ports, with carefully crafted sets and original preserved trawler interiors as well as the sights, sounds and smells that capture the essence of this remarkable way of life (fishingheritage.com).

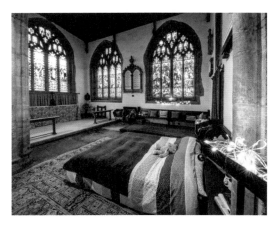

Hadrian's Wall, Northumberland

Stonehenge is the jewel in the crown of English Heritage, but there are over 400 other wonderful historic monuments, buildings and places that the conservation organization manages, from prehistoric sites and abbeys to grand medieval castles and Cold War bunkers. One of the most fascinating is the series of Roman forts along Hadrian's Wall in Northumberland, where you can find out what life was like on the frontier of Roman Britain (english-heritage.org.uk).

Silbury Hill, Wiltshire

One of the most understated of English Heritage's attractions, it's the largest artificial mound in Europe (comparable in size to the Egyptian pyramids) that archeologists think was probably completed around 2400 BC. Its purpose and signficance remain unknown (english-heritage.org.uk).

Greenway, Devon

The National Trust cares for over 200 historic houses as well as many industrial monuments, lighthouses, pubs and barns. One of the most scenic journeys to their properties is to Greenway – the holiday home of the author Agatha Christie, on the River Dart (she described it as 'the loveliest place on Earth'). The house is in a woodland garden, which drifts down to the banks of the river. Travel there by ferry from Dartmouth Quay or Dittisham on the Greenway and Dittisham Ferry (greenwayferry.co.uk), which travels across the river to the Greenway Quay. Stay at one of four holiday cottages on the estate, including the quaint ferry cottage on the riverside (nationaltrust.org.uk).

Harlech Castle, Gwynedd

CADW is the Welsh Government's historic environment service that cares for historic buildings and places ('Cadw' is a Welsh word meaning 'to keep' or 'to protect'). It manages over 120 places, from ancient burial chambers and monuments to abbeys and castles. One of the most impressive is Harlech Castle, set on a spectacular sheer rocky crag overlooking the dunes of Cardigan Bay (cadw.gov.wales).

The Innocent Railway, Edinburgh

Historic Environment Scotland manages over 300 properties, from well-known places like Edinburgh Castle to little-known archaeological gems and relics of its industrial heritage. One of its industrial heritage projects is the Innocent Railway in Edinburgh, which was the first railway tunnel in Scotland. It has now been reopened as a cycle path (from St. Leonards to Brunstane) forming part of the National Cycle Network Route 1. The top of the tunnel can be accessed by following the signposts in the Newington area of Edinburgh; the easiest access is from Holyrood Park Road, just before entering the park (historicenvironment.scot).

The frontier of Roman Britain at Hadrian's Wall

The beautiful architecture of the Alhambra palace and fortress, Grenada

Tullymurry House, Co. Down

The Irish Landmark Trust manages over 30 heritage properties from lighthouses and schoolhouses to castles and gate lodges across the island of Ireland. Tullymurry House is a characterful seventeenth-century country farmhouse overlooking the Mourne Mountains in Northern Ireland, which the Trust has renovated and now lets out as a holiday home, sleeping up to eight in this Area of Outstanding Natural Beauty (irishlandmark.com).

Paradores de Turismo, Spain

Hotels operated by Paradores de Turismo de España have helped preserve some of Spain's most historic buildings, including castles, monasteries, fortresses and palaces. There are over 90, including Parador de Santiago de Compostela in Galicia, reputedly the oldest hotel in the world, Parador de Las Cañadas del Teide high up in the mountains of Tenerife, but perhaps the grandest is Parador de Granada, which is among the splendid gardens of the magnificent Alhambra (parador.es).

World Heritage Sites

A World Heritage Site is a cultural or natural landmark that has been recognized by the United Nations Educational, Scientific and Cultural Organization (UNESCO) as being deemed worthy of preservation due to their 'outstanding value to humanity'. There are over 25 cultural heritage sites in the UK, including the Blaenavon Industrial Landscape; the City of Bath; Durham Castle and Cathedral; and the Old and New Towns of Edinburgh. In France there are 39, including the Canal du Midi, the decorated Cave of Pont d'Arc at Ardèche, Mont Saint Michel and the Routes of Santiago de Compostela. In Spain, cultural heritage sites include the Alhambra in Grenada, the Catalan Romanesque Churches of the Vall de Boí, and the Cave of Altamira and Paleolithic Cave Art of Northern Spain, while in Portugal there are 16, including the cultural landscape of Sintra, the historic centre of Évora, and the Alto Douro Wine Region. Italy has the most World Heritage Sites (an accolade shared with China), including the City of Verona, Syracuse and the Rocky Necropolis of Pantalica, and the historic centre of Urbino (whc.unesco.org).

10 of the best

Renovated and unique places to stay

Upcycling comes in all shapes and sizes. Thanks to the creativity of an increasing number of entrepreneurial hoteliers and landowners, redundant buildings, vehicles, storage units and spaces are being repurposed into a wide range of quirky places to stay, from buses and railway carriages to lighthouses and shipping containers. Some are fashioned using makeshift, Heath Robinson-esque contraptions, while others are born of architectural innovation creating state-of-the-art, designer-led abodes that have appeared on prime-time TV shows like *Grand Designs* and *This Morning*. All are in wonderful locations and show how you can reuse almost anything to create a unique eco escape.

1 The conker
There's room for two at this off-grid, high-tech, copper-clad orb high on a hill on a private estate in Powys, Mid Wales. Designed in collaboration with an engineer from Bentley Motors, the spherical hideaway has a double bed, an innovative air-recirculation heating system and an adjacent Scandi-style log cabin bathroom (chillderness.co.uk).

2 The airship
A slightly bonkers but brilliant aluminium-clad capsule with wonderful views of the Ardnamurchan peninsula over the Sound of Mull in the Highlands of Scotland. Inside there's a four-poster bed, wood stove and shower (outoftheblue.uk.com).

3 The chrysalis
'Fall asleep as a caterpillar and wake up a butterfly' says the owner of this wonderful cocoon of comfort among the treetops in the heart of the Vendée countryside south-east of Nantes in the Pays de la Loire, France. You can dine here too, feasting on fresh local products, including goat cheeses, cold meats and seaweed tartare, washed down with biodynamic wine (terragora-lodges.com).

4 The lighthouse
Perched at the end of one of Ireland's longest peninsulas in Co. Down, St John's Point Lighthouse has been helping guide boats along the north side of Donegal Bay from the entrance up to Rotten Island since 1831. It is now fully automated and no longer manned, but the Irish Landmark Trust has renovated the former lightkeepers' cottages into two characterful places to stay, SJ Clipper and JP Schooner, which both sleep up to four (irishlandmark.com).

5 The harbour
New life has not just been breathed into a small, salty-sea cabin, but an entire nineteenth-century harbour has been rescued and maintained as a tranquil, picture-perfect hideaway in Dunbar on the east coast of Scotland. Access is through a short tunnel within the cliffs that opens out onto the harbour with the cabin and one other building in splendid isolation at the far end. Swim in the protected waters of the harbour, and keep an eye out for the fishermen who still work out of the harbour and can sell you their latest catch of crab and lobster (bluecabinbythesea.co.uk).

6 The railway station
Staying at this beautifully restored station master's house (sleeps four) at Ribblehead station in the Yorkshire Dales on the scenic Settle–Carlisle line means you can do day trips by train to explore the Three Peaks country of Ingleborough, Whernside and Pen-y-ghent. It's one of 45 converted railway station cottages in the UK that you can book at railwaystationcottages.co.uk.

7 The school bus
Curl up by a log burner in a beautifully converted American school bus on a smallholding between the hills of Yr Eifl and the Irish Sea in the Llŷn Peninsula Area of Outstanding Natural Beauty in North Wales. Friends could join you camping among a wildflower meadow or in a Scandinavian-inspired cottage, and you can all eat together for breakfast and dinner with food gathered by hand from the owners' garden, foraged locally and sourced from local suppliers (bertskitchengarden.com).

8 The shipping container
An open-plan surf shack (sleeps two) imaginatively upcycled from a huge shipping container on the stunning Causeway Coast Area of Outstanding Natural Beauty in Co. Antrim, Northern Ireland. The interior is clad with reclaimed wood and decorated with vintage surfboards, plus there's a small kitchenette and a bathroom in an outhouse. Nearby is the World Heritage site at Giant's Causeway, the Carrick-a-Rede rope bridge established by salmon fishermen in 1755, and the Bushmills Irish Whiskey Distillery (airbnb.co.uk).

9 The floating cabin
For families who like to be close to water, these off-grid, nest-like cabins, shaped like coconuts with a fig-like roof, float above the water (reached along a pontoon or by boat) among 200 acres (81ha) of forest in the great lakes area of Franche-Comté in eastern France (cabanesdesgrandslacs.com).

10 The railway carriage
Take the train to Cornwall on the GWR main line from Plymouth to Penzance and you'll get a discount to stay in one of five imaginatively renovated historic train carriages alongside the railway stations at St Germans in the south-east and at Hayle in the far west (railholiday.co.uk).

Slow travel

Enjoy life in the slow lane, savour regional, seasonal cuisine, make the most of the great outdoors on foot or by bike, and immerse yourself in local culture on a slow travel journey that allows you to enjoy the rhythms and patterns of everyday life at your own pace.

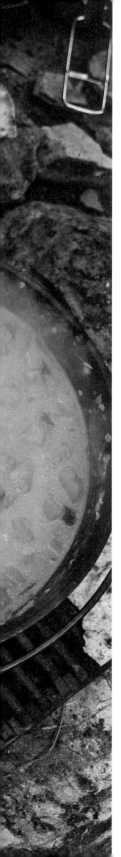

As I checked in as a foot passenger for the ferry at the port at Bonifacio on the southern tip of Corsica, the sun was shining, the sea was shimmering blue, and the white yachts lining the harbour, flanked by a ninth-century fortress, looked magnificent against the bright sky. I boarded the smart blue and white Moby Lines ferry *Giraglia* and headed out across the Strait of Bonifacio on the one-hour crossing to Santa Teresa di Gallura in the north of Sardinia. They were near-perfect sailing conditions, I spent most of the crossing on the top desk enjoying the fresh, salty sea air and wonderful views of Sardinia's historic coastline.

I'd come to Corsica on a three-week overland adventure from the UK. After the Eurostar to Paris, I'd taken the night train down to Nice, the ferry to Corsica and the rickety trinichellu ('trembling') train across Corsica (the locals call it, ironically, the TGV – Train à Grandes Vibrations), as it rumbles over the forest mountains of Corsica providing glimpses of the Mediterranean far below. It is one of the most scenic rail journeys in Europe. I walked across the Désert des Agriates in northern Corsica, and stayed at Hotel Monte d'Oro near Vizzavona, a characterful fin de siècle hotel with a wonderful ivy-clad restaurant serving traditional Corsican food and wine. After the ferry crossing to Sardinia, I hiked up to a Bronze Age village tucked into a cave near the top of Mount Tiscali in Sardinia's Supramonte mountains, then crossed to Sicily by ferry to stay at Il Paesino (long-travel.co.uk), a 123-acre (50-ha) olive agritourism site just outside the ancient city of Syracuse, while I explored the beautiful villages of south-east Sicily among the prehistoric caves of Pantalica Gorge and the Cava Grande del Cassibile nature reserve. At the end of the three weeks, I took the train back to mainland Italy across the Straits of Messina (the train is actually carried on an extraordinarily long ferry), followed by the train up to Rome and high-speed train to Paris for the Eurostar to London.

A multi-week, no-fly adventure like this allows you to really immerse yourself in the places you visit. It's the kind of journey known as 'slow travel', taking its influence from the slow food movement, which is all about using the time to savour the care and attention of local provenance of food. Slow travel is about taking the time to enjoy the journey, and learn about the history, food, language and people along the way. It's become a movement in its own right. Here are some examples of how you can enjoy life in the slow lane, discover a sense of place, and savour these memorable moments.

Slow Ways

A national network of walking routes that connects all of the UK's towns and cities, as well as thousands of villages. It is designed to make it easier for people to imagine, plan and go on walking journeys using existing paths, ways, trails and roads, to walk or wheel between neighbouring settlements, and combine them to create longer distance trips. Route testing was first carried out during the Covid lockdown of spring 2020, during which 700 volunteers mapped out 7,000 routes covering over 62,000 miles (100,000km) and more are being added all the time (slowways.org).

Pilgrimage walks

Throughout Britain there are many long-distance walks to holy places, often following ancient pagan pathways that became ritualized routes in Celtic, medieval and early modern Christianity. This ancient tradition has been on pause since Henry VIII and Thomas Cromwell banned it in the sixteenth century but The British Pilgrimage Trust (britishpilgrimage.org) is helping to revitalize it, broadening the concept to encourage people of all

ages, faiths and incomes to tread their own paths across the country's historic holy sites in search of physical, mental and spiritual wellbeing. The charity arranges for volunteers to test the routes to holy places (in the spirit of opening modern pilgrimage to all, its definition of 'holy places' includes prehistoric burial sites, trees, wells and hilltops, as well as mosques, synagogues and Buddhist monasteries). So far over a hundred have been documented, such as the 80-mile (130-km), five-day Anglesey Pilgrimage, which tracks the journey from the Roman stronghold of Caernarfon Fort to Caer y Twr, the mountain top of Holyhead, the holiest place in prehistoric druidic culture; and the 62-mile (100-km), 6–7 day St Cuthbert's Way from Melrose on the Scottish Borders to Lindisfarne on the north-east coast of England, the eventual resting place of Saint Cuthbert and the site of his original shrine.

The British Pilgrimage Trust's flagship project is the Old Way, a 250-mile (400-km) route from Southampton to Canterbury, passing ancient churches and a 1,000-year old mulberry tree, as well as the dramatic Solent Way shoreline, the majestic Arundel Castle, a stretch of the South Downs, and the coastal towns of Winchelsea and Rye, before finally arriving at the World Heritage Site of Canterbury Cathedral – the seat of the Archbishop of Canterbury.

If you prefer not to walk alone, you can join other walkers on one of several annual guided pilgrimages organized by the Trust. These range from one-day hikes to month-long journeys, and many link with sites run by its partner organization English Heritage and are designed to introduce more people to British pilgrimage, as well as to raise funds for its voluntary work.

The slow boat

Thanks to the incredible network of canals built in the eighteenth century, there are more than 2,000 miles (3,200km) of British waterways. The emphasis of these trips has to be on slow travelling as the maximum speed you're allowed to travel is just a horse-plodding 4mph (6.4km/h) – when calculating routes, you'd be advised to allow for 3mph (plus 15 minutes per lock). Some of the most scenic routes are the Kennet and Avon Canal between Reading and Bristol; the Llangollen Canal, which crosses the border between England and Wales and includes crossing the magnificent Pontcysyllte Aqueduct, a World Heritage Site that is the tallest navigable aqueduct in Britain; the Monmouthshire and Brecon Canal between Brecon and Pontypool; the Leeds and Liverpool canal; the Trent and Mersey Canal between Cheshire and Derbyshire; and the Forth and Clyde Canal. For information on canal boating, including details of boat hire in England and Wales, see canalrivertrust.org.uk; for Scotland see scottishcanals.co.uk.

The Falkirk Wheel is the world's first rotating boat lift that lifts boats between the Forth and Clyde Canal and the Union Canal allowing you to travel coast to coast across central Scotland. It's eco-friendly design means that just 1.5kWh is required to turn the wheel (the same energy needed to boil eight kettles).

The slow routes of France

The high-speed TGVs of France are the quick and efficient way of travelling overland between cities, but if you want to enjoy the joys of a more sedate ride, there are lots of minor routes on the French rail network that can take you on some wonderful scenic journeys. TER (Trains Express Régionaux) is a train and coach service that operates many of these routes; it's managed by local governments and can run over fairly long distances. Often these slower routes run across the country, west to east, rather than the faster north to south lines.

One of my favourite TER routes is from Lalinde to Sarlat-la-Canéda in Nouvelle-Aquitaine, where the single-track line crosses the Dordogne River several times, including across the stunning seven-arched stone bridge at Mauzac, as the track winds itself through the beautiful countryside of the Dordogne to the medieval town of Sarlat-la-Canéda, which reputedly has more listed buildings per square mile than anywhere else in Europe.

I also love the journey on the TER train and coach from Toulouse to Bagnères-de-Luchon in the heart of the Pyrenees. Out of the windows on the left-hand side of the train, you first catch sight of the snow-capped mountains looming in the distance on the way to Montréjeau, where you change to a coach that travels along the valley that is the border between the Haute Pyrenees and the Haute Garonne, all the way into the mountains. The coach stops outside a church at the head of the main street of Bagnères-de-Luchon, an ancient spa town that's a hub for skiing in winter and hiking, biking, climbing, canoeing and kayaking in summer. At the far end of the tree-lined boulevard Allées d'Etigny, where cafes and restaurants spill out on to the pavement, there's the town's historic Roman baths where you can spend hours soaking in the age-old waters and geo-thermal caves (luchon-bien-etre.fr).

Farm stays and Agriturismos

The idea of staying on a working farm started in Italy where farm-based rural retreats, known as agriturismos, developed from farmers letting out a few rooms, often based in their outbuildings, so that they could earn an alternative source of income while guests got to experience the sights and sounds of a working farm. The farmers might sell some of their own produce, including meat, fruit and vegetables, so guests are assured of authentic farm-to-fork meals. Guests might help out on the farm or at least see the farm in action, from feeding the animals and milking the cows, to collecting hens' eggs and looking after the horses, while the children go on donkey rides. Some extend the activities to making foods such as jams, yoghurt and cheeses, to handicrafts, including learning how to make natural decorations or aromatic oils, experimenting with pottery, and also visiting festivals connecting with farming, such as wine harvests, shepherds' fairs and sheepdog demonstrations.

Nowadays the concept of an agriturismo (in the UK it's known as a farm stay) is applied more loosely to almost any kind of country retreat, including farms that have been converted in stylish rural abodes – even boutique hotels where the closest thing to cattle is likely to be the cowhide in front of the reception desk. The rooms are more stylish than rustic, but guests still get to stay in traditional buildings in rural locations not just in Italy, but all over Europe. In Italy, the website agriturismo.it lists over 6,000 properties, while in Spain the website ecotur.es lists several hundred in Spain and Portugal. In the UK, the website farmstay.co.uk lists over 400 farm stays and country escapes that range 'from self-catering holiday cottages with hot tubs; B&Bs to glamping with a view'.

The Slow Travel People

Inntravel is a tour operator, based in York, that bills itself as the 'Slow Holiday People' specializing in carefully crafted, self-guided walking, cycling and activity holidays in the UK and Europe. It focuses on delicious regional cuisine and authentic, characterful family-run hotels. Many of its holidays are in remote, rural places where depopulation is a threat to the local economy, so holidaying in these regions helps to bring employment and regeneration to these areas. Furthermore, many of its walking and cycling routes also help to keep open traditional drovers' roads and other ancient paths. It provides a wealth of information on the history and gastronomy of its chosen regions, helping to promote maintain local cultures and traditions (inntravel.com).

sloWays, Italy

A small tour operator in Italy that organizes walking and cycling holidays, mostly in Italy, but also in other countries in Europe. It was founded by Alberto Conte, a pioneer in slow travel in Italy, and began with tours along the Via Francigena, a collection of routes to Rome that have been used since the Middle Ages. Its trips are designed so that customers can easily reach the starting point of the tour by public transport (sloways.eu).

The Slow Cyclist

The Slow Cyclist is a specialist tour operator that runs guided cycling holidays, typically 6–7 days, to Georgia, Transylvania, northern and southern Greece. It aims to help customers get under the skin of the local culture, spending the days cycling in stunning locations and stopping off to enjoy food and wine at local restaurants and staying overnight in comfortable locally-run lodgings (theslowcyclist.co.uk).

Wanderlust Gypsy Caravans

Trundle along quiet country lanes in a quirky horse-drawn gypsy caravan to beautiful locations in and around Cumbria and the Eden Valley, between the Lake District National Park and the North Pennines. You'll set up for the evening at a secluded off-grid camp where you'll paddle in streams and cook over an open fire, before bedding down for the night in the cosy caravan (wanderlusts.co.uk).

Foraging courses

Joining a foraging course is a great way to learn about the abundance of nature's free larder while spending time in the great outdoors. Adhering to the foraging code, you'll learn how to recognize, gather and sustainably harvest wild foods with confidence, including those found along the coast, such as seaweed and shellfish, as well as in forests, including edible plants, berries, seeds, mushrooms and truffles – depending on what's in season. The duration of the courses varies from just a few hours to a weekend, or multi-day residential courses where you can also learn how to prepare and cook the delicacies you find in the wild.

1 Galloway Wild Foods
Mark Williams has been teaching foraging for 30 years across a range of Scottish habitats, from high mountains and forests to hedgerows, urban settings and at the coast, introducing aspects of health and nutrition, traditional and modern medicinal uses, survival and bushcraft. Mark also runs online one-to-one courses and webinars as well as outdoor adventure trips, such as a three-day kayaking, wild camping and shore-based foraging trip along the coast of Galloway (gallowaywildfoods.com).

2 Coastal Foraging
Craig Evan's Costal Foraging courses explore the coastline of south-west Wales, from Pembrey in Carmarthenshire to St Davids in North Pembrokeshire, covering three habitats: beach, rockpool and rocky shore; tidal mudflats and estuaries; and sand dunes. The courses focus on edible seafood, including clams, mussels, oysters, plants, marsh samphire and sea vegetables – where to find and catch them, with a bit of local history thrown in (coastalforaging.co.uk).

3 Forage Fine Foods
This company is run by Liz Knight at Nant y Bedd Gardens, a beautiful wild forest garden high up in the Grwyne Fawr valley near Abergavenny. Her day courses run from 10.30am–3pm, but you can also book her for 2-hour foraging walks (for up to five people) or combine with one of the workshops on topics such as making wild drinks, seasonings and beauty products. Liz is also the wild food tutor at Humble By Nature in Monmouth, Eckington Manor in Worcestershire, and Brompton Cookery School in Shrewsbury (foragefinefoods.com).

4 Brecon Beacons Foraging
Adele Nozedar has written several books on foraging. Her half-day courses in the Brecon Beacons focus on finding and recognizing plants, fungi and wildlife. She also runs courses specifically for children (aged 6–12), looking at fewer plants than on the adult courses, but including outdoor, on-the-spot cooking and some bushcraft activities (breconbeaconsforaging.com).

5 Taste the Wild
Chris and Rose Bax set up their company to promote wild foods as exciting ingredients to use in innovative ways. Their courses are held in the north of England and cover a variety of subjects, including foraging for flowers, herbs and wild berries, picking hedgerow fruit and preparing wild game, as well as a day's foraging for edible mushrooms in autumn, and a day's foraging for edible seaweeds and plants in pools and gullies and around the pretty village of Robin Hood's Bay on the Yorkshire coast (tastethewild.co.uk).

Find a forager near you
foragers-association.org

6 Wild Food UK
The team at Wild Food UK organize foraging courses covering much of England and Wales, including Cambridgeshire, Surrey, Yorkshire Dales, Ross-on-Wye, Cardiff, and Carmarthenshire. The courses are typically a half-day and aim to teach you how to identify, pick and eat whatever is in season, including tasty edible wild plants, mushrooms, fruits, roots and flowers (wildfooduk.com).

7 Le Manoir du Lys
Spend an autumnal weekend mushroom foraging at Le Manoir du Lys, a smart country inn near the spa town of Bagnoles-de-l'Orne in Normandy. After an afternoon's foraging in the nearby forest, a mycologist will help you identify what you've found over a refreshing glass of pear cider, and Michelin-starred chef Franck Quinton will give you a masterclass in how to make delicious mushroom-based dishes. If you go in late September, head east to the town of Bellême for the annual four-day International Wild Mushroom Festival (manoir-du-lys.com).

8 Eat Weeds
These plant-based foraging courses held in Devon, Dorset, Kent, Sussex and London are run by author Robin Harford, who will teach you how to identify wild edible plants as well as tell you the stories of wild plants, their uses as food and medicine, and their folklore and history (eatweeds.co.uk).

9 Tours By Locals
If you're new to the world of truffles, Tours By Locals runs an introductory half-day truffle hunt 40-minutes outside Barcelona in the countryside of the pre-Pyrenees where you'll learn how to keep, cook and eat this national delicacy (toursbylocals.com).

10 Kanela & Garyfallo
After decades working for WWF and volunteering for Greenpeace in Canada, Vasilis Katsoupas returned to Greece to run foraging and ecology trips in the beautiful Zagori region of Greece. Afterwards, you can taste uniquely mushroom-inspired dishes at his restaurant, Kanela & Garyfallo, in the village of Vistra (kanela-garyfallo.gr).

City breaks

Make the most of a green city break overland by rail or ferry from the UK.

Busy, anonymous, resource-hungry they may be, but some of the most colourful cities in Europe are a great choice for a green break. An increasing number of pragmatic local authorities are implementing the circular economy to create sustainable transport, housing and economic development policies that are accelerating their transition to net zero, which has the knock-on effect of improving the experience for green travellers. For example, regenerative wetlands and connected green spaces help manage storm water, air quality and improve biodiversity, but also provide wonderful green sanctuaries that are great for appreciating urban nature or for just chilling out in parks and gardens across urban villages. Innovative high street businesses too are designing out waste and pollution by using material that can be reused, recycled or composted: restaurants that turn surplus food into delicious dishes; food markets that sell novel jams and chutneys made from odd-shaped, 'wonky' fruit and veg that would otherwise be discarded; fashion outlets that repair, reuse and refurbish clothes; and transport facilities, such as bike rental and car-pooling, which promote the concept of sharing rather than owning.

If you add in travelling door-to-door by train, city breaks become all the more convenient. Most railway stations are in the city centre, so there's no need to transfer from an out-of-the-way airport, and they're often designed as transport hubs connected to bus stations, cycling lanes and other railway stations that makes onward journeys seamless. When you arrive on the station concourse, instead of the hassle of baggage reclaim and endless duty-free sales, you pass by bistros, buskers and bike racks, as you emerge into the heart of city life. You already feel like you're travelling like a local. And if you know where to look away from the tourist hotspots, you can always find places those special places embedded within the local community, such as neighbourhood bakeries that makes the freshest pastries, characterful hostels furnished with local art, community-run cafés, live music venues and community-run gardens, as well as off-the-beaten-track cycleways and organic markets selling the best fresh, seasonal fare. Here are three suggestions for green breaks in cities, all reachable by train and/or by ferry from the UK.

Caen la Mer, France

This is a destination often overlooked by ferry motorists driving past it on their way through France. What they miss are the wonderful green spaces and rich medieval history of this port city in the heart of historic Normandy.

If you arrive by ferry, don't miss the year-round daily fish market at Ouistreham harbour bustling with traders selling their wares, including shiny mussels and sea snails, silvery mackerel, slabs of sole, crimson gurnard and crabs still flexing their pincers. In Caen, head to Caen Castle, founded by William the Conqueror in 1060; it's one of the largest medieval fortresses in Europe. In the heart of the city, there's Cimetière des Quatre-Nations, one of Caen's 'sleeping' cemeteries no longer used for burials – walk through the empty, leafy avenues of headstones and ivy-draped memorials. François Truffaut's *La Chambre Verte* was filmed here, and it sums up the city itself: green, with bags of history, bearing the scars of the past, but a secret worth discovering.

Where to stay: At Zest'Capade, a 'zero waste' bike-friendly B&B for up to four people, just south of the city. Breakfast includes fresh fruit from the market, locally roasted fair-trade coffee and crusty bread (facebook.com/zestcapade).

Where to buy calvados: La Boîte à Calva, a treasure trove of regional specialities on one of the oldest streets in the city (cave-pepins.com).

How to get there: Eurostar to Paris then transfer to Paris Gare St-Lazare for 2-hour train to Gare de Caen. Alternatively, by train to Portsmouth Harbour, ferry to Ouistreham and catch a 40-minute shuttle bus (Bus Verts du Calvados line 1), which is scheduled to meet ferry arrivals at the port and run to Caen's main railway station. If you come over on the ferry with a bike, you could cycle the 10 miles (16km) from Ouistreham to Caen on La Vélo Francette, a traffic-free route along the canal.

Amsterdam, Holland

There's so much more to this green city than its famous cycle-friendly culture; the city is leading the way in developing a circular economy, plus there are world-class vegetarian restaurants, organic food markets, sustainable fashion outlets and eco boutique hotels. There's no shortage of green spaces too in the 30 parks and gardens, from the creative vibe at Westerpark to the beautiful sculptures at Oosterpark and free concerts in Vondelpark. And then there's the exemplary cycling infrastructure – over 185 miles (298km) of cycle lanes so you can reach pretty much anywhere in the city on two wheels.

Where to stay: The stylish but unfussy Ecomama hostel is just around the corner from Centraal station, it's the sister hostel to Amsterdam's first boutique Hostel Cocomam, with private double rooms, family rooms, small cabins and dorms, with cradle-to-cradle furniture, natural stone heating, and an eco water system (ecomamahotel.com).

Where to eat: Restaurant Instock rescues leftover surplus food from local growers, such as odd-shaped carrots or slightly damaged fruit, and turns them into delicious dishes. It's open seven days a week for breakfast, lunch and dinner (instock.nl).

How to get there: Eurostar direct from London.

Barcelona, Spain

The Spanish capital is reachable in a day from London by train. It was the first city in the world to be given Biosphere status, and away from the famous streets and attractions, there are plenty of open-air spaces, including over 80 parks and gardens and over 3 miles (5km) of beaches. There's also lots to do outside the high season. Don't miss the wonderful views of the city from the sea on board the 150-seater Eco Slim electric catamaran that runs 50-minute tours from Barcelona Port (barcelonanavaltours.com).

Where to stay: The budget option is Twentytú High-tech Hostel, close to Plaça de les Glòries (only three stops on the Barcelona Metro from the centre of the city), with over 60 rooms for 2–4 people, all with ensuite bathrooms and wonderful views of the city from the rooftop bar (twentytu.com). For more creature comforts, head to Hostal Grau, a smart eco-minded hotel in the centre of Barcelona, a 3-minute walk from the Barcelona Museum of Contemporary Art (hostalgrau.com).

Where to eat: Restaurant Green Spot, a restaurant in Port Vell (near the harbour and beaches) with a modern monastic vibe, curved white ceilings and stripped-back wood panelling. It specializes in an assortment of plant-based food, including Asian-influenced soups and a wide-ranging menu of salads using seasonal local ingredients, such as kale and quinoa salad with cherry tomatoes, hazelnuts and white miso vinaigrette (encompaniadelobos.com/the-green-spot).

How to get there: Eurostar to Paris then transfer to Gare de Lyon for the direct train to Barcelona (if you get the early Eurostar, you can do this journey in a day, arriving in Barcelona in the evening). There should be enough time for you to have lunch at the wonderful Train Bleu restaurant at Gare de Lyon while you're waiting for the train south (le-train-bleu.com).

Green cities

● **Edinburgh** is home to the UK's first eco-powered green space at Saughton Park, whose glasshouse, buildings and café are all run from two ground source heat pumps. Don't miss the audio-visuals at Dynamic Earth, which tell the story of planet Earth (dynamicearth.co.uk).

● **Bristol** is a Fairtrade City, the UK's first Cycling City, home of the sustainable transport charity, Sustrans, the Soil Association, Ecotricity and any number of vegan restaurants, so it's no wonder it has become known as a green hub. There's also We The Curious, a family-friendly centre that's home to the UK's first 3D planetarium and explores the relationship between science, art, people and ideas.

● **Angers**, **Nantes**, **Metz** and **Lyon** frequently make it in the top tier of France's greenest cities index, according to the Green Cities Observatory (observatoirevillesvertes.fr), which has been ranking French cities since 2014 based on 25 criteria, including the amount of green space, waste management, and commitment to biodiversity conservation.

● **Zurich**'s electricity mostly comes from renewable energy, nearly half of all waste is recycled and nearly three-quarters of its hotels have received some sort of sustainable certification. Don't miss swimming in the city's rivers and lakeside lidos: there's mixed bathing at Flussbad Oberer Letten close to Zurich main station; the Art Nouveau bathhouse at Frauenbad am Stadthausquai is ladies-only

while the timber-box boathouse at Freibad am Schanzengraben is men-only; both open as trendy 'bars-under-the-stars' in the evening for both sexes.

● **Ljubljana**'s cycle-friendly city centre has been car-free since 2008. Don't miss the views of the city from the wooded hill at Rožnik, a short walk up from the city's largest park, Tivoli, or paddle-boarding through the heart of the city as you admire the architectural heritage of Jože Plečnik.

● **Copenhagen** From organic eateries, to car-sharing, sustainable fashion and eco hotels, the Danish capital has it all. There's even a 'green wave' for cyclists where the cycle traffic lights are coordinated so that if you travel at the average speed, you can cycle all the way into the city centre without stopping (gogreendanmark.dk).

Bristol hosts an international hot-air balloon fiesta every summer

10
of the best

Green places to stay in gateway cities

Many northern European cities are within reach of the UK within a day by train, but if you're looking to go further afield – and there isn't a connecting overnight sleeper service – you might need to stay the night in one of the gateway cities and catch the onward train or ferry the following morning. Or you could plan to stay in these cities anyway and make the detour part of the journey. Railway stations are usually in the city centre and are surrounded by any number of hotels, but it's not always easy to find green options, so here are ten eco-friendly suggestions to rest your head on a green getaway.

1 Paris
Mob Hotel is in the heart of St Ouen, just a few miles north of Gare du Nord and close to the Garibaldi metro station. The hotel is all about being socially engaged within its neighbourhood (the artistic creations of local craftspeople are everywhere), but it also has strong eco credentials, such as water jugs rather than plastic bottles, refillable toiletries and organic cosmetics in the rooms. The restaurant is fully organic with a seasonal menu that draws on produce from farming cooperatives or direct from local producers (they also make their own honey and beer). There is another Mob Hotel planned for the up-and-coming Confluence area of Lyon (mobhotel.com).

2 Lille
Hotel du Croise is a quiet, comfy little three-star hotel near the famous racecourse of Marcq en Baroeul and a short trip by tram from Lille Europe – the gateway to long-distance SNCF trains to Lyon, Valence, Marseille and other cities in the south of France. The 11 rooms here are simply and neatly furnished, and each offers its own small terrace. It has been awarded Clef Verte accreditation for its environmental policies (hotelducroise.com).

3 Munich
Both a hostel and a hotel, the 4You is just 5 minutes' walk from Munich railway station. For the budget traveller, there are beds in dorms or for those who want more privacy there are individual single, double and triple rooms with bathrooms. There's a small bar and restaurant serving local Bavarian food in a quiet courtyard. Bike hire available (the4you.de).

4 Nice

Conveniently located along a short walk between the city's main railway station and the port, Hotel Florence Nice is a great option if you're looking to travel the next day on the ferry out to Corsica or for bus or rail connections along the Cote d'Azur. The hotel has the EU Ecolabel for its efforts to reduce its waste, energy and water consumption – and don't miss tasting the honey that's produced from its rooftop beehives (hotel-florence-nice.com).

5 Milan

Hotel Milano Scala is an eco-boutique hotel in the historical district of Brera, a 10-minute walk from Milan Central railway station – the gateway to Bologna, Rome, Naples, Florence, Turin, Lake Como and Venice. It has a range of clever energy-saving devices and a farm-to-table restaurant with fruits, flowers, vegetables and herbs from the sixth floor's garden terrace. Sip on organic wine while enjoying the fabulous views of the Dome of Milan and the city's skyline from the Sky Terrace (hotelmilanoscala.it).

6 Hamburg

The three Superbude hotels dotted around Hamburg are all easily reachable from on foot, on the U-Bahn or S-Bahn trains from the city's main railway station – the gateway to the Nordic countries as well as to the Rostock ferry port for travelling up the Baltic Sea to Stockholm and Helsinki. All the hotels have installed a range of eco-friendly initiatives from energy-efficient lighting and reduction of water consumption to drawing on renewable energy suppliers and plastic-free cups, straws and bags (superbude.com).

7 Amsterdam

There are four Conscious Hotels in Amsterdam that are elegant but unfussy, and all the materials they use in their hotels are certified cradle-to-cradle, recycled or second-hand, plus they serve an excellent organic breakfast. Hotel Westerpark is a 20-minute bus ride (or 30-minute walk) from Centraal station, while the other three are a short ride by tram: the 112-room Hotel The Tire Station and 81-room Hotel Vondelpark are both near to the leafy Vondelpark, while the boutique 36-room Hotel Museum Square is in the heart of the museum district (conscioushotels.com).

8 Berlin

The 75-room Almodóvar Hotel is a smart, modern hotel with an organic, vegetarian-vegan deli restaurant (bistrobardot.de) in the trendy Friedrichshain district: take a short train ride from Berlin's main railway station to Berlin Ostbahnhof, then it's a few minutes' ride on Bus 240 towards Storkower Straße, where you get off at Boxhagener Straße/Holteistraße (almodovarhotel.de).

9 Marseille

Hotel Bellevue is in the Old Port of Marseille overlooking the busy harbour and Notre Dame de la Garde, just a few minutes' walk from the city's main railway station and a stone's throw from the ferry departure point for services to several ports on Corsica and Algeria. It was the first hotel in the city to be certified by Green Key and has a magnificent, listed iron staircase (hotelbellevuemarseille.com).

10 Copenhagen

Hotel Ottilia is a boutique hotel on the site of a former Carlsberg brewery, two stops on the intercity B line train from Denmark's Copenhagen Central station - the overland gateway to Sweden and Norway. It's part of the Brøchner group of hotels that are leading the way in green hospitality in Denmark; they're certified by Green Key and give excess products such as soap and shampoo (as well as donations of furniture and inventory) to the homeless. There's a terrific organic breakfast and if you've time, don't miss the ancient thermal baths next door (brochner-hotels.com).

Long distance journeys

There's no need to automatically reach for the 'book flight' button when planning a long-haul journey, there are plenty of lower carbon ways of travelling long distance: by train, coach, electric car, tall ship and yacht, or even by taking a ride on a cargo boat.

Taking the early-morning ferry across the Straits of Gibraltar from the Spanish port of Algeciras, we cruised past the famous Rock of Gibraltar before slipping into the port of Tangiers in Morocco. The journey had only taken an hour, just enough time to wipe the sleep from my eyes and pinch myself – I was in Africa.

Travelling overland by train from London to Morocco is like a long, slow teleport to another world. Of course, it's much quicker to fly, but the journey down through France and Spain is a real treat. After taking the Eurostar to Paris, with lunch at Le Train Blue restaurant, then the efficient, high-speed trains from Paris to Madrid and south to Algeciras, I watched the world whizz by: the rivers, hilltop villages and wide open expanses of the French countryside; the mountainous border at the Pyrenees, and then the Spanish countryside from north to south as it morphs into its Moorish influence. Travelling on the ferry from Algeciras mostly with Moroccans returning from work in Spain, I already felt my trip to Morocco had begun. On arrival at Tangiers, although we were met by the heat and humidity and the customary onslaught of taxi drivers touting for business, I already felt as though I'd acclimatized, that the long journey here had help me adjust to the change of culture. When you fly, it can take days for this to happen.

Thanks to Europe's extensive rail network, it's possible to reach almost every corner of the continent by train, to southern Italy, Greece, Turkey, the Nordic countries, Eastern Europe and Russia. One of my most memorable long distance journeys was travelling by train to Rostock in northern Germany where I caught the ferry up the Baltic Sea to Helsinki and then took the ferry across to Estonia. If you want to venture even further, the Trans-Mongolian Express can take you from Moscow all the way to Beijing in seven days. But long journeys don't have to be done just by train, here are a few other ways to travel long distance over land or sea:

Road trips for electric vehicles

With the range of electric cars improving every year, and electric charging networks being rolled out across Europe, it's now perfectly possible to plan a long-distance journey by electric car. There are an increasing number of dedicated scenic routes designed specifically for electric vehicles: the organizers indicate where the charging stations are along the way. An example is the E-Grand Tour of Switzerland (myswitzerland.com), a nine-day 1,000-mile (1,600-km) round trip from Zurich (where there are over 300 charging stations), which takes in a range of wonderful sights, including the Rhine Falls (the most powerful waterfall in Europe), the alpine resort town of St Moritz, Lausanne and Interlaken. Another road trip for electric vehicles is the Grand Tour of Catalonia (grandtour.catalunya.com), which is designed to visit a range of scenic places where you can get to know the art, history, gastronomy, landscapes, people and traditions of this special part of Spain between the Mediterranean and the Pyrenees. There are 13 stages, starting out from Barcelona and travelling south past the magnificent mountain at Montserrat to Tarragona, then across the vineyards of Priorat, along the coast up to Lleida and then into the mountains across to La Seu and Figueres, and then back down the coast to Barcelona.

Crewing on a yacht

Joining someone's sailing voyage is a wonderful way to travel long distance, for instance from the UK to southern Portugal or from the Canary Islands west across the Atlantic to the Caribbean or the USA. If you're looking to cross the Atlantic the low carbon way, sailing is a wonderful way to make the journey. The voyage across the Atlantic can take 2–4 weeks depending on the conditions and how fast the yacht can sail. There are plenty of unpaid opportunities for recreational crew on leisure boats or yachts that are used for non-commercial activities, such as amateur sailing, racing, sports, fishing and diving. In return for your passage, you'll have to follow instructions from the skipper or captain and help out where required in safe running of the vessel. Just make sure you find out before you hit the high seas exactly what will be expected of you, whether you need to contribute to costs, such as food, fuel, and mooring, and whether there are any reimbursed expenses for pre-agreed costs. There are several websites that help pair up interested crews with yachts, including findacrew.net and cruiserlog.com.

Working on a tall ship

Whether you want to take part in a regatta or just go sailing on an historic vessel in the style of great explorers, tall ships are an adventurous way to travel long distance. Sail Training International (sailtraininginternational.org) is a hub for tall ship sailing, it organizes races, regattas and adventure holidays, pairing up crew with the tall ships all over the world. There are also several other organizations that offer tall ship holidays: Windseeker (windseeker.org) runs sail training adventures on board tall ships for young people aged 15–25. Classic Sailing (classic-sailing.com) runs a variety of long-distance tall ship holidays, including 8–14-day taster trips on small ocean passages to the Canaries and Cape Verde, and a 1,300-nautical mile (2,400-km) trip through the waters of Spain, Portugal, France, Cornwall, Wales, Ireland and the Scottish Hebrides. The Tall Ships Youth Trust (tallships.org) takes anyone aged 18–80 on a range of tall ship adventures, from a day's sail in the Solent to a transatlantic crossing.

Travelling by cargo boat

Not quite as poetic a way to travel as under sail, travelling by cargo ship can be a convenient way to travel very long distances. Facilities can be limited: a room and access to a dining room and lounge, but there can also be basic gyms and a swimming pool. The first port of call for this kind of transit is The Cruise People (cruisepeople.co.uk), who since 1992 have been arranging passenger trips on board freighters run by shipowners from the UK, France, Germany and Italy. Voyages can be anything up to 125 days, although typical short round-trip voyages are 28 days, such as between France and the Caribbean, or 35 days between Southampton and the Mediterranean. It also arranges voyages on ten-passenger container ships operating between Southampton and the Far East and China, as well as between Singapore and Australia. Other agencies are: cargoshipvoyages.com, freightlink.co.uk and Berlin-based Slowtravel (langsamreisen.de).

Railway station restaurants

In the golden age of European rail travel in the nineteenth century, city centre railway stations were at the hub of urban life and were often architecturally exceptional. Many of these impressive buildings survive, and now that there's a renaissance in rail travel across the continent, new life is being breathed back into these relics of living heritage. Not only have the buildings been restored but facilities and amenities fit for the twenty-first century have been installed, including gastro bars, bistros and fine dining restaurants. Even in remote rural areas, there are an increasing number of railway stations with outlets selling quality local food. While you pass the time waiting for an onward connection, sit back, enjoy a fabulous meal with a drink, and watch the world go by.

1 Le Train Bleu, Paris
The epitome of railway dining in style and sophistication, you may want to plan your onward connection based around when you can reserve a table at this gourmet Belle Époque restaurant inside Hall 1 of the Gare de Lyon, named after the traditional summer escape of Parisians to the Cote d'Azur and beyond (le-train-bleu.com).

2 Brasserie La Consigne, Paris
It doesn't match the grandeur of Le Train Bleu, but this fabulous Art Deco restaurant inside the Gare de l'Est has its own unique sense of old-world travel as the historical gateway for the Grand Est. Feast on superfood salads or traditional French dishes, from croque monsieur/ madame to roasted salmon (en.brasserie-laconsigne.fr).

3 The Booking Office, London
Set off for a European rail adventure in style with a meal at this best-of-British restaurant in the former booking office of the wonderfully renovated St Pancras International railway Station. Open for breakfast, lunch and dinner (booking-office.co.uk).

4 Corrour Station House Restaurant, Inverness-shire

Billed as 'the UKs remotest restaurant', the intimate Corrour Station House Restaurant is also the highest (at 1,339ft/408m) and can only be reached by train on the West Highland Line or a 20-mile (32-km) walk. If you make it this far, you might as well stay for its famous 14-hour slow-cooked local venison stew, the Scottish smoked salmon platter, or delicious seasonal and vegetarian dishes (corrour.co.uk). See also p71.

5 Waterside Seafood Restaurant, Dornie, Ross-shire

Within The Dornie hotel at the end of the line at the terminus of the Kyle of Lochalsh Line on the north-west coast of Scotland, this local favourite has a daily changing menu of freshly caught fish and shellfish – queenies, langoustines, salmon and crab landed from its own fishing boat Green Isle that's skippered by the owner Neil MacRae. Dornie is where three lochs meet – Loch Duich, Loch Ash and Loch Long – nearby is Eilean Donan Castle and it's just 8 miles (13km) to the Isle of Skye (watersideseafoodrestaurant.co.uk).

7 To Treno Sto Rouf, Athens

At Rouf railway station, just 5 minutes on the train from Athens main station, dine in one of several refurbished antique 'wagons', including one that was used on the Orient Express. Time it right and you can enjoy musicals and plays while you feast on salads and pizzas, washed down with signature cocktails (totrenostorouf.gr).

7 Bistrot Milano Centrale, Milan

Come here for organic fair-trade coffee and freshly squeezed juices, panini, pizza and focaccia made with sourdough baked daily on site. A variety of street food and traditional Italian pasta dishes using seasonal ingredients are available at this smart bistro in the heart of Milan's main railway station (bistrot.com).

8 Buffet de la gare, Céligny

This is a delightful little restaurant on the train line just north of Geneva with a naturally shaded terrace, run by the same couple for over 20 years, who make the most of seasonal ingredients and a celebrated recipe for perch fillets from Lake Geneva. Famously a favourite of Richard Burton (buffet-gare-celigny.ch).

9 Grand Café Restaurant 1e klas, Amsterdam

Head to platform 2B in Amsterdam Central station for brasserie-style dining at this nostalgic fin-de-siècle restaurant in the splendid former first-class art deco waiting rooms. Designed by architect Pierre Cuypers, the grand renovated space is adorned with huge arched windows, high ceilings, ornate floral decorations and scenes from literature. Visit for coffee and breakfast pastries, lunchtime sandwiches and omelettes, or a waiter-served three-course fish, meat or vegetarian dinner (restaurant1eklas.nl).

10 Orient Express Restaurant, Istanbul

A little oasis that has been a refuge for travellers away from the hustle and bustle of the busy Sirkeci station since 1890 (it's where the Orient Express would set off from on its way to Paris). A good place for just a strong Turkish coffee in a nostalgic setting or to feast on a variety of moderately priced Turkish dishes, from grilled chicken and meatballs to fish of the day, followed by seasonal fruits. (en. orientexpressrestaurant.net).

Volunteering

Give your time and use your skills to help with conservation or a range of development projects, from community service to medical support.

Each morning on the island sanctuary of Île aux Cocos in the Indian Ocean, we'd walk past an adorable white-tailed tropicbird chick nesting at the foot of a tree on our way to where we were monitoring the nests of lesser noddies, another seabird species native to this part of the world.

The other volunteers and I watched the chick develop a little more each day, growing from a tiny baby into a comically plump fledgling. One day, however, as we passed the same spot, all we could see were its white-grey down feathers scattered around the unprotected nest. The chick had gone, and the nest was such a mess, it looked as if it had been taken by a predator. It was such a sad sight, and we wondered if we could have done more to protect it, even though this was the natural way a tropicbird nested. Later that day, however, while we were collating our recordings from the day, we suddenly heard a familiar 'kek-kek-kek' bird call overhead, and looked up to see two magnificent white-tailed tropicbirds flying across the blue sky, followed by a third smaller bird trailing a little further behind – it was the fledgling chick on one of its first flights. Its progress may have been a little awkward, but it looked magnificent.

This simple but powerful experience gave me my first practical understanding of how tourism can be a tool for conservation. The trip was part of a ten-week voluntary expedition to Mauritius and Rodrigues. Long term volunteering for more than a month with respected organizations like the one I was on, organized by Raleigh International (raleighinternational.org) and others, such as Project Trust (projecttrust.org.uk) and Azafady (madagascar.co.uk), provides much needed skills and resources for developing countries. They are a unique way to develop life skills such as teamwork, communication and decision-making, and to work with people your same age from other cultures, while providing a positive impact on important conservation work and international development.

Here are three examples of other projects where the work of volunteers can help make a significant difference to important local conservation work.

Turtle conservation

Work for at least a month alongside scientists to protect one of the most important loggerhead sea turtle nesting habitats in the Mediterranean. Help treat injured turtles and in the breeding season protect nests and collect data (dekamer.org.tr).

Voluntary services underseas

Help rebuild tropical fisheries or mangrove 'blue forests' to protect coastal ecosystems and livelihoods. NGO Blue Ventures has been working in Madagascar for 20 years to increase the resilience of vulnerable coastal communities, many of whom live in precarious conditions, lacking access to basic services, and are reliant on fishing for survival (blueventures.org).

Rainforest regeneration

Work on rainforest regeneration in a bio-hotspot by joining a well-established programme of research carried out at the Manu Learning Centre within a remote area of 643 acres (260ha) of regenerating rainforest in the Amazon. Minimum duration four weeks (travel-peopleandplaces.co.uk).

Tell me and I will forget;
Show me and I may remember;
Involve me and I will understand.

Chinese proverb

Tips on volunteering abroad

Committed, long-term volunteering abroad requires preparation so make sure you plan well ahead. There are hundreds of volunteering organizations, but some are more transparent than others on how your money is spent and how your work will benefit the destination. Here are a few questions to ask yourself and the organization:

CAN I AFFORD IT?

The listed price of a placement typically covers accommodation, food and local transport, but don't forget that volunteering abroad, especially to developing countries, might incur extra charges, such as vaccinations and visas, as well as the cost of travelling there.

HOW EXACTLY DOES THE PLACEMENT FEE BREAK DOWN?

Ask what proportion of the money you spend goes on internal administration costs, staff wages, your food and accommodation and training, and how much actually goes on the project itself.

WHAT WORK WILL I BE DOING?

Find out exactly what sort of work you'll be doing (not just in general terms) as well as how many hours a day and how many days a week you'll be expected to work.

Also, check that the volunteer work you'll be doing couldn't be done by locals who would actually earn a wage from doing the work instead of you.

WHAT IS THE IMPACT OF THE WORK?

Does the organization monitor and evaluate the efficacy of the project to ensure it really is making a genuine difference, whether that's to biodiversity conservation or community development?

HOW DID THE PROJECT COME ABOUT?

The most worthwhile projects often originate from local people who have sought out specific help from international agencies to select volunteers on a committed long-term basis. The organization should match your skills to relevant projects, so be wary if there's no selection process or if the organization doesn't try and find out who you are and about your interests and skills. Ask

whether you'll be working with a local NGO or charity, and if someone from that organization will be involved in the day-to-day running of the project.

WILL THEY GIVE YOU SUPPORT?

Good organizations usually offer pre-departure training and provide further training, support and guidance during the project. Make sure there is someone at the destination who has direct responsibility for you and can help should any issues arise.

WHAT'S THE FEEDBACK LIKE FROM OTHER VOLUNTEERS?

Check the social media channels of the organization and read what previous volunteers have posted about the placement using relevant hashtags. Also, try and speak to someone who has been on the trip and, ideally, worked on your specific project, and ask to see the feedback forms of previous volunteers to see what challenges they faced.

Volunteering in the UK

Local volunteering can be a rewarding way to meet new people, gain new skills and experience, and make a significant difference to your community. There's a wide range of opportunities available, from wildlife, conservation and environmental projects to lending a hand to a local charity or community group. The work can be anything from a few hours during the week or over a weekend, such as helping out with your local wildlife trust (wildlifetrusts.org) on tasks like community gardening, species surveying, plant identification and GPS mapping, to a longer commitment that can include staying overnight in some fabulous locations. Example of these kinds of residential opportunities, include a 'Conservation Week' revitalizing the wild forests of the Highlands with Trees for Life (treesforlife.org.uk) or even as much as a month-long stint at a National Nature Reserve run by NatureScot (nature.scot) where you can get involved in monitoring habitats, birdlife and trees, or perhaps working in the visitor centre and helping to lead groups.

WWOOF

Founded in 1971, World Wide Opportunities on Organic Farms is a worldwide movement that links volunteers with organic farmers to help support ecological farming, including in the UK. In return for helping out on the farm, you receive free board and lodging (wwoof.net).

There are several online databases that can point you to local volunteering opportunities:

The website Do-it.org has links to more than a million volunteering opportunities in the UK that you can search by interest, activity or location and then apply online.

The Conservation Volunteers brings people together to care for green spaces, from local parks and community gardens to local nature reserves and Sites of Special Scientific Interest. tcv.org.uk

The website of the National Council for Voluntary Organisations has a search facility that enables you to find your nearest volunteer centre that tries to match potential volunteers with a suitable role with a local charity of voluntary organization. ncvo.org.uk

10
of the best

Citizen science projects in the UK

There are many surveys that take place across the UK each year where you can help provide valuable information for research scientists and conservationists. The idea is that the experts draw on your work to collect large amounts of data from across the country and create an overall snapshot, which they couldn't possibly do on their own. Most involve simply recording what you see and uploading the information to a website or app and you can then see how your data is part of the bigger picture. Here are ten citizen science opportunities where you can make a considerable contribution to taking the pulse of the nation's natural world.

1 Big Garden Birdwatch
Spend just an hour counting the birds in your garden (or local park or other green space) each winter to help provide the RSPB with a vital snapshot of the UK's birds. Even if you don't see a single bird, the information is still highly valuable (rspb.org.uk).

2 Big Butterfly Count
Find a spot in your garden in July and August and for just 15 minutes record how many butterflies you see and upload the information to an app. These beautiful flying insects are a vital indicator species of the health of an ecosystem as both pollinators and important components of the food chain, so tracking their numbers is crucial for understanding how to conserve the natural world (bigbutterflycount.butterfly-conservation.org).

3 Project Puffin (Puffarazzi)
Join the #Puffarazzi to record sightings of what puffins are eating at colonies across the UK, including Skomer, the Farne Islands and the Isle of May. Puffin numbers have plummeted, and they're now threatened with global extinction, which the RSPB thinks may be partly

down to lack of food, so they need to find out how the food puffins carry in their bills is changing over time (**rspb.org.uk**).

4 **The Great British Beach Clean**
During a week-long event every September, collect litter from any one of hundreds of beaches in the UK, and record all the items of rubbish you find in a 100-m stretch. The data helps drive the conservation work of the Marine Conservation Society, which feeds into the work of the International Coastal Cleanup (**mcsuk.org**).

5 **Planet Patrol**
Record evidence of any litter, such as single-use plastic, that you find to the #planetpatrol app whose 'litter map' is helping experts at Nottingham Trent University and the University of Glasgow to uncover insights into the trends and patterns of litter to help create solutions to prevent the problem at source (**planetpatrol.co**).

6 **Shoresearch**
Participating in this survey involves some basic training so that you can identify and record the marine wildlife in the intertidal zone at shores across the UK. The data collected helps experts understand the effects of pollution, climate change and invasive alien species, and has been key to designating many of The Wildlife Trusts' Marine Conservation Zones (**wildlifetrusts.org**).

7 **Big Seaweed Search**
For an hour, you're asked to take a photo and record what seaweeds you can find in a small patch of seashore

so that the Natural History Museum can assess the effects of rising sea temperatures, non-native species and ocean acidification on Britain's sealife (**nhm.ac.uk**).

8 **Shorewatch**
Carry out regular 10-minute surveys of whales and dolphins at over 35 specific sites off the north and north-west coasts of Scotland. The data helps Whale and Dolphin Conservation (WDC) understand how human behaviour affects these sentinels of ocean health to help influence policy makers and advise developers to ensure better protection for them (**uk.whales.org**).

9 **The Big Forest Find**
Contribute to a national record of forest biodiversity using the iNaturalist app every time you visit a forest. Recordings can be of anything, from lichen and fungi to birds, butterflies and mammals, which will help ecologists, scientists and rangers care for the forest wildlife (**forestryengland.uk**).

10 **Nature's Calendar**
Record the signs of the changing seasons near you, from leaf buds bursting to birds arriving and blackberries ripening, to help the Woodland Trust predict how wildlife will be affected as the climate changes (**naturescalendar. woodlandtrust.org.uk**).

People power

Find a citizen science project at home and abroad using Zooniverse, which lists a wide range of projects, from recovering hidden weather data to tracking the Northern Lights and exploring the secret life of the Mont Blanc massif (**zooniverse.org**).

Positive-impact adventures

Choose pioneering holidays that contribute to regeneration, rewilding and nature conservation work as well as humanitarian efforts and global citizenship.

I hadn't anticipated that coming face to face with a 6ft (1.8m), 2-ton rhinoceros would be so heart-wrenching, but this was no ordinary rhino. Sudan – the last male of his species – was living out his final days at the Ol Pejeta Conservancy, a wildlife sanctuary in Kenya's Laikipia County.

Sudan's ranger, Joseph Wachira, led me to his shaded enclosure, sensitively approaching Sudan and stroking his enormous head tenderly while whispering something reassuring in his ear. I stood for a long time just gazing at Sudan, purely in admiration of such a magnificent animal. A year later, I learnt that he had died, aged 45, from complications to a leg infection. He was the very last male northern white rhinoceros on the planet.

As Richard Vigne, the Managing Director of Ol Pejeta pointed out to me on my visit: 'Sudan represents a failure of conservation.' By the time Sudan was transferred to Kenya from a zoo in the Czech Republic, it was becoming too late, the chances of him reproducing with either of the two remaining females had all but vanished. Yet in the face of this tragedy, there are many more hopeful stories of conservation at Ol Pejeta, where the team have been able to intervene in the survival of other species before it is too late. As well as looking after other rhinos, Ol Pejeta is a sanctuary for chimpanzees rescued from the black market. The majority of visitors to Ol Pejeta are Kenyans, but the funds generated by international visitors help significantly with its crucial conservation work. It's no surprise David Attenborough visited while filming for *Seven Worlds, One Planet*.

Part of the success of Ol Pejeta is because it doesn't rely solely on tourism to survive. 'We could lose tourism overnight', Richard Vigne explained, 'so we have to build in a strategy to manage that risk. And we've done that by introducing and managing other businesses within the conservation space. For example, keeping livestock further supplements and expands our revenue

base, meaning that we always have the ability to finance the fixed costs of conservation irrespective of what happens to tourism.' It's a successful model that can be replicated at other wildlife sanctuaries.

Below is a selection of other postive impact initiatives that are greatly contributing to biodiversity conservation and humanitarian efforts. In order to reach them, it's most likely you will have to fly (some are in very remote places), so as long as flying continues to be a large emitter of carbon, you do have to weigh up the advantages of supporting their work with the pollution of your flight. The longer you can stay, the more your visit will benefit the work in these destinations.

Preserving rainforests

Following decades of tree clearing for agriculture and livestock production, in the 1980s the Costa Rican government implemented policies that have halted and reversed this deforestation. Today, over half of Costa Rica's land is covered by forest, compared to just 26 per cent in 1983, allowing it to make the most of the biodiversity in its rainforests and pioneer the concept of ecotourism, which is defined by the International Ecotourism Society as, 'responsible travel to natural areas that conserves the environment, sustains the well-being of the local people, and involves interpretation and education.' Small-scale, high-end eco lodges have contributed to the conservation of its rainforests, such as the sister lodges of Pacuare and Lapa Rios that protect nearly 2,000 acres (800ha) of pristine rainforest. Guyana is also developing community-based eco-tourism to fund the protection of its rainforests. Lodges such as Iwokrama River Lodge, Rewa Eco-Lodge, and Surama Eco-Lodge enable visitors to enjoy the country's incredible biodiversity, while contributing to its conservation and to the livelihoods of remote communities.

Protecting mountain gorillas

The entire population of wild mountain gorillas lives in just two regions of Central Africa – in the Virunga Mountains region that borders Uganda, Rwanda and the Democratic Republic of Congo, and the Bwindi Impenetrable National Park in south-west Uganda. Despite years of civil unrest in the region, gorilla numbers have actually grown in recent years to over 1,000 thanks to concerted anti-poaching and conservation efforts, helped by the income from tourism. In order to visit the gorillas, you have to purchase a permit, most of which is for conservation, while some goes to the government and a small proportion is earmarked for local communities. There are several local operators that run trips, such as Rwanda Eco-Tours (rwandaecotours.com), while Expert Africa can organize staying at luxury lodges, such as Sabyinyo Silverback Lodge and Virunga Lodge, which are also a major driver of socio-economic development in the area (expertafrica.com).

Conserving biodiversity

The Long Run is a global alliance of nature-based tourism businesses who collectively conserve over 23 million acres (9 million ha) of biodiversity. Members include many trailblazing retreats that are embedded in their local community, such as Borana Conservancy at the foot of Mount Kenya, which is home to black and white rhino and many other endangered species – guests are encouraged to get involved in conservation initiatives tracking rhino with the scouts on foot, monitoring lion movements, and engaging in local community projects. Other members of The Long Run include Caiman Ecological Refuge in Brazil's vast pantanal wetlands, home to jaguars, blue-fronted parrots, and caiman crocodile; Misool, in Raja Ampat, Indonesia, which protects some of the world's most biodiverse corals reefs; and Grootbos Private Nature Reserve in South Africa, which protects 790 plant species, many of which are found nowhere else on Earth (thelongrun.org).

Numbers of mountain gorillas have increased in recent years

GHE's solar grids have helped bring light to many remote Himalayan villages

Lighting up Himalayan villages

One of the main reasons for poverty in remote mountainous areas in the Himalayas is the lack of access to energy, so for the past decade Global Himalayan Expeditions (GHE) has used the funds generated by its adventure expeditions to the region to finance the installation of solar grids in over 130 indigenous villages. Its trips involve multiple days trekking at relatively high altitude in remote valleys and visiting the villages that benefit from the installation of the solar technology. Its 8-day 'Women Leaders Expedition' includes a bike ride on the dirt trails of Ladakh visiting innovation centres that GHE has set up to provide students with access to experiential education (ghe.co.in).

Village Ways is another pioneering sustainable tourism organization in the region, which operates walking holidays from village to village in India and Nepal. Walk among the breathtaking scenery of snow-capped peaks, verdant pastures and terraced hills, and learn about traditional village life, while bringing local economic and social benefits, including employment for young people who might otherwise migrate to cities. The income complements rather than replaces other sources of revenue so that households do not abandon traditional work such as farming (villageways.com).

Empowering global citizenship

Orbis Expeditions works to establish positive long-term social impact, global citizenship and business development in Africa. It works with local partners, such as Ripple Africa, which runs large scale community-based environmental projects 'by providing a hand up, not a hand out'. You can help support the work by joining one of its forthcoming study tours and education expeditions (for youths) or sporting adventures (for families) in Malawi, or women-only adventure expeditions in other countries, including Jordan, Morocco and Ghana (orbis-expeditions.com).

Community-run enterprises

Tapping into community-run ventures and social enterprises is a great way to get into the heart and soul of a place while giving back to the places you love to visit, helping them with their running costs so they can maintain and improve their resources and character. Some of these hubs are run as non-profits, others are groups, charities and associations run by passionate local people and volunteers, which wouldn't exist without their commitment. Here are ten inspiring community-run initiatives where you can get great service while helping to spread the pound around.

1 The pub
The Pack Horse Inn is a seventeenth-century pub in the village of South Stoke on the outskirts of Bath that was given a makeover when it was bought by the local community in 2016. The interior has a wonderful olde English charm with inglenooks and ancient beams, while outside there's a lovely beer garden from where you can feast on locally inspired dishes and sup cider and local ale looking out over the glorious Midford Valley (packhorsebath.co.uk).

Pub is the Hub

Inspired by Prince Charles in 2001, Pub is the Hub is a not-for-profit organization that works to strengthen the connection between pubs and their local communities. There are over 150 across the UK, including many that have diversified into other retail outlets, such as delis, bakeries, farm shops, and village stores, such as The Raven Inn, Clwyd, the King's Arms, Shoudham, West Norfolk, and the Fleece Inn, Hillesley. To find one near you, search **pubisthehub.org.uk**

2 The restaurant
Brigade Bar + Bistro is in a beautiful old Victorian fire station building near London Bridge serving brunch, lunch and dinner. It's run by a social enterprise that helps homeless people get into work by giving them work experience in the kitchens and training them to become chefs (thebrigade.co.uk).

3 The café
The Forest is a vegetarian café that helps fund a volunteer-run, collectively owned arts and events project in Edinburgh where the space is used for a variety of performances from music and theatre to dancing and poetry recitals (blog.theforest.org.uk).

4 The hostel
The Smugglers Hostel is a 20-bed hostel in the village of Tomintoul in the Cairngorms National Park and reputedly the 'highest hostel in the Scottish Highlands'. It's an independent hostel run by a local community development trust where all profits are ploughed back into the community (thesmugglershostel.co.uk).

5 The lodge
The Mourne Lodge in Cnocnafeola, Co. Down is an eco-friendly, purpose-built community enterprise in the Mourne Mountains between Spelga Dam and the Silent Valley. It provides simple, unfussy accommodation for those looking to explore one of Northern Ireland's Areas of Outstanding Natural Beauty (themournelodge.com).

6 The arts centre
Dartington Trust is an arts, ecology and social justice charity, which runs a social-enterprise hub for retreats, festivals and summer schools as well as a visitor centre on a 1,200-acre (486-ha) estate near Totnes in South Devon. There's a campsite, hostel-style rooms and a fisherman's cabin next to the River Dart. Explore the glorious gardens and deer park trails and dine on local food in the medieval Great Hall (dartington.org).

7 The art gallery
Run by volunteers, the Fry Art Gallery in the market town of Saffron Walden is home to a large number of paintings, prints, books and ceramics showcasing the art of the twentieth and twenty-first-century heritage of north-west Essex (fryartgallery.org).

8 The village shop
In the historic Somerset village of Mells, the shop and post office is run by a team of about 50 volunteers, rotating shifts, job-sharing, fundraising and caring for the window displays and plants. It supports a wide range of local producers, including cold meats from Thorner's of Somerset and home-baked cakes from Frome Country Market, as well as the work of local artists, including earthenware pottery from Philip Wood of Whatley and work by Katharine Pollen – another local potter. The community also raised funds to build a café next door to the shop, which was opened by Mary Berry, serving hearty breakfasts, home-cooked lunches and teas to residents, walkers and cyclists, seven days a week (mellsvillage.co.uk).

9 The museum
The Diving Museum in Gosport is the UK's only museum dedicated to underwater diving. Run by a charity that relies entirely on admission fees and support from donors, it is a treasure trove of diving equipment, including diving bells, chambers, the Hall Rees helmet that featured in the silent film *20,000 Leagues Under the Sea* (1916), and the prototype helmet that the Deane brothers used to perfect their diving helmet for the world's first commercial dive off the Isle of Wight in 1832 (divingmuseum.co.uk).

10 The heritage centre
Maidenhead Heritage Centre is run mainly by volunteers to showcase the history of the town, particularly the operations of the Air Transport Auxillary, whose headquarters was at White Waltham Airfield during the Second World War. The star attraction is the Spitfire Simulator Experience, where you can sit in the pilot's seat of a Spitfire rigged up to a wide-screen electronic simulator and get a taste of the thrill of flying these awesome machines (maidenheadheritage.org.uk).

Index

Acknowledgements

The Green Traveller wouldn't have happened if it hadn't been for the wonderful designer, Tina Hobson, who is a joy to work with. We have had the good fortune to have been edited by Sophie Allen who has given us the freedom to craft the book we wanted, fashioned by her expert eye and exceptional team, including copy editor Katie Hewett and proofreader Karen Fick.

This book is a testament to the many who have contributed to greentraveller.co.uk since it was established in 2006, particularly Anouk Van Den Eijnde, Lucy Symons, Florence Fortnam, Emma Smith, Catherine Mack, Holly Tuppen, Paul Miles, Paul Bloomfield, Sarah Baxter, and Yvonne Gordon. I'd like to thank Andy Phillipps and Matt Witt for providing me with the benefit of their wisdom and ready advice over many years, and to the Guardian's Andy Pietrasik and Isabel Choat who commissioned me to write a regular slot about green travel long before it was fashionable. Thanks also to those who have advised and supported me over the years: Graham Miller, Richard Hearn, Noel Josephides, John Telfer, Simon Wrench,

Maria Pieri, Jeremy Lazell, Jane Dunford, Kate Quill, Cath Urquhart, Steve Keenan, Alastair Sawday, Tom Hall, Martin Dunford, Sophie Campbell, Julia Spence, Gillian Monahan, Susie Aust, Kate McWilliams, Sue Ockwell, Nicola Forsyth, Ann-Charlotte Carlsson, Steve James, Hannah Gilbert, Jason Freezer, Jackie King, Michael Cullen, Jonny Keeling, Tim Martin, Miranda Krestovnikov, Lucien Clayton, Neil Courtis, Jamie Drummond, Alan Dangour, Chris Gregory, Julian Matthews, Neil Birnie, Delphine Malleret King, Richard Denman, Mark Smith (Man in Seat 61), Xavier Font, Ben Lynam, Jeremy Smith, Sally Davey, Susanne Becken, Sophie Poklewski-Koziell, the late Roger Diski, and the communication teams past and present at Brittany Ferries, Eurostar and Rail Europe.

Finally, I have had incredible support from my family – from my brilliant wife Rhiannon whose determination to seek out the green and gorgeous has no equal, and from my late parents whose love, kindness and laughter live on in our two little green travellers, Osian and Owen.

Picture credits